WORLD HISTORY BY ERA

Ancient Civilizations

VOLUME 1

Don Nardo, *Book Editor*

Daniel Leone, *President*
Bonnie Szumski, *Publisher*
Scott Barbour, *Managing Editor*

Greenhaven Press, Inc., San Diego, California

T 26230

Every effort has been made to trace the owners of copyrighted material. The articles in this volume may have been edited for content, length, and/or reading level. The titles have been changed to enhance the editorial purpose.

Library of Congress Cataloging-in-Publication Data

Ancient civilizations / Don Nardo, book editor.
    p. cm. — (World history by era; vol. 1)
    Includes bibliographical references and index.
    ISBN 0-7377-0645-7 (pbk. : alk. paper) —
ISBN 0-7377-0646-5 (lib. : alk. paper)
    1. Civilization, Ancient. I. Nardo, Don, 1947– II. Series.

CB311 .E16 2002
930—dc21   2001016156
                                                         CIP

Cover inset photo credits (from left):
Corel Professional Photos; Photodisc; Corel Professional Photos; Corel Professional Photos; Planet Art; Digital Stock; Photodisc
Main cover photo credit: © Massimo Listri/Corbis

Copyright © 2002 by Greenhaven Press, Inc.
10911 Technology Place, San Diego, CA 92127

Printed in the USA

CONTENTS

Prologue: In the Mists of Time: Humanity Before Cities and Writing

1. Humans in the Stone Age: A Fight for Survival

Life in the Paleolithic era, or "Old Stone Age," was
sometimes difficult and often uncertain, as primitive
humans fought to survive in hostile environments;
yet they managed to spread their cultures across
most of the earth's surface.

2. Life Among the Hunter-Gatherers

Before humans learned to grow their own food, they
had to rely on hunting game and gathering wild
fruits and vegetables. The lifestyle of modern hunter-
gatherers casts fascinating light on that of their prehistoric counterparts.

3. The Emergence of Agriculture and Raising Livestock

The transition from hunting and gathering to agriculture and pastoralism (raising livestock) was one of
the most far-reaching social and cultural changes in
human history, for it led to permanent settlements
and village life.

Chapter 1: The Great River Civilizations

1. The Sumerians Establish the World's First True Cities

The earliest large-scale cities appeared on the fertile
plains of Mesopotamia (northwest of the Persian
Gulf), which was called "the land" by the first city-
dwellers, the Sumerians.

Every year the Nile River gently flooded over its banks, laying down a fresh layer of fertile soil in which the ancient Egyptians planted their crops. The river's cycles also helped to regulate other aspects of daily life for one of the world's great early civilizations.

vanced, vigorous pre- or proto-Greek cultures, one
centered on the island of Crete, the other on the
Greek mainland.

2. The Hardy Celts Spread Across Europe

The vigorous tribal Celts inhabited the wilds of central and northern Europe for over a thousand years,
long predating the classical Greeks and Romans, who
later came to look on their northern neighbors as
"barbarians."

3. One God: The Emergence of the Hebrews and Monotheism

Among the major bulwarks of Western and Near
Eastern culture is the rich legacy of religious ideas
and stories originating with the early Jews, who established the concept of monotheism (one god),
which was later also adopted by Christians and Muslims.

4. The First Kingdom of Israel

The ancient Hebrews established the first kingdom of
Israel in about 1000 B.C., almost three centuries before
the founding of Rome. Its early rulers, David and
Solomon, subsequently came to play major roles in
the Judeo-Christian Old Testament.

5. The Phoenicians: Pioneering Traders of the Mediterranean

Beginning at the dawn of the first millennium B.C.,
the Phoenicians, skilled sailors and enterprising
traders, pushed outward from their home cities on
the coast of Palestine and established commerce with
peoples across the Mediterranean world.

6. Italy's Mysterious, Splendid Etruscans

The origins of the Etruscans, a vibrant, inventive, fascinating early Italian people, are still not well understood. Most of the relatively little that is known about
their culture comes from excavations of their tombs.

Chapter 5: Early Greek Culture: The Birth of the West

The late 1980s were a time of dramatic events worldwide. Tragedies such as the explosions of the space shuttle *Challenger* and the Chernobyl nuclear power plant shocked the world out of its complacent belief that humankind had mastered nature and firmly controlled its technological creations. In U.S. politics, scandal rocked the White House when several high-ranking officials in the Ronald Reagan administration were convicted of selling arms to Iran and aiding the Nicaraguan Contra rebels. In global politics, U.S. president Ronald Reagan and Soviet president Mikhail Gorbachev signed a landmark treaty banning intermediate-range nuclear forces, marking the beginning of an era of arms control. In several parts of the world—including Beijing, China, the West Bank and Gaza Strip, and several nations of Eastern Europe—people rose up to resist oppressive governments, with varying degrees of success. In American culture, crack cocaine and inner-city poverty contributed to the development of a new and controversial music genre: gangsta rap.

Many of these events were unrelated to one another except for the fact that they occurred at about the same time. Others were linked to global developments. Greenhaven Press's World History by Era series provides students with a unique tool for examining global history in a way that allows them to appreciate the seemingly random occurrences as well as the general trends of human progress. This series divides world history—from the time of ancient Greece and Rome to the end of the second millennium—into ten discrete periods. Each volume then presents a collection of both primary and secondary documents that describe the major events of the period in chronological order. This structure provides students with a snapshot of events occurring simultaneously in all parts of the world. The reader can then see the connections between events in far-flung corners of the world. For example, the Palestinian uprising (*Intifada*) of December 1987 was near in time—if not in character and location—to similar protests in Beijing, China; Berlin, Germany; Prague, Czechoslovakia; and Bucharest, Romania. While these events were different in many ways, they all involved ordinary citizens striving for self-autonomy and democracy against governments that were attempting to impose strict controls on their civil liberties. By making the connections between these events, students can see that they comprised a global movement for democracy and human rights that profoundly impacted social and political systems worldwide.

Each volume in this series offers features to enhance students' understanding of the era of world history under discussion. An introductory essay provides an overview of the period, supplying essential context for the readings that follow. An annotated table of contents highlights the main point of each selection. A more in-depth introduction precedes each document, placing it in its particular historical context and offering biographical information about the author. A thorough chronology and index allow students to quickly reference specific events and dates. Finally, a bibliography opens up additional avenues of research. These features help to make the World History by Era series an extremely valuable tool for students researching the rise and fall of civilizations, social and political revolutions, cultural movements, scientific and technological advancements, and other events that mark the unfolding of human history throughout the world.

THE REVOLUTIONARY RISE OF THE EARLIEST CIVILIZATIONS

T he history of human civilization is still far from complete, not so much because humanity has a future (hopefully a long and bright one) still ahead of it, but rather because frightful gaps exist in our knowledge of past cultures. This is especially true of the earliest civilizations, which rose and fell in the long ages before the classical cultures of Greece and Rome transfigured Europe. We do not know exactly where and when the invention of agriculture took place, for instance, or who the first king was, or the certain identity of the first city, or where and when the biblical great flood occurred, or the date that the Egyptians began using the Nile's annual floods to aid in the growing of crops, or from where the Sumerians, Etruscans, and many other important ancient peoples originated. On these and thousands of other burning questions about the peoples and events that shaped civilization, we must be content to make only educated guesses.

In spite of our ignorance about the past, however, it must be said that the history of human civilization, as imperfect as it is, could not have been written before the nineteenth and twentieth centuries. There were some ancient historians, of course, including the Greeks Herodotus and Thucydides, Josephus the Jew, and the Romans Livy and Tacitus. But their accounts dealt with the recent figures and events of their own and a few neighboring societies. Moreover, most of what they wrote about prior ages was based on thirdhand accounts, hearsay, and myths. Because the systematic search for and preservation and study of past civilizations did not yet exist, they had little or no idea about the true identity and achievements of the peoples that preceded them. Only with the development of the science of archaeology in the past two centuries has the silent earth begun to release a torrent of information about the long and magnificent human pageant. As scholar Gilbert Highet puts it,

> Until then scarcely anyone, however learned and imaginative, had conceived the notion that the dead past was everywhere around us, beneath our feet, waiting for resurrection. Since then the past has in large measure been reborn. . . . Egypt, Iraq, Cambodia, Turkestan, Peru—from all of them mighty monuments of human will and imagination have been unearthed. With infinite effort lost languages have been recovered, forgotten scripts have been read. . . [and] vanished masterpieces of Greek poetry have emerged from the rubbish heaps of Egypt.[1]

Besides the thousands of individual relics and facts that have come to light about past civilizations, some general, overriding historical realities have become apparent. One of the most important is that the earliest human societies often had a cultural impact on one another; and that their lifestyles, customs, and discoveries profoundly influenced and shaped later cultures and nations, which, in their turn, passed on the torch of civilization. And in that way, the modern world became what it is. "The history of a single nation is unreal," says Highet, and

> the history of one civilization is incomplete unless it also includes the impacts of other nations and cultures upon it and describes their effects. . . . Half of history is the history of distinct civilizations. The other half is the story of cross-culture conflicts and cross-culture fusions.[2]

This realization—that our identities as people and as nations are a complex composite of habits, customs, ideas, institutions, and discoveries accumulated since humans began making tools and crude shelters—is more than sufficient justification for looking back on the earliest human civilizations.

The stark and somewhat humbling fact is that the human species is vastly older than human civilization. Just how much older depends somewhat on one's definition of *civilized*. Some would say that humans became civilized when they adopted a settled existence and began growing their own food (the so-called agricultural revolution); meanwhile, others hold that civilization did not begin in earnest until the first cities and writing systems appeared several thousands of years later. Former Purdue University scholar Herbert J. Muller advocates the second of these views, writing,

> *Civilization* means literally the making of cities and city life, and it is literally impossible without them. . . . The rise of the city has been the historic sign of a society on the march; it stimulated further adventure by bringing people together, pooling their efforts, promoting change by exchange, enlarging the world through contact with other peoples and cities. The great city became the center of unrest and disorder because it remained the center of creative activity. . . . Although civilization has always rested on the labor of the village world, its history is the history of Babylon, Jerusalem, Athens, Rome, Constantinople, Paris, London.[3]

Whatever starting point one chooses for civilization, there is no escaping the fact that it came late in the human story. One convenient way of looking at it is to represent the entire span of time that has elapsed since humans first began making tools (perhaps about 2 million years ago) as the face of a clock with the hands sweeping through the hours and minutes from noon till midnight. In this analogy, the beginnings of agriculture do not begin until three minutes before midnight; the first cities and writing occur somewhere around one and a half minutes before midnight; and the Industrial Revolution in Europe happens about four or five seconds before midnight. During the first eleven hours and fifty-seven minutes of the twelve hours, therefore, humans have no settled homes, no writing skills, and must rely on primitive stone tools and weapons to scratch out a living. This perhaps gives some idea of just how recent, revolutionary, and special the rise of the earliest civilizations actually was.

FROM HUNTER-GATHERERS TO FARMERS

Indeed, for hundreds of thousands of years before the advent of agriculture our human ancestors lived a simple and virtually unchanging hand-to-mouth existence. Scholars refer to this long period, in which people used stone tools, as the Paleolithic, or the Old Stone Age. (For convenience, the Paleolithic period is divided into the Lower, Middle, and Upper, the latter encompassing the period from about 40,000–30,000 to 10,000 B.C.) All available evidence suggests that those who lived in these times were nomadic hunter-gatherers, who roamed from place to place following herds of game and foraging for roots, berries, and other edible flora. As for the places they chose to live, University of Lancaster scholar John Haywood writes,

> The Upper Paleolithic people preferred to live in sheltered valleys close to fords [in rivers] which perhaps were used as regular crossing places by migrating herds. Where possible they chose south-facing caves or rock shelters to catch the warmth of the sun as much as possible. Tents and screens of hide were built to make these drafty sites more comfortable. In areas like central Europe and the steppes of the Ukraine and Russia where there was little shelter and no trees, sturdy huts were built of mammoth bones on promontories [high places] overlooking rivers. One of the most important of these sites, at Mezhirich, in the Ukraine, was occupied . . . [during] the coldest period of the last glaciation [about 16,000 B.C.]. The settlement consisted of five round huts, varying in size from 13 to 22 feet in diameter. The huts were built with an intricate framework of mammoth bones and were probably covered with mammoth hide. . . . Between the huts, pits dug into the permafrost were used as deep freezers for storing meat.[4]

It is important to emphasize that even when several such huts clustered together, as they did at Mezhirich (which may have had a population of fifty or more people), such settlements were temporary. When the herds moved on, so did the hunters and their families. Therefore, it would be misleading to describe these early settlements as true villages, a term that suggests permanence. To make it viable for successive generations to live in the same place, it was necessary to have a steady, more or less reliable and permanent food supply. And that required the domestication of plants and animals.

Identifying the exact beginnings of agriculture and pastoralism (raising and herding livestock) is difficult, partly because these developments evidently occurred several times independently, in different regions and at different times; also, each farming culture emphasized its own characteristic staple crops. As the late, noted historian Chester G. Starr put it,

> Agriculture seems to have developed independently in more than one area. In eastern Asia [i.e., China and other parts of the Far East] people began raising millet, yams, and rice. In the New World, beans, squash, potatoes, and corn were cultivated in Central America and Peru. The most important step by far was the domestication of wheat and barley by the peoples of the Near

East; from this region the idea of deliberately raising
animals and plants spread outward to most of Eurasia
and Africa.[5]

Most modern scholars agree with Starr and place the earliest
large-scale development of agriculture in the Near East perhaps
around nine thousand or ten thousand years ago. This marked
the beginning of the Neolithic, or New Stone Age. (Experts define Neolithic cultures as those that practiced agriculture but still
used stone, rather than metal, tools and weapons.) The initial
zone in which the first Near Eastern farmers and herders appeared ran through the wide belt of foothills surrounding the
plains of Mesopotamia (the region lying between and around the
Tigris and Euphrates rivers, in what is now Iraq). This belt, often
referred to as "the Fertile Crescent," stretched in an arc from
Palestine northward through Syria and eastern Anatolia (or Asia
Minor, present-day Turkey), eastward across northern Iraq, and
into the Iranian Plateau.

THE FIRST PERMANENT VILLAGES

With the growth of agriculture in the Fertile Crescent, it is not
surprising that permanent settlements arose in this region and
that these quickly matured into villages with sophisticated social
structures. Simply put, agriculture and herding provided more
food, which in turn stimulated population growth and increased
the size and complexity of human settlements. "The activities of
farming and shepherding required an intensification of group organization," says Starr. "A phenomenal increase in physical possessions resulted from the needs of more developed life, much
greater population, and more sedentary routines."[6]

By the eighth or seventh millennium B.C., some of these early
Near Eastern settlements had begun to protect themselves with
defensive walls of brick and stone. The most famous early example is the town of Jericho, in the Jordan Valley in Palestine (the
region occupied today by Israel, Jordan, and Lebanon), featuring
stone defenses enclosing an area of eleven acres. A larger fortified village, covering some thirty-two acres, flourished in the seventh and sixth millennia B.C. at Çatal Hüyük in southeastern Anatolia. (In fact, Çatal Hüyük is the largest Neolithic site in the Near
East.) The town's "square, flat-roofed houses," writes noted archaeologist Trevor Watkins,

> were built side by side like a pile of children's building
> blocks, pushed together. Access to each house was by
> means of a door at roof-level, from which a steep lad-
> der led down into the living area. Circulation [move-

ment] around the settlement was across the flat roofs. The edge of such a settlement would have presented a solid, blank wall to any intruder or attacker. Once the ladders . . . were drawn up, the settlement would have been impregnable.[7]

Unfortunately, the social and political organization of early Near Eastern settlements like Jericho and Çatal Hüyük remain largely uncertain. But some evidence suggests that religion played a prominent role in the life of the community. At Çatal Hüyük, for example, excavators discovered the remains of small shrines dating to about 6150 B.C. Bulls, and perhaps an early form of the mother goddess, were apparently worshiped at these primitive altars.

THE SETTLEMENT OF MESOPOTAMIA AND EGYPT

Eventually, probably by about 5500 B.C., the population of the upland regions of the Fertile Crescent had grown great enough to stimulate expansion southward into the Tigris and Euphrates plains. "People may have perceived that their villages were getting too crowded," suggests Near Eastern scholar Daniel C. Snell, "even if they may not have been crowded at all by later standards. And so they moved out into the forbidding frontier area, which turned out to be extremely productive agriculturally."[8]

Another, more provocative and tantalizing cause for these crucial migrations was recently proposed by a group of scholars that includes Columbia University scientists William Ryan and Walter Pitman. They point to evidence showing that before the sixth millennium B.C. the Black Sea, located directly to the north of the Fertile Crescent, was a large freshwater lake. Today, that sea is joined to the Aegean and Mediterranean Seas via two straits, the Bosphorus and the Dardenelles; originally, however, the Bosphorus was blocked by a huge earthen dam and the lake's level was hundreds of feet lower than that of the seas beyond. In about 5600 B.C., the dam burst and mighty torrents of water rushed into the Black Sea lake, flooding its shores for many miles inland. Because the date of this catastrophic event roughly coincides with that of the initial migrations of peoples southward into Mesopotamia, Ryan and Pitman suggest that these population movements were set in motion by large numbers of refugees fleeing their lakeside villages and farms. (They also speculate that the memory of the disaster gave rise to the legends of the great flood mentioned in several ancient Near Eastern texts, including the Old Testament.)

The identities of the peoples who inhabited the Mesopotamian plains in the next few millennia remain unknown, largely because they left behind few artifacts and no written records. The first important identifiable people in the area were the Sumerians, who inhabited the flatlands of southern Mesopotamia just northwest of the Persian Gulf at least by the late fourth millennium B.C. (The name *Sumer* comes from the later Babylonian name for southern Babylonia, the old Sumerian heartland. The Sumerians themselves called this region *Kengir,* meaning "Civilized Land.")

Agriculture, pastoralism, and settled life also made their appearance in another Near Eastern region, Egypt, somewhat later than in the Fertile Crescent and Mesopotamia. Hunter-gatherers had lived in the Nile River Valley since late Paleolithic times. And over time, migrants from Palestine, Lybia (west of Egypt), and Nubia (south of Egypt) entered the area. Small-scale farming may have begun in the Nile's marshlands early in Egypt's predynastic period (ca. 5500–3100 B.C.), but large-scale farming along the banks of the river, taking advantage of its yearly floods, did not begin until about 4000 B.C. or somewhat later. As had happened in Mesopotamia (and would happen again in other parts of the world), agriculture and settled life stimulated rapid and significant developments in social organization and the production of new tools, utensils, stone vessels (and eventually pottery ones), and other artifacts. During the fourth millennium B.C., two distinct cultures evolved, one in the south (called Upper Egypt because it lay closer to the Nile's source), the other in the north (Lower Egypt).

CITIES, CITY-STATES, NATIONS, AND EMPIRES

The Sumerians and Egyptians are credited with several major milestones in the development of civilization. Among the most crucial of these was the creation of the first cities, city-states, nation-states, and empires. The first cities appeared in Sumer shortly before 3000 B.C. Perhaps the first city was Eridu, then located very near the shore of the Persian Gulf (which has since that time receded about 125 miles southeastward). Uruk, farther north, is also a candidate for the first city. It is possible that Eridu was an older site used mainly as a ceremonial center and that Uruk was the first actual urban center supporting a large population. Other important Sumerian cities included Ur, Lagash, Larsa, and Nippur. These had begun as small villages, probably, like Jericho and Çatal Hüyük, covering only a few dozen acres at most. Under the Sumerians, however, their size increased manyfold. Between 3000 and 2700 B.C., for example, Uruk became a city of tens of thousands of inhabitants enclosed by a circuit wall six miles in circumference.

These early cities, like all in Mesopotamia for hundreds of years to come, were not dependent units within a larger Sumerian nation but rather independent city-states, each in a sense a tiny national unit in its own right. In the third millennium B.C., a typical Mesopotamian city-state consisted of a densely populated central town surrounded by dependent villages and farmland. Evidence shows that the Sumerian cities periodically fought among themselves for various reasons. Often, one would amass unusual power and prestige and dominate most of the others for a generation or a century or so; then the balance of power would shift and another city-state would rise to prominence. This process, in turn, helped to accelerate the development of the institution of kingship.

In Egypt, by contrast, the separate societies (or kingdoms) of Upper and Lower Egypt coalesced into a single nation-state. This achievement of unification, credited to the first pharaoh, Menes (or Narmer), occurred around 3100 B.C.[9] To hammer home the importance of unity, Menes established a new city, Memphis, at the boundary between the former rival kingdoms, making it his capital; he also adopted a crown that combined the main features of the crowns worn by the leaders of those kingdoms.

The trend toward unification and larger political units took a different, more violent course in Mesopotamia. Amidst its array of competing city-states, it was only a matter of time before one strong ruler, from either Sumer or Mesopotamia's northern reaches, was able to conquer the entire region and create an empire. That ruler was Sargon the Great, who was born in about 2370 B.C. in Akkad (the region of northern Mesopotamia in which Assyria would later rise). Not long before, a number of Akkadian rulers had managed to unite the central Mesopotamian cities into a national unit. Now Sargon founded the city of Akkad (or Agade) and went on to attack and absorb all of the Sumerian city-states. In this way, the lower and upper halves of Mesopotamia were united into what was more or less a single nation.

Sargon and his immediate successors then expanded eastward and westward beyond the plains, conquering neighboring sections of the Near East and creating the world's first empire. For the first time in human history (and unfortunately not the last), imperialism—one nation's drive to dominate and control its neighbors—had come to operate on a grand scale. The Sargonid empire became a model followed by other Near Eastern peoples in the centuries that followed. Fairly consistently, the main rivals in the region were the Assyrians, based in Mesopotamia's northern hills and plains; the Babylonians, whose power was centered in the southeast, the former Sumerian heartland; and the Egyptians; although from time to time other groups and peoples entered the fray and vied for supremacy along with them.

EARLY PEOPLES OF THE FAR EAST AND EUROPE

During the late third and early second millennia B.C., as these peoples struggled to control the Near East, other early civilizations were flourishing far to the east and west. As in the cases of the Tigris-Euphrates and Nile, two great eastern cultures grew up along major rivers. In India, the Indus River gave rise to what modern scholars call the Harappan culture, named after one of its two largest cities, Harappa (the other being Mohenjo Daro). Each of these impressive cities was over a square mile in extent and featured well-planned main streets up to thirty feet wide and thousands of brick houses. According to noted Australian scholar A.L. Basham, the crops and animals that sustained these cities included

> wheat, barley, peas, and sesamum, the latter still an important crop in India for its seeds, which provide edible oil. There is no clear evidence of the cultivation of rice, but the Harappan people grew and used cotton. It is not certain that irrigation was known, although this is possible. The main domestic animals known to modern India had already been tamed—humped and humpless cattle, buffaloes, goats, sheep, pigs, asses, dogs, and the domestic fowl. The elephant was well known, and may also have been tamed.[10]

Still farther east, in China, a civilization grew up along the banks of the Huang Ho, or Yellow, River. As in Mesopotamia, the advent of agriculture stimulated the growth of a settled population; by 2000 B.C. (or perhaps earlier), numerous small independent city-states had risen along the river and its main tributaries. In the 1500s B.C. a dynasty of rulers called the Shang conquered a large number of these states, just as the Sargonids had in Mesopotamia a few centuries before.

In the same years the Shang were conquering their neighbors in China, thousands of miles to the west Europe's first high civilization was flourishing on Crete. This large island, located in the eastern Mediterranean Sea several miles southeast of the Greek mainland, was then inhabited by a people that modern scholars call the Minoans (after a legendary king named Minos). During the first half of the second millennium B.C., the Minoans dominated seagoing trade in the area; examples of their pottery and other artifacts have been found as far away as Egypt and Palestine.

The Mycenaeans, who originally inhabited the Greek mainland and overran the Minoan sphere in the fifteenth and fourteenth centuries B.C., were also vigorous traders. Indeed, Mycenaean trade routes extended westward to Italy and Sardinia.
These enterprising, warlike people, who spoke an early form of
Greek, were also prodigious builders. "Their palaces," said the
late, great classical scholar C.M. Bowra,

> were built within formidable citadels with walls 10 feet
> thick, and some of their royal tombs were enormous
> beehive structures made of stones weighing, sometimes,
> as much as 120 tons. They were also immensely wealthy,
> especially in metals, and most especially in gold. . . . In
> Mycenaean tombs, diggers have found death masks and
> breastplates of gold. . . . Decisions of the Mycenaean
> king and his court were carried out by an officialdom
> consisting, in diminishing order, of military leaders, ad-
> ministrative officials, charioteers, and mayors of the
> group of villages that surrounded the city.[11]

CIVILIZATION: A COOPERATIVE EFFORT

The Mycenaeans' prosperous civilization collapsed, along with
several other cultures in Anatolia and other parts of the Near
East, circa 1200–1100 B.C. The cause or causes of this catastrophe,
in which large numbers of cities were destroyed, never to be rebuilt, is uncertain.[12] What is more definite is that Greece sank into
a dark age of poverty and illiteracy.

However, the political and commercial vacuums created by the
upheavals were quickly filled in other regions of the Mediterranean and Near East by enterprising peoples. By the late
eleventh century B.C. the Phoenicians, a maritime people inhabiting the coast of Palestine, had taken over the lucrative Mediterranean trade routes once monopolized by the Mycenaeans. At the
same time, in Palestine, David and Solomon, the early Hebrew
kings later immortalized in the Judeo-Christian Old Testament,
were creating the first kingdom of Israel and erecting the first version of the great temple in Jerusalem. These early Jews could not
have foreseen that their then unusual religious concept of a single,
invisible god, an idea almost all other ancient peoples rejected out
of hand, would become the basis for three of the world's great
faiths—Judaism, Christianity, and Islam. Ancient Israel split into
two kingdoms—Israel and Judah—in the tenth century B.C. In 722
B.C. the Assyrians, who were then enjoying their greatest burst of
conquest and expansion, conquered and absorbed Israel, leaving
Judah to survive precariously in Assyria's shadow a while longer.

At the moment that Assyrian troops were laying waste to Israel's cities and farms and carrying out aggressions against other Near Eastern peoples, the neighboring continent of Europe may have seemed relatively quiet by contrast. Nowhere in Europe had large cities or powerful, aggressive nation-states yet come into being. But beneath the surface, momentous forces were at work. Slowly and inexorably, the peoples who would later come to dominate not only that continent, but also, through their descendants, much of the rest of the world, were establishing their religious and cultural identities. In Greece, the Dark Age had given way to a great age of invention (writing and literature), expansion (overseas colonization), and political experimentation (the first steps on the road to democracy). Meanwhile, in central Italy a group of crude farming villages were coalescing to form a single city called Rome. At this time it was a small, dingy, rather unimpressive place; in later centuries, however, it would rise to dominate the entire Mediterranean world. The eventual fusion of Greek and Roman societies would come to be known as classical civilization, which would eventually provide the cultural underpinnings of modern Europe.

However great and splendid Greco-Roman civilization may appear to people today, it is essential to realize two important and humbling facts. First, like all peoples before them, the Greeks and Romans began as simple, largely uncultured farmers and villagers. Second, and even more important, they did not invent from scratch all of the skills and ideas that eventually made them so successful and influential. Instead, many aspects of their cultures were borrowed from older civilizations, which had themselves built on the concepts developed by even older cultures. Archaeologists are still engaged in an arduous but exciting attempt to trace and reconstruct the origins of tool making, language, farming and animal raising, religious worship, writing and literature, various arts and crafts, and all the other crucial bits and pieces of what we call human civilization. The more they learn, the more they realize that its creation has been a cooperative effort, with input from many peoples in many places and ages.

NOTES

1. Gilbert Highet, introduction to *The Light of the Past,* ed. Marshall B. Davidson. New York: American Heritage, 1965, p. 6.

2. Highet, *Light of the Past,* p. 6.

3. Herbert J. Muller, *The Uses of the Past.* New York: New American Library, 1952, p. 58.

4. John Haywood, *The Illustrated History of Early Man*. New York: Smithmark, 1995, p. 71.

5. Chester G. Starr, *A History of the Ancient World*. New York: Oxford University Press, 1991, pp. 17–18.

6. Starr, *A History of the Ancient World*, pp. 18–19.

7. Trevor Watkins, "The Beginnings of Warfare," in *Warfare in the Ancient World*, ed. Sir John Hackett. New York: Facts On File, 1989, p. 16.

8. Daniel C. Snell, *Life in the Ancient Near East, 3100–332 B.C.* New Haven, CT: Yale University Press, 1997, p. 14.

9. The term *pharaoh* is an ancient Greek version of the even more ancient Egyptian phrase *per-aa*, meaning "great house." It originally referred to the royal palace and was not used by the Egyptians themselves to describe their kings until the New Kingdom (which began in 1550 B.C.).

10. A.L. Basham, *The Wonder That Was India*. New York: Taplinger, 1967, p. 18.

11. C.M. Bowra, *Classical Greece*. New York: Time-Life, 1965, pp. 31–32.

12. Historians have advanced a number of theories to explain this widespread catastrophe. Some think that rapid local population growth among the semibarbarous tribes inhabiting the vast steppes north of the Black and Caspian Seas caused them to migrate southward in search of new lands, destroying all in their path. Others suggest that climatic factors, such as a prolonged dry spell, caused these mass migrations. Another theory holds that a large portion of the destruction was caused by civil conflicts, economic collapse, and other crises within the Near Eastern states themselves. And still another view, advanced recently by Robert Drews of Vanderbilt University, is that military innovations among the "periphery" peoples living near the borders of these kingdoms suddenly gave their foot soldiers the ability to defeat the chariot corps that had for centuries been the mainstay of Near Eastern armies. For a detailed discussion, see Robert Drews, *The End of the Bronze Age: Changes in Warfare and the Catastrophe ca. 1200 B.C.* Princeton, NJ: Princeton University Press, 1993.

In the Mists of Time: Humanity Before Cities and Writing

— PROLOGUE —

HUMANS IN THE STONE AGE: A FIGHT FOR SURVIVAL

CHESTER G. STARR

The late, great historian Chester G. Starr, of the University of Michigan, composed the following tract outlining the major developments of the Upper, or late, Paleolithic period. Paleolithic means "Old Stone Age." Experts generally define it as the age in which the first humans made and used simple chipped stone tools, beginning about two million years ago. The period is usually subdivided into the Lower, Middle, and Upper Paleolithic. As Starr explains, the last of these three divisions, beginning about 30,000 B.C. (or earlier) and ending with the emergence of agriculture about 10,000 to 8,000 B.C. (the beginning of the Neolithic, or "New Stone Age"), witnessed the most concentrated amount of material and social progress among primitive humans. Human culture spread all over the globe; the earliest examples of community, religious, and artistic expression emerged; and stone-age hunters began to pose a serious threat to other animal species.

M an is the oldest domesticated animal. His culture, a term which has been well defined as meaning "all those things which are *not* inherited biologically," has been a powerful force in determining his development. Throughout the Paleolithic period the outside physical world underwent great changes in temperature, elevation of mountains along with volcanic activity, and the spread or retreat of mammoth ice sheets;

and mankind adapted its ways of life as best it could to suit this rugged environment.

Commonly men lived in the open. At least by the Gravettian era [ca. 22,000–18,000 B.C.] in Upper Paleolithic times they built lean-tos and other simple skin tents, but evidence of this type of habitat has rarely survived. In cool climates, in winter, or in dangerous terrain our primitive ancestors were at times driven to dwell in caves; this custom was particularly evident in Neanderthal times [about 110,000 years ago]. Cave dwellers preferred sites with a southern exposure, a good source of water nearby, and a view of adequate hunting grounds. Here men might dwell for long periods and build up large deposits of garbage, into which their tools would fall and in which their own remains were interred casually or carefully. . . . Man early knew fire, but the first certain evidence on this point comes from France about 230,000 years ago.

Paleolithic men made their living by gathering food. Adult males probably hunted; females and children sought out edible berries, plants, and fruits. Their basic needs could probably have been met, to judge from modern simple societies, by only a few hours of work each day. Across the long Paleolithic period only stone tools have survived in any quantity. These are enough to support very significant conclusions. First, early mankind did not everywhere use the same types of objects. Second, progress at first was extremely slow as men fought to survive, but speeded up toward the end; and, third, by this latter point new ideas as to how to make tools were certainly transmitted from one area to another.

ADVANCES IN TOOL-MAKING

The various assemblages of stone tools which were used in different regions or succeeded earlier patterns in the same district have been patiently analyzed by anthropologists. Generally men preferred stones that could be worked by fracture with some precision, for example, flint (which is harder than steel) or obsidian. In the manufacture of tools either flakes were struck off, or a suitable piece of stone was reduced to a core; both methods of producing tools were used concurrently.

The earliest men in Africa and Asia made crudely chipped pebbles of lava, quartz, or quartzite. By the early part of the second (Mindel) ice age [about 125,000 years ago] the inhabitants of Africa, western Asia, and southern Europe had learned to process cores into a distinctive, all-purpose cutting and scraping tool. This is commonly but incorrectly called a hand-ax; beside it appear rude flake tools, stone balls, and other items. The culture of this era, named Abbevillian in its first phases and then Acheulian from French sites, was remarkably uniform from the Cape of Good Hope to England on the one extreme and to India on the other. Alongside it, however, were peoples (now called Clactonian, Tayacian, etc.) who did not use hand-axes proper and perhaps did not hunt but gathered food instead. For hundreds of thousands of years men everywhere lived in the same general ways with these types of tools. Then, by the third interglacial period (Riss-Würm), which ended about 70,000 B.C., the Eurasian cultures of the Lower or Early Paleolithic gave rise to assemblages of more specialized flake tools, which are collectively termed Mousterian. This is the culture of Neanderthal man, who dominated the Middle Paleolithic era and was a skillful hunter with wooden spears and stones.

Within the fourth (Würm) glacial period, human beings speeded up their progress remarkably in making tools and in other respects. This rise in tempo, which produced the Upper Paleolithic about 30,000 B.C., corresponds roughly with the arrival of modern man, though it is by no means certain that the two events were interconnected. What is visible is that improved social organization and technical equipment allowed man to exploit nature not just by scavenging but by hunting reindeer, bison, and other animals. Ornaments such as beads began to appear in such profusion as to suggest to some scholars the beginnings of social differentiation. Whereas the Lower Paleolithic had known only a few types of tools, which were widely used over Eurasia, a large variety of Upper Paleolithic cultures can be distinguished in Europe alone, in addition to other well-defined cultures in Asia and Africa. As man progressed, it is more obvious that there was no *one* way by which he must live.

The European sequence in the last stage of the Paleolithic age can be approximately dated. First came the Chatelperronian, which mingled with earlier Mousterian forms, and then the more significant Aurignacian cultures (to about 22,000 B.C.): the discoveries at Cro-Magnon in France attest the presence of *Homo sapiens sapiens* in this era, and fishing surely appears. Then, after the Gravettian (22–18,000) and the Solutrean (18–15,000) eras, there arises the marvelous stage of Magdalenian culture. The latter covers about 15,000–8000 B.C. Throughout these successive stages changes can be observed in many aspects. Craftsmen worked their stone tools ever more skillfully; the symmetrical, finely chipped laurel-leaf points made in the Solutrean technique, in particular, are justly famous. At the end of the era the employment of microliths, small stones set in bone or attached to arrows, was borrowed from Africa. Other examples, too, attest the diffusion of techniques and materials; shells have been found, for instance, in burials in central France, which originated along the Mediterranean coast 200 miles away. Hafted tools appeared more commonly from the Aurignacian era onward; stone flakes were worked into gravers and scrapers, tools with which yet other tools could be made by sawing, grinding, and boring out of bone and antler. In Magdalenian times came needles and harpoons, which attest improvement both in clothing and in fishing.

INTELLECTUAL DEVELOPMENT

Besides this material advance we can begin to see, though only dimly, swifter intellectual progress in the Upper Paleolithic period. To speak of progress over the course of human history may seem dangerous, if one is depressed today about the present situation of mankind; but there is no better corrective to undue pessimism than to see how many difficulties our ancestors surmounted. From the first the use of tools is an impressive testimony to the unique ability of man to reason out a solution to a problem of life and to fashion means of protecting himself from the brute forces of nature. While he perhaps came to many of his discoveries by accident, the role of deliberate curiosity and intent cannot be disregarded.

One of the most fascinating developments in the Upper Paleolithic era is the appearance of visible testimony that man lived to do more than simply hunt for food. Beads and other jewelry were made of animal teeth, shells, ivory, and so on; tattooing apparently was practiced. Bone flutes and other instruments now turn up to indicate the existence of music and probably of the dance. Some bone and ivory carvings seem to have been made purely for the joy of creation. Figurines of women with pronounced sexual characteristics but almost without facial features, the so-called Venuses in ivory, stone, and clay which appear from Gravettian times on may also have represented early man's ideal of womanhood or may have had religious significance as part of a cult of generative forces.

Even more tantalizing are the carvings on rocks in Europe and in parts of the Sahara now uninhabitable and also the paintings which have been found on cave walls in France and Spain. Beginning about 28,000 B.C., men ventured deep into hidden recesses, torch in hand, and painted animal after animal; at Lascaux some 400 oxen, deer, horses, bison and other figures survive. The artists' palette included brown, yellow, red, and black. In its superb, direct realism the drawing of animals was not to be matched for millennia. Men on the other hand are shown in distorted, shorthand form, and the symbols used in rock carvings were sometimes almost geometric and conventionalized.

The purpose of this work was surely not always artistic self-expression, and modern students initially assumed that it was basically magical. By drawing pictures of the animals they hunted men must have felt they would have a better chance of finding them in the real world. Sometimes the artist showed a spear or dart sticking out of the animal; at other times painting and sculpture reveal indentations as though they had been hit by a spear. While faith in the presence of spirits, which is called animism, recurs often in later societies, the objectives of cave painters may have included a variety of other purposes, such as the commemoration of social gatherings. Another branch of religious beliefs alongside those created by problems of subsistence and the generation of human life is attested by the deliberate burial of the dead, at times with objects to be used after death, which occurs from Neanderthal times. Sometimes the bones of the dead are covered by red ocher, perhaps to represent the life-giving qualities of blood; one Neanderthal burial has been proven to have been strewn with wild flowers, though no graves of this era have any beads.

COOPERATION AND COMMUNITY

On other important, nonmaterial aspects of early life we can only speculate. The development of speech did not leave visible marks, though it is most unlikely that culture could have progressed far until men used language. There is no evidence either that cave men secured their mates by force or that the mothers were the dominant element in primitive societies, to cite another modern theory. Women, true, must have been economically as important as were men, as gatherers of wild plants; but anthropologists feel that the monogamous, enduring family patterns of most later societies may have evolved only slowly. The long period of human dependence in childhood, as well as the risks of illness and injury, surely forced human beings to live together fairly permanently in packs rather than in single family cells. Yet from early time men had to learn to channel purely instinctive emotional and sexual urges if they were to emerge out of an animal state and form successful social groups. Since the packs lived by food-gathering, the total population was extremely small, perhaps not more than one person on the average per square mile even in good territories; but the presence of large masses of animal bones at the foot of cliffs shows that communal hunts took place by the Late Paleolithic stage.

A famous English philosopher, Thomas Hobbes, once defined the life of early man as "solitary, poor, nasty, brutish and short."

Others have, with equally little justification, idealized our first ancestors in a cult of the Noble Savage, not yet beset by the cankers of advanced civilization. Two specific discoveries in recent years may perhaps suggest that the attitudes of men toward each other varied as much in the Paleolithic era as in more recent times. One is the skeleton of a Neanderthal male, arthritic and with only one arm from childhood, who apparently tended the communal fire in an Iraq cave for his fellows. The other is likewise a Neanderthal skeleton, from the Mt. Carmel caves of Palestine, which was clearly marked by the impress of a spearpoint. In any case life was indeed short; examples of early modern man show that 54 per cent died by 20 and 35 per cent between 21 and 40. If one considers just those people of the Neanderthal and early *Homo sapiens sapiens* periods who lived past 20, most women were dead by 30 while most men lived past that age.

HUMANS SPREAD ACROSS THE GLOBE

Even as a food-gatherer, man had spread over the entire globe. In North America skeletal remains go back at least 12,000 years, but evidence for an earlier date is mounting. In the Upper Paleolithic period men had devised a material and social structure capable of supporting them wherever they went in pursuit of game.

To us they may still look primitive, but certainly they had become exceedingly dangerous to all other forms of animal life. Over the hundreds of thousands of years we have already considered, the biological and cultural evolution of mankind had given it considerable physical and mental dexterity and also a useful complement of tools by which men could extend their powers. Many of our basic social attitudes and views of the surrounding world were surely formed in these distant ages.

As a result of the quickening tempo of development in the Upper Paleolithic stage, men achieved an intellectual and technical level far beyond anything in the past. They were, at least in some areas, ready to take a giant step forward. In doing so they may have been encouraged by the climatic changes after 8000 B.C. As the glaciers began that retreat which is still going on, the climate in Europe proper turned rainier, the forests grew, and the fauna moved northward. Northern Africa and western Asia had a damp climate; not until later did the Sahara and parts of the Near East begin to dry up as the rain-bearing winds shifted northward. Similar physical developments, however, had occurred frequently in earlier periods; only now was man sufficiently advanced to change his mode of life so as to fit the altered natural surroundings.

The transitional phase at the end of the Paleolithic era is sometimes given the name of the Mesolithic period. In the Near East it may extend from about 10,000 to 8000 B.C.; but in central and northern Europe it reached on down to about 3000 B.C. Like all transitional epochs this period is marked by an uneven speed of advance, as different peoples gave up their old ways more or less reluctantly; and the rise of new ways of life is difficult to detect in the first stages. Archeological interest in the era is so very recent that we may be sure any preliminary conclusions today about the emergence of agriculture will have to be revised extensively in the next few years.

Over most of the earth it is clear that men simply continued to hunt their food. The brilliant Magdalenian stage in Europe collapsed as the climate changed and fauna moved accordingly. In the duller age that followed, the inhabitants of north-central Europe near the Baltic, called Maglemosian from a Danish site, improved further their food-collecting techniques and elaborated their physical equipment for life. Here men turned to exploit the resources not only of the land but also of the seacoast, which grew longer as the seas rose at the end of the ice age. Eventually they collected and ate oysters with such enthusiasm that they left kitchen middens or banks of oyster shells many feet thick. Maglemosian men also fished from canoes with nets and hooks, gathered nuts and fruits, and hunted with bow and arrow as well as with the spear. Thanks to their intensive exploitation of available food resources, such people could become more sedentary. Perhaps as a result they domesticated the dog and tended to polish stone tools so that they could work wood better with adzes, chisels, and gouges.

ON THE BRINK OF A REVOLUTION

Cultures like that of the Maglemosian area represented a dead end, from which further progress would be limited and slow. To break out of the inherent limitations of the food-gathering society required a veritable revolution. This was the discovery of agriculture, which took place primarily in the area now known as the Near East.

In this district, stretching from the eastern end of the Mediterranean inland along the hills at the northern edge of Mesopotamia to Iran, men had lived since earliest times. A fairly large number of Neanderthal-type specimens have been found in the area; by shortly after 10,000 B.C. an almost sedentary population resided in the caves of the region, from Mt. Carmel in Palestine to the Caspian Sea.

The inhabitants of the Carmel rock-shelters and the nearby open settlements of Palestine, whom we may take as an example, are called Natufians. They lived in the same locality so continuously that they could adorn the terraces in front of their rock-shelters with low stone structures, the purpose of which has not yet been fathomed, and they rebuilt their huts several times on the same spot. They also employed a fairly extensive equipment of physical objects, both useful and decorative. Their dead, for instance, were carefully buried with beads and head-dresses. These people must have had an assured food supply. In large part they were hunters and fishers with the usual Mesolithic equipment of harpoons, fishhooks, spears, bows, and so on; but they seem to have been on the verge of discovering agriculture. Natufian man certainly reaped the wild grasses of the neighborhood with straight bone sickles set with small flint teeth, and then processed the kernels with milling and pounding stones; huts at times had built-in storage places and fireplaces.

In the hills of Iraq people in a similar state of development lived in pit houses which were grouped in regular villages. The ancestors of both wheat and barley grew wild in these upland districts, which enjoyed a regular, adequate rainfall; root vegetables, which may have been more useful before baking and brewing were discovered, were also available. Men of this area, as in Palestine, were sufficiently advanced in social and technical organization to settle down. The next step, to raise food deliberately, may seem inevitable, but it was nonetheless an amazing break with earlier customs.

LIFE AMONG THE HUNTER-GATHERERS

JOHN HAYWOOD

For hundreds of thousands of years during the Old Stone Age (Paleolithic times, ending about 10,000 years ago), humans obtained their life-giving food supplies by hunting and gathering. Researchers are not completely certain about their methods, lifestyles, and attitudes. However, in this illuminating essay, University of Lancaster scholar John Haywood shows how studies of the societies of modern hunter-gatherers have helped to shed light on their prehistoric counterparts. He makes the point that all early hunter-gatherers were nomadic. He then describes their hunting strategies, basic social unit (the band), diet, division of labor, and other important elements of everyday life.

P aleolithic humans all depended on hunting and gathering to provide the essentials of life. Many of these Paleolithic hunter-gatherer groups have left rich archeological remains, but there is only so much that these can tell us about an ancient pre-literate society. Interpreting artifacts which had a symbolic meaning, such as art, a burial, or a ritual structure, is very difficult because the people whose minds carried and understood that meaning are gone. At least with artifacts we can see what they looked like and make an intelligent guess at their meaning or purpose but some of the most important aspects of human behavior leave few material traces. How were Paleolithic hunting parties organized? What kind of family structures did they have? How did they see their place in the world? What were relations between the sexes like? How were disputes settled? The list could be a long one.

One way to get an insight into the ways of life of Paleolithic hunters and gatherers is by drawing analogies from the behavior of the few hunter-gatherer societies which survived into the modern age. Anthropologists recognize two types of hunter-gatherer societies, the nomadic "generalized hunter-gatherer" and the rarer sedentary "complex hunter-gatherer." All Paleolithic hunter-gatherers were of the generalized variety, complex hunter-gatherer societies did not evolve until after the Ice Age [which ended about 10,000 years ago].

We need to be careful in the conclusions we draw from modern hunter-gatherer societies. Although the generalized hunter-gatherer way of life is well over a million years old, it is not static. The behavior of hunter-gatherers is in fact very flexible and adaptive (it has to be) and their customs, habits, and beliefs may often be of relatively recent origin. Modern generalized hunter-gatherers are largely confined to environments which Paleolithic man would have regarded as marginal, such as rainforests, coniferous forests, and deserts. Arctic hunters, like the Inuit, live in conditions which are not dissimilar to those which must have been experienced by Upper Paleolithic man in Europe and Siberia but most of the big game which flourished on the Ice Age tundras is now extinct. Modern hunter-gatherers may then live more uncertain lives than the majority of their Paleolithic forebears did. However, modern generalized hunter-gatherers do share the same basic problems that faced Paleolithic hunter-gatherers, so it is likely that they also shared similar social and economical arrangements. "Shared" is the operative word because there are now no pristine hunter-gatherer societies left in the world: those few peoples who continue to live in this way have all in recent decades been exposed to the strong and usually destructive and demoralizing influence of Western civilization.

THE FIRST AFFLUENT SOCIETY?

For many centuries, hunter-gatherers were believed by Europeans to lead lives of extreme hardship and deprivation. According to the seventeenth-century English philosopher Thomas Hobbes their state could be summarized thus: "No arts; no letters; no society; and which is worse of all, continual fear and danger of a violent death; and the life of man, solitary, poor, nasty, brutish, and short." Therefore, when anthropologists finally began to take hunter-gatherer societies seriously in the post-war period, it came as something of a shock to discover that their lives were not like that at all. Hunter-gatherers rarely went short of food and what was more, even in the marginal environments to which they had been confined by the twentieth century, they did not have to work very hard to get it. The Dobe !Kung people of the Kalahari desert, for instance, are able to provide all the basics of life for themselves by about two to three hours work a day, depending on the season. The rest of their time is to be spent at leisure, either gossiping and socializing, telling stories, playing games, or resting. This compares very favorably with the modern affluent lifestyle in which commuting, shopping, cooking, and household chores must be added to a 40-hour working week before leisure can begin. Not for nothing, though with some exaggeration, have the hunter-gatherers been styled the "first affluent society."

REDUCING COMPETITION

Hunter-gatherer affluence has been achieved by social adaptations which are designed to suppress competition for resources. Competition, so we are told, is a good thing in an industrialized society but it is potentially deadly to the hunter-gatherer. The main problem faced by hunter-gatherers is how to obtain reliable food supplies in a world where the availability of plants and animals is unpredictably variable. Hunter-gatherers are totally dependent on the natural productivity of the environment, they cannot, as farming or industrialized peoples can, step up production to meet increased demand. Uncontrolled demand for resources would quickly lead to their overexploitation and starvation for all (this may yet happen to our industrialized society, of course). Hunter-gatherers therefore limit population growth and have an economic system based on sharing resources to reduce damaging competition.

Hunter-gatherers have learned that if their lifestyle is to be sustainable, they must maintain their numbers well below (usually between 20 and 60 percent of) the theoretical maximum carrying capacity of their environment. This ensures that under normal conditions everyone in the group can live well for very little expenditure of effort and that in bad years nobody starves. In practice this means that hunter-gatherer societies go to great lengths to limit their population by discouraging early marriage, weaning infants late to suppress fertility, and exposing [leaving outside to die] surplus babies. The latter might seem harsh but parents know that the survival of their existing children could be threatened by too many new mouths to feed. Also, generalized hunter-gatherer bands need to be mobile and it is impractical for a mother to have more than one infant to carry at a time. These measures are usually successful in restraining population growth below 0.001 percent per year and typically hunter-gatherer population densities are very low. A tundra environment, for instance, can sustain a theoretical maximum hunter-gatherer density of no more than 0.05 people per km^2 (0.3861 square miles) and in practice only 20–60 percent of this. Put another way, a band of 30 Inuit caribou hunters would need a range of around 3000km^2 (1158.3 square miles). Even in richer environments such as savannahs, steppes, prairies, and the game-rich tundras of Upper Paleolithic Europe, population densities could rarely have exceeded 0.1 people per km^2 (i.e. a band would still need around 300km^2). Historically, their small numbers and need for a great deal of space has made hunter-gatherers very vulnerable to encroachment by more numerous fanning peoples, to the extent that the hunter-gatherer way of life is now almost extinct.

THE BAND FORMS THE BASIC SOCIAL UNIT

The typical unit of social organization among generalized hunter-gatherers is the band. Bands are usually between 30 and 50 strong. A larger band than this would exhaust the local food sources so quickly that it would be forever on the move; a smaller band would find it hard to raise enough adult men for a successful hunting party. Archeological sites from many parts of the world show that this has been the average band size since at least Upper Paleolithic times. Bands are always egalitarian and exhibitionist behavior or attempts to coerce other band members against their will are always suppressed. Because of their power to communicate with the spirit world, shamans or witch-doctors are normally the most feared and influential people in hunter-gatherer society. All food and property is shared within the band and if anyone asks for anything, it is always willingly given. This is not generosity but enlightened self-interest. A hunter will, on average, make a kill only once every 4–10 days. If a hunter kept the whole of his kill to himself, he would have more than he could eat some of the time and nothing at all at others. By sharing his kill with others, the hunter can be confident that others will do the same with him: if he has a run of bad luck he knows that he will not go hungry nor is he forced to compete for game with other band members, so reducing the chances of over-hunting. Some people inevitably contribute more food than others but anyone who abuses the system and tries to live off the labor of others will simply be excluded from the band.

Generalized hunter-gatherers do not belong to tribes as such (by definition a tribe has leadership) but bands do form wide-ranging alliances with other bands. These alliances serve the same function at an inter-band level as food-sharing does within the band: it suppresses competition for resources and evens out irregularities in food supplies. If one band has a bumper crop of nuts or other plant food in its territory, it will invite allied bands to come and share it. Likewise, if animal migration routes change unexpectedly, a band will share its hunting grounds with its allies, as the Chippewayan Indians of Canada did. If a band is faced with a critical food shortage in its own territory, it can simply go and visit an allied band and ask to be fed. These alliances are essential to the survival of hunter-gatherer bands in bad years and they are continually maintained by a complex social life. All the bands may come together for a short time every year to celebrate religious festivals. Shamanistic rituals induce an ecstatic trance-like condition in worshippers and shared religious experiences of this kind create particularly strong emotional ties between individuals. Festivals were also occasions to exchange gifts of stone for toolmaking and luxuries like decorative seashells or beads. It is thought that some of the most important sites of Upper Paleolithic cave art in Europe served as similar ritual centers. There is also a constant to-ing and fro-ing of visitors between bands during the year, maintaining individual friendships. European settlers in Australia misinterpreted the Aboriginal habit of "going walkabout" as mere aimless wandering, when it was in fact an important part of their adaptive strategy. Another means of cementing alliances is by arranging marriages to create kinship links between bands. So important is this that it is rare for hunter-gatherer societies to permit marriage within the band (this helps prevent inbreeding too).

Disputes over women are the most common cause when alliances break down. Violence is usually limited and peace is easily patched up as soon as one side has proved itself the stronger. Feuds with bands outside the alliance network are not uncommon and though they are rarely prosecuted with great vigor, hostilities can continue for generations. Disputes within bands are usually settled by peer group pressure but in serious cases the dissident minority may leave to join another band or try to survive alone. Crime is virtually unknown and there is no motive for theft as one only has to ask for something for it to be given and it is, in any case, impossible to accumulate more possessions than can be carried. Violently disruptive people may be expelled from the group, in which case they would probably starve, or in extreme cases they might be killed by their fellows.

MOBILITY IS ESSENTIAL

The technology of hunter-gatherers is determined largely by the environment and the need for mobility. Most hunter-gatherers need to move on to find new food sources about once a month, so they cannot acquire much in the way of possessions and their technology must be lightweight and easily portable. This is not a problem for those living in warm climates as they need neither clothes nor shelter: an Aborigine needs only spears, spear thrower, throwing sticks, and bags to carry a few tools. On the other hand, to cope with the demanding arctic environment, the Inuit's survival depends on a complex technology of spears, bows, harpoons, fishing tackle, multi-layered clothing, stone cooking pots, sledges, and skin boats. However, as they can store food easily they do not need to be as mobile as other hunter-gatherers. It is not surprising that in warm climates hunter-gatherers waste little effort building shelters which they know they will soon abandon but this is also the case in cold climates. For example the Athabascan Indians of the Yukon relied only on surprisingly flimsy tents to survive savage winter weather. Only relatively sedentary hunter-gatherers, like the Northwest Coast Indians of North America who exploit rich salmon rivers, build substantial dwellings. The same is true of artistic traditions. Many hunter-gatherers from Upper Paleolithic Europe to twentieth-century Australia have painted cave walls, and body ornaments are almost universal, but only complex sedentary hunter-gatherer societies have developed any monumental art. For a long time, the simplicity of hunter-gatherer technology blinded Europeans to the richness of these peoples' oral traditions of myth and sto-rytelling, which are often very sophisticated.

OBTAINING THE PROPER DIET

Generalized hunter-gatherers exploit the widest possible range of food sources as insurance against any one of them failing. The Dobe !Kung could recognize over a hundred plant foods and could order them in a hierarchy from most to least nutritious. As far as possible, the most nutritious foods, such as the mon-gomongo nut (enough of which can be gathered and processed in half an hour or so to provide a day's nutrition), were exploited first and the least nutritious only in times of hardship. Main-taining a correct balance of protein and carbohydrate in the diet is essential because proteins cannot be digested properly with-out the energy provided from carbohydrates: it would be quite possible to starve to death on a diet which consisted only of lean meat. Obtaining carbohydrates is relatively easy for hunter-gatherers in tropical environments where a wide range of seeds, nuts, and roots is available, but it is a greater problem in higher latitudes where most carbohydrates must come from animal fat. By late winter wild animals are carrying very little fat, so hunters suffer annual carbohydrate crises until animals begin to fatten again on spring growth. The Upper Paleolithic hunters of Europe must certainly have experienced similar problems. As wild animals always carry less fat than domestic animals, even at the best of times fat may be in short supply and it is always eaten with relish by hunter-gatherers. The hunters with the least problems on this score are the Inuit on the shores of the Arctic Ocean who obtain enough fat from the blubber of marine mammals not only to eat but to provide winter heat and light.

In tropical environments where food is available all year round, hunter-gatherers rarely store food even overnight, such is their confidence in their knowledge of the environment. In higher latitudes storage becomes essential and hunter-gatherers had to learn to dry meat and fish for winter supplies. Arctic dwellers like the Inuit are the most fortunate hunter-gatherers in this respect as almost unlimited amounts of food can be stored in natural deep freezes such as pits dug in the permafrost.

DIVISION OF LABOR

Men and women in hunter-gatherer societies have clearly differentiated roles: the men hunt while the women, whose child rearing responsibilities make them less mobile, gather vegetable foods near the camp. In tropical environments where plant foods are abundant, it is the women who provide most of the band's food. Among the Dobe !Kung the men spend more time talking about hunting than actually doing it but the women gather every day. Nevertheless, despite the fundamental importance of plant foods to the !Kung, meat is regarded as the most prestigious food by both men and women. Away from the tropics where plant foods are very seasonal, or even absent altogether, it is the men who provide most of the food. The (now extinct) Yahgan people of Tierra del Fuego had few plant foods but in coastal areas the women were able to make a significant contribution of food by gathering shellfish on the seashore. Among the Inuit, who have no plant foods at all, virtually 100 percent of the food is provided by the men (the women have plenty of other work to occupy their time, however). This division of labor is likely to be of very long standing and was probably a characteristic of early hominid societies. Apart from the different sex roles, there are no other specialized roles in generalized hunter-gatherer societies, everybody, even the shamans, must be a jack-of-all-trades.

THE EMERGENCE OF AGRICULTURE AND RAISING LIVESTOCK

WILLIAM H. McNEILL

Humanity's momentous transition from being a mere predator within nature to a shaper of natural forces began with the development of agriculture and pastoralism (raising livestock). The author of the following tract, former University of Chicago historian William H. McNeill, calls it "the most basic of all human revolutions." When it occurred, about seven to nine thousand years ago, the nomadic hunter-gatherer societies of Paleolithic (Old Stone Age) times gave way to the more sedentary, settled villages of the Neolithic (New Stone Age) era.

D uring the Paleolithic . . . age man had already become master of the animal kingdom in the sense that he was the chief and most adaptable of predators; but despite his tools, his social organization, and his peculiar capacity to enlarge and transmit his culture, he still remained narrowly dependent on the balance of nature. The next great step in mankind's ascent toward lordship over the earth was the discovery of means whereby the natural environment could be altered to suit human need and convenience. With the domestication of plants and animals, and with the development of methods whereby fields could be made where forests grew by nature, man advanced to a new level of life. He became a shaper of the animal and vegetable life around him, rather than a mere predator upon it.

This advance opened a radically new phase of human history.

Excerpted from *The Rise of the West: A History of the Human Community*, by William H. McNeill. Copyright 1963 by The University of Chicago. Reprinted by permission of the University of Chicago Press.

The predator's mode of life automatically limits numbers; and large-bodied predators, like early men and modern lions, must perforce remain relatively rare in nature. Thus larger populations, with all the possibilities of specialization and social differentiation which numbers permit, could only be sustained by human communities that found ways of escaping from the natural limits imposed by their predatory past. This constituted perhaps the most basic of all human revolutions. Certainly the whole history of civilized mankind depended on the enlargement of the human food supply through agriculture and the domestication of animals. The costs were real, however; for the tedious labor of tilling the fields was a poor substitute for the fierce joys, sharp exertions, and instinctive satisfactions of the hunt. The human exercise of power thus early showed its profoundly double-edged character; for a farming folk's enlarged dominion over nature, and liberation from earlier limits upon food supply, meant also an unremitting enslavement to seed, soil, and season.

INDEPENDENT DISCOVERIES OF AGRICULTURE

Archeological discovery cannot yet tell us much about this fundamental transformation of human life. Even proto-men may unwittingly have begun to affect the distribution and speciation of certain plants that attracted their attention. Hunters probably valued especially those plants from which dyes, narcotics, stimulants, or poisons could be derived. Perhaps the first efforts to control the growth and reproduction of plants centered rather upon these than upon the later staples of ordinary agriculture."

Domestication of plants was a process rather than an event. Genetic combinations and recombinations, cross-breeding between cultivated and wild varieties, and selection by human action—both conscious and unconscious—meant, in effect, an unusually rapid biological evolution of certain types of plants toward a more effective symbiosis with man. In some cases, domestication proceeded so far that the very survival of the plant depended on human actions—as with maize. Reciprocally, human survival came in time to depend no less absolutely upon the crops.

It is probable that agriculture was invented more than once. The fact that the crops of pre-Columbian America were botanically quite different from those of the Old World has persuaded most students of the question that agriculture developed independently in the Americas. Even within the Old World, agriculture probably originated in at least two different areas. The principal evidence for this is the basic contrast which until recently divided Eurasian agriculture into two distinct styles. Field agriculture, depending on reproduction by seed, dominated Europe and the Middle East, where grains constituted the principal crop. On the other hand, garden farming, involving propagation of crops by transplantation of offshoots from a parent plant, pre-vailed in much of monsoon Asia and the Pacific islands, where root crops were of major importance. Such differences are fun-damental and may stem from independent discoveries of the possibility of raising vegetable food by deliberate human action. Yet the contrast may also arise merely from an Intelligent ex-ploitation of varying local flora under conditions imposed by di-verse climates.

The grain-centered agriculture of the Middle East provided the basis for the first civilized societies. Careful work by archeologists permits us to know something of the natural conditions which made the development of that agriculture possible. Radiocarbon dating suggests we should look for the beginnings of Middle Eastern agriculture at about 6500 B.C., when the icecap had van-ished from Continental Europe, and the earth's climatic zones were probably distributed more or less as at present. In western and central Europe this meant the appearance of heavy forests. . . . Farther south, desiccating trade winds had already begun to form the Saharan, Arabian, Gedrosian, and Thar deserts in re-gions that had previously been important centers of human pop-ulation. Between lay a zone of transition, where the trade winds blew only part of the year, while in winter cyclonic storms from the Atlantic brought life-giving precipitation. This was the zone of Mediterranean climate, within which lies most of the Middle East. Here the vegetable cover was thinner than in the better wa-tered lands to the north; but before men and their domesticated animals had denuded the landscape, the plains supported a scat-tered growth of trees, among which grasses luxuriated in the spring, withered in the summer drought, and revived with the winter rains. By contrast, rain-catching hillsides and mountain slopes were often thickly wooded on their windward side.

DOMESTICATION OF WILD GRASSES

Such a varied landscape was eminently suited to mankind. Food resources unavailable in the deciduous northern forest offered themselves for human exploitation in the Middle East. The seed-bearing grasses ancestral to modern cultivated grains probably grew wild eight or nine thousand years ago in the hill country between Anatolia and the Zagros Mountains, as varieties of wheat and barley continue to do today. If so, we can imagine that from time immemorial the women of those regions searched out patches of wheat and barley grasses when the seeds were ripe and gathered the wild harvest by hand or with the help of simple cutting tools. Such women may gradually have discovered methods for assisting the growth of grain, e.g., by pulling out competing plants; and it is likely that primitive sickles were invented to speed the harvest long before agriculture in the stricter sense came to be practiced.

A critical turn must have come when collectors of wild-growing grain came to understand that allowing a portion of the seed to fall to the ground at harvest time assured an increased crop in the following year. Perhaps this idea was connected with concepts of the spirit of the grain, propitiation of that spirit, and the reward that befitted a pious harvester who left part of the precious seed behind. A second breakthrough occurred with the discovery that by scattering seed on suitably prepared ground, women could create grain fields even where the grasses did not grow naturally. Yet the laborious practice of breaking ground with a digging stick and covering the seed to keep it from birds may well have spread slowly, even after the prospective rewards for such labor were well understood; for hunting communities seldom remained long enough in one locality to engage in extended tillage.

Nonetheless, the development of agriculture in the Middle East was rapid as compared to the earlier progress of mankind. The spread of grain fields so enlarged human food resources that men began decisively to transcend their predatory past, escaping the limits upon number and density of population that had hitherto made humankind relatively rare in the balance of nature. No date can confidently be assigned to this tremendous departure; and indeed, no completely satisfactory archeological evidence for the transition has yet come to light. But assuming that as new food-producing methods proved their advantage, they spread far and wide among the wild-grain gatherers of the Middle East; and assuming further that enlarged food resources resulted in comparatively rapid population growth, then it is probable that this earliest agriculture did not much antedate 6500 B.C. Village sites, created by the necessity for a more sedentary existence when fields had to be cultivated and guarded against browsing animals, have not been found dating from before about 6250 B.C. (plus or minus 200 years), but become increasingly numerous for later periods.

FROM HUNTING TO STOCK-RAISING

Middle Eastern agriculture must at first have been conducted on a small scale, and was women's work. Hunting remained the task of the menfolk; but by discovering even rudimentary agriculture, women rudely upset a delicate ecological balance. Human hunters became too numerous; game animals within range of the pullulating grainfields must quickly have been almost exterminated. As this happened, agriculture gradually displaced hunting from the center of community life. Men, whose bows had lost much of their usefulness, may have been persuaded to take on part of the work of the fields—fencing to keep out animals, harvesting in the precious days when the grain must be gathered before it scattered its seeds irreparably on the earth; and at last, as food for the year came to depend mainly on the size of the cultivated plot, men may in some communities have taken spade or hoe reluctantly in hand to work the fields side by side with their womenfolk.

But there was another possibility. Men could tame some of the beasts upon which they were accustomed to prey. It was logical for intelligent hunters confronted with a dwindling game reserve to protect their potential victims from rival predators and to conserve the herds for their own future use. This still falls short of full-scale domestication, however, which implies exploitation of the living animal for its milk, wool, and even its blood.

No one really knows how or by what stages a hunting-collecting way of life retreated before agriculture and stock-raising. Perhaps the first fully domesticated animals were used to decoy their wild fellows within the reach of hunters; and other uses for them may have been discovered only gradually, as the numbers of wild herds decreased. No doubt the innovators failed to foresee how domestication of animals would transform their familiar customs. Reason presumably had little scope in this transformation, for the whole relationship of man to animals was saturated in magical conceptions. Ritual slaughter of captured beasts played a part in the religions of some hunting peoples; and perhaps protecting and nurturing herds of potential victims in the hope of assuring better hunting through more regular and sumptuous sacrifices seemed the only proper answer to an increasing shortage of wild game.

All that can be said with certainty is that men in the Middle East did succeed in domesticating goats, sheep, pigs, and cattle at an early stage of their agricultural development, and were able thereby to secure a continued and perhaps even an enlarged supply of meat and other animal products. Conceivably, domestication of animals may have begun even before agriculture caused human population to increase beyond the level that could be maintained by predation; but even if so, domesticated flocks and herds can have had only a very limited importance before hunters found their accustomed prey becoming scarcer. As long as hunting continued to bring in the usual amount of food, why abandon a way of life inculcated by the practice of untold generations and sanctified by firm religious and moral values?

TRANSITION TO VILLAGE LIFE

Discoveries in the Middle East suggest that once agriculture had begun to transform human life, the range of material equipment at the disposal of the new farming communities rapidly increased. The apparent suddenness with which new accouterments appear in the archeological strata may partly be due to gaps in the record. Yet the new routines of daily life must have called for new tools and methods; and the human response to such new needs may have been relatively rapid. Presumably the drastic transformation implicit in the shift from hunting to agriculture and stock-raising temporarily freed men's inventive capacities from the bonds of custom. Normal resistance to innovation was reduced for a time, until a series of brilliant inventions and adaptations of old methods provided the basis for a new and satisfactory way of life, which then in its turn formed a stable, customary pattern: that of the Neolithic village community.

Archeology permits us to know something of the technical and material side of this social mutation. Tillage and stock-raising were associated with brewing, weaving, and the manufacture of pottery and polished stone tools. Some pre-pottery sites have been discovered where traces of agriculture are discernible; and no doubt some centuries were needed before the mature assemblage of what archeologists call "Neolithic" tools had been worked out and adopted by the primitive farming communities of the Middle East.

Once a community had come to rely on cereal foods, its members automatically became far more firmly rooted to a given spot than had been the case in the days of hunting economy. Throughout the growing season, at least part of the community had to protect the fields from browsing animals; and even during the rest of the year the difficulty of transporting harvested grain, together with the need to work old fields and clear new ones, must have kept the women of the community tied to a fixed location for nearly the whole circle of the seasons.

With the establishment of permanent settlements, it became possible to accumulate bulky, heavy, and fragile household goods. Clay pots, for example, became suitable substitutes for the lighter and less fragile containers made from animal skins, gourd shells, and woven willow withes that had been used previously. The first departure from older types was minimal. Much early pottery suggests that it had been copied in clay from basket and gourd shapes; and it is tempting to imagine that the first pots were made when it became necessary to coat such earlier containers with a fireproof and waterproof layer of clay in order to cook newfangled cereal porridge. Meat, after all, could be roasted on a wooden spit; but to cook cereals required a container both fire- and waterproof: required, in short, a pot.

The earliest known traces of cloth come from Neolithic sites. This does not prove that cloth was previously unknown, for clothmaking, like potmaking, had its Paleolithic antecedents in basketry. But until flax came into cultivation and hair and wool from domesticated animals became available, the supply of fiber must have been too scant to allow much clothmaking, even if the skills of spinning and weaving were familiar. Agriculture and the domestication of animals, however, so enlarged the supply of fiber that woven cloth became an important adjunct to the new way of life.

Polished stone tools, particularly axes, constitute the hallmark of every Neolithic site. Flint, chipped and flaked in a fashion to produce sharp cutting edges, had been perfectly adequate for the arrowheads, knives, and scrapers needed by hunters; but flint was too brittle for stripping the bark and branches from trees or cutting them down. Usable axes could only be made from tougher kinds of stone, which could not be shaped by traditional methods of flint-knapping. The solution to this difficulty was found by transferring to the harder medium of stone the methods of rough-hewing and polishing which had long been in use for shaping bone and horn implements. Polished stone axes and other tools therefore became characteristic of agricultural settlements; and the conspicuous difference between them and the older flints caused archeologists to name such remains "Neolithic" long before the connection between the technique of tool manufacture and the changed requirements of the community was understood.

DEVELOPMENT OF MIXED ECONOMIES

The first agriculturalists were not fully sedentary. Soil repeatedly cropped lost its fertility after a few years, so that if harvests were to be maintained, old fields had to be abandoned and virgin soil broken in from time to time. The sort of land that lent itself to primitive agriculture was thickly wooded ground where the tree cover prevented heavy undergrowth. In such areas, once the trees had been killed by stripping their bark, the soil beneath lay relatively open and might easily be worked with digging stick, spade, or hoe by going around the stumps. After a season or two of cropping such soil, fertility could be renewed by burning the dried limbs and tree trunks and scattering their ashes. By contrast, natural grassland offered stubborn resistance to wooden digging sticks; and it was almost impossible to prevent the native grasses from growing up through the grain and crowding it out. Hence the earliest agriculturalists, like eighteenth-century American pioneers, preferred the woodlands and clung at first to the slopes and foothills of the Middle East where trees grew naturally. It was probably this style of slash-and-burn agriculture, involving a semi-migratory pattern of life, which was practiced by the "mature" Neolithic villages of the ancient Middle East, as it still is today by primitive farmers in tropical rain forests and in subarctic birch and spruce forests on the fringes of the agricultural world.

As agriculture evolved in the Middle East, mixed economies, combining cereal-cropping with stock-raising, became characteristic. No doubt some communities put more emphasis upon the one or the other activity. At lower altitudes along the margins of the woodlands, where grasslands shaded off into desert, the domestication of animals made possible a predominantly pastoral mode of life; and just as Abraham set out from Ur of the Chaldees with his flocks and herds and human followers, so many another group must also have done, both before and after his time.

Since pastoral peoples leave few traces for archeologists, it is uncertain when a distinct divergence between pastoral and agricultural modes of life first developed. The occupation of the steppe and desert was gradual. Indeed, the full potentiality of pastoral nomadism was not realized until men learned to ride horseback habitually—not before about 900 B.C.; while the earliest peoples who followed their flocks onto the grasslands also cultivated favorable patches of ground, so that the difference between the two ways of life was at first rather of emphasis than of kind.

In all probability, pastoralism was divorced fully from agriculture only by communities that had remained hunters until the migratory expansion of stock-raising farmers brought the new style of life to their attention, perhaps by usurping some part of their accustomed hunting grounds. Clearly, hunters would find the labor of the fields little to their liking; whereas the arts of the herdsman fitted smoothly and easily into traditions of the hunt. Hence, if for any reason hunters had to modify familiar routines, it is not difficult to believe that they might accept domesticated animals eagerly but repudiate crop tillage as unworthy of free men. It was therefore toward the margins of the earliest centers of agricultural life—in the steppes of Europe and central Asia and in northern Arabia, where natural grasslands made cultivation difficult at best—that pastoralism found its principal home.

The occupation of the grasslands by pastoral peoples meant that two divergent styles of human life, partially interdependent and capable of endless interaction, came to exist side by side in the Middle East. As they still do today, pastoralists must from the earliest times have brought their animals to feed on the grain stubble. No doubt from the beginning they entered into trade relations with farming populations, for the surpluses produced by farmer and by herdsman naturally complement each other; and the more mobile life of the pastoralist made it easy and natural for him to act as carrier of such special and precious goods as hard stone for axes, shells for decoration, and valued perishables which have not left archeological traces. Finally, the perennial warfare between peasant and herdsman, symbolized in the biblical story of Cain and Abel, must have brought recurrent violence into the lives of Neolithic peoples.

Communities of hunters, whose way of life was essentially uniform throughout wide areas, and whose skills were exquisitely adapted to the existing environment, could find little stimulus to social change from contact with neighboring human groups. But with the development of agriculture and pastoralism, ways of life were no longer uniform. A new and fertile stimulus to fresh departures had arrived on the human scene. Once men had started re-creating their environments to suit themselves, older limits to social change were removed, and the spectacular ascent to our contemporary level of skill in manipulating the forces of nature began.

The Great River Civilizations

CHAPTER 1

THE SUMERIANS ESTABLISH THE WORLD'S FIRST TRUE CITIES

MICHAEL WOOD

This informative essay by popular scholar, writer, and filmmaker Michael Wood explores the first cities, which grew up on the fertile plains lying northwest of the Persian Gulf, in Mesopotamia. The people who inhabited this region in the fourth and third millennia B.C. have come to be called the Sumerians. Wood focuses on the Sumerian settlement of Uruk (called Erech in the Old Testament), perhaps the world's first large-scale urban center. Like other Sumerian cities, it had a ziggurat (a temple constructed in stepped levels), a long defensive circuit wall, and surrounding farmland to provide needed food and livestock.

Not long before 3000 BC, the first true cities in the world arose in Mesopotamia. Later Sumerian written tradition names the first place in Sumer, the earliest shrine: Eridu. Lost to the world for over two thousand years, Eridu was identified in 1853 by John Taylor, the British Vice-Consul in Basra who also did pioneering archaeological work at Ur, the city of Abraham. Twelve miles out into the desert beyond Ur, the mound of Eridu was called by the local nomads Abu Shahrein, 'Father of the Two Crescent Moons.'. . .

Excerpted from *Legacy: The Search for Ancient Cultures*, by Michael Wood (New York: Sterling Publishing, 1995). Copyright © 1992 by Michael Wood. Reprinted by permission of BBC Books, a division of BBC Entertainment Limited.

THE FIRST GREAT RELIGIOUS SHRINE?

Eridu is lonely, windswept and abandoned today. . . . But it was one of the most famous places in the history of Mesopotamia. The Sumerians believed that it was the site of the mound of creation, the first land which rose from the primal sea at the beginning of time. They thought that kingship—that is political society—first came down to earth here. Their myths also describe how the arts of civilization were initially possessed by Eridu before any other city. It originally stood at the edge of a great sea of fresh water stretching out to the south, the Apsu, from which apparently comes our word 'abyss.' The great temple here, the most ancient shrine in Sumer, was also named Apsu. This was the dwelling place of Enki, the archaic god of the waters, the god of wisdom, named after that primeval ocean of sweet water out of which all human life and all natural life came, as they believed. Indeed, at least as late as the tenth century AD there were still old sects in the southern marshes and coasts who worshipped the waters and whose myths and cosmologies incorporated Sumerian myths. . . .

Eridu had to wait till 1949 before there was a full-scale excavation deep into the mound below the platform of the temple ziggurat built in 2000 BC by the kings of nearby Ur. When the archaeologists dug into the temple hill they uncovered nineteen levels below the ziggurat, going back to the founding of the shrine around 5000 BC. At the bottom was a little sand mound surrounded by a reed fence with a tiny chapel, marking the site of the mythical mound of creation. If anywhere, then, here is the origin of the Biblical story of the garden of Eden. For what the Bible calls paradise, Eden, was simply the Sumerian word *Edin*, the wild, uncultivated grassland of the south, the natural landscape which lay outside the artificial landscape of the city. And picking over the debris of paradise, it is hard not to see the psychological truth of the Bible story: that the very beginning of our ascent to civilization was also the fall, when we tasted the fateful fruit of the tree of knowledge: the means by which we would become masters of the earth and yet eventually gain the power to destroy it and ourselves.

Such speculations become all the more pointed when we look at the layers of Eridu which superseded the early Ubaidian village with its primitive mud and reed shrine. For around 4000 BC a dramatic change came over the hill. Massive ceremonial buildings were constructed, a huge shrine in a monumental style of architecture. Grand tombs for an élite suggest class divisions were now in existence. Gold and metal-working and imported luxuries hint that the élite now controlled Eridu's surplus wealth.

Several thousand people now lived around the hill. Perhaps in these clues we can see the very moment when 'kingship came down to earth' and political power fell into the hands of the few.

The Eridu myths then perhaps are reflections of a real historical process, from the creation of organized communities in the south of the plain, to the arrival of the temple, the city, and kingship. These, in sum, were the key arts of civilization which Sumerian myth believed originated in Eridu and were passed on by the gods to future ages from Eridu to the first true city on earth, Uruk.

URUK: CITY IN THE SAND

To get to Uruk from Eridu today, you cross southern Iraq. . . . You cross the Euphrates beyond Samawa, then head south-east into the desert, where you enter a lunar landscape, a wasteland swept by gales of sand. Immense mounds loom out of the haze in a furnace heat. It can be 135° Fahrenheit out here in the summer. Finally you come to a city gate, still visible after nearly five thousand years, its approach silted with a deep tide of pottery and bones. This is where [the English excavator] William Loftus stood in 1849.

Still 50 feet high, the line of eroded walls curves round to the horizon. The centre of the city is dominated by the ruins of a great stepped tower, a ziggurat on which once stood the temple of the city's goddess, Inanna, whom we know as Ishtar. The first city may have begun as a religious centre, perhaps a shrine for the herders of the plain, in the quarter known as Kullaba, the sky god's shrine. The goddess's sanctuary came later. From the top of the ziggurat you can see what is left of the rich landscape of Sumer. Once fertile fields criss-crossed by canals, lined with palm groves, the territory of Uruk is now parched, wind-blown desert. To the north-east, beyond a dried bed of the Euphrates, is a huge cone-shaped tomb from the Persian period. All over the desert are the signs of human habitation: ruined irrigation canals, broken pottery, twisted slag. Beyond are the tell-tale mounds of ancient cities, some of which the ancients believed had existed even before the Flood. On the horizon, lit by the setting sun, you can just make out the mound of Larsa. Further out are Umma, one of the oldest cities in Sumer, and Tel Jidr, which survived into the Middle Ages. Out of sight to the north across huge sand dunes is Shurrupak, home town of the Sumerian Noah. There are, surely, few more extraordinary landscapes in the world.

From the top of the goddess's ziggurat the full extent of Uruk becomes apparent, with its walled circuit of more than six miles. There were two settlements here before 4000 BC, a sizeable city during the next millennium; but modern archaeology has shown that the walls were built at the end of a period of remarkable expansion when Uruk increased four times in size in just a few generations from about 3000 to 2700 BC. Presumably then, tens of thousands of people were moving in from the countryside to this new city life. There are distant parallels for this kind of large-scale change from rural to urban life. In China between 1100 and 1250 AD, southern cities like Hangchow increased five times in population, fed by a revolution in agriculture. In England during the industrial revolution, the population increased more than four times in a single century before 1800. In some parts of medieval Europe, too, between 1100 and 1300, a tenfold population increase occurred in regions where new land could be opened up through land reclamation and irrigation. In Europe this seems to have gone hand-in-hand with a lowering of the marriage age, which has the effect of accelerating the birth rate by lessening the gap between generations.

THE RAPID GROWTH OF CITIES

Bearing such ideas in mind we can see how a combination of similar factors could have worked in the early third millennium BC. Improved irrigation and land reclamation created more land; intensive cultivation produced more food; larger walled settlements brought more security; more land, more food and better security encouraged people to leave the countryside and to live in the cities, moving from the uplands into the southern plain. The inexorable pull of the cities' markets with their necessities and luxuries must have made them additionally attractive, as cities have been throughout history. Then, once powerful rulers were able to impose their control, whether kings, priesthoods or noble families (or a combination of all three), they were no doubt able to place heavy burdens on the poorer peasantry; for some among the masses in old Sumer, the 'urban miracle' may have been as grim as it was in the nineteenth century industrial city. For the answers to many of these questions we are still in the dark, not least about the social and power structures which brought about this great historical change, and in particular in the origins of kingship. But like their nineteenth century successors they were in no doubt as to the greatness of their achievement: 'Look at the walls of Uruk, gleaming like burnished bronze; inspect its inner wall, the like of which no man can equal! Go up on the wall of Uruk and walk around: examine its foundation, look at its brickwork—even the inner core is kiln-fired brick. Didn't the Seven Sages themselves lay out its plans?' [*Epic of Gilgamesh*]

Another Sumerian poem, the story of Etana, gives us an imagined bird's-eye view of such cities, and conveys something of their dizzying effect on the imagination of those early generations who lived through this first urban miracle. Looking down on the plain from miles up, on the brown desert and the blue sea, on the warrens of houses, and on their populations with 'the business of the country ceaselessly buzzing like a myriad insects,' Etana is lost in admiration at humankind's ability to reshape its environment.

In the peak period of the third millennium BC there were some forty cities in Sumer and Akkad, which together made up the Babylonian plain, mainly independent city states. They were densely settled. A big city state like Lagash had 36,000 male adults, Uruk perhaps the same. They were closely organized and controlled. In Nippur at a later period, there were 200 subsidiary villages in its territory, clustered around five main canals and sixty lesser ones, joined by a web of countless small irrigation ditches, all of which were subject to rules, duties and control, a constant source of litigation!

LAND EXHAUSTION AND THE DECLINE OF CITIES

As for the physical make-up of the city itself, according to the Epic of Gilgamesh, Uruk was one-third built up, one-third gardens, one-third temple property. Excavated streets in Ur and Nippur look just like the warrens of houses still visible in old Irbil, Kirkuk, Tel Afar, or at the sacred city of Najaf. In today's Irbil the 4000 people who still live inside the now decaying citadel belong to three wards, one to each gate; each has a small shrine, bath and souk; each too had its scribe or writer. These arrangements are an exact echo of ancient Ur or Nippur. The design of houses in the ancient cities was identical to that used up till the advent of air conditioning, with central courtyards, windcatchers, and serdabs (sunken rooms) to keep the ferocious summer heat at bay. The pattern of streets also served to create shadow and allow the breeze to blow through: only in the last twenty years has this older Iraq disappeared.

At the centre of the ancient city was the temple, as the mosque is today, and they were no doubt run in the same manner as now. In Nippur for example in 2000 BC, the Ur-Meme family administered the Inanna temple for generations. Just so, in Irbil today, the Al-Mulla family have run the main mosque for the last 600 years, producing distinguished poets, astronomers and scholars. . . .

But there is another way in which the Mesopotamian city resembles its modern counterpart: it was parasitical of the soil and the environment. The plain around Uruk was once big wheat country with grain yields as high as the Mid-West and Canada; today it is salt-encrusted and barren as far as the eye can see. The need for more land and for more intensive cultivation to feed an ever-growing population eventually devastated the landscape. We know now that civilization inevitably destroys the environment, but they discovered it here for the first time. The most telling proof of this is that there is virtually no continuity in land use between the great periods of Mesopotamian history, between the ancients, the Hellenistic and Sassanian, the Islamic and the modern. Improved irrigation and fertilization, better use of fallow periods, and especially the cutting of huge new dykes by the Sassanians and the Arabs all enabled some landscapes to regenerate and live on. But essentially each of these great epochs had to open up new areas for cultivation, leaving the old land, now exhausted, to return to desert.

So it is a salutary experience today to walk the weathered gullies of 'wide-wayed Uruk,' littered with testimony to the long ascent of man, if such it is. Here were enormous temples as big as cathedrals, their façades decorated with blue glazed tiles, just as can be seen today on the mosques of Iraq. Still visible are the platforms of the vast shrines rebuilt in traditional Babylonian style in the third century BC under the Greek successors of Alexander the Great, when Uruk was still rich and populous, and perhaps still a major centre of pilgrimage. At that time the cities of Old Sumer still preserved their own civil customs and organization and were still built in the old way, still worshipping the old gods. As late as the Christian period there was some life left in the old place. . . .

With the ups and downs of any living organism, the city of Uruk and its institutions lasted through to about 300 AD. A small settlement outside the walls survived till the Arab conquest. Indeed, even in the eighth century the local Christian bishop still called himself 'Bishop of Uruk and Kaskar.' But by then it was dead, after a life of over five thousand years.

EGYPT ACQUIRES UNITY AND NATIONAL GOVERNMENT

H.W.F. SAGGS

Although the first true cities seem to have appeared in ancient Mesopotamia in the late fourth millennium B.C., they long remained politically independent of one another. It was further to the west, in ancient Egypt, where cities and their landholdings first came together to form a true country with a centralized national government. As summarized here by noted University of Wales scholar H.W.F. Saggs, about 3000 B.C. King Menes, leader of Upper Egypt, united that region with Lower Egypt, forming the nation-state that would be a major player in Near Eastern affairs for many centuries to come.

T he crucial political change in early Egypt came at about 3100 or 3000 BC; different scholars use different chronologies. Then, according to tradition, Menes, the king of Upper Egypt, conquered Lower Egypt and made the two kingdoms into one. But history shows that a stable major state does not come about suddenly as the result of a single incident of conquest. The innovation which we call the unification of Egypt must have been the final stage of a long period of convergence. Yet even if not as sudden as tradition represents it, it did mark a major step in deliberate social organization; by it, Menes made all Egypt into a single political and economic unit—a good half millennium before any comparable development in Mesopotamia. Admittedly there were those in ancient Egypt who might have denied that Menes made the whole into one kingdom, since to the end the Pharaohs preserved the pretence of the duality of the system, not only in their title 'King of Upper and Lower Egypt', but also in wearing a composite crown which incorporated separate crowns for the original two kingdoms; but in practical terms the country was undoubtedly one. To emphasize the essential unity, Menes created a new capital, Memphis, at the point where the two former kingdoms met. Tradition, recorded by Herodotus but not otherwise proved, recounts that Menes built a dyke to change the course of the Nile, and founded Memphis on the land so reclaimed. Even if this tradition was not literally true, it at least implied a very early explicit recognition that life in Egypt depended upon regulation of the flood waters. . . .

THE KING'S WILL

Rule by one man depends upon the existence of sanctions so powerful that the rest of the population are willing to accept his direction unquestioningly. In ancient Egypt the sanctions were religious and had prehistoric origins. In many primitive societies, the central figure is a magician who is believed to be so intimately linked with the supernatural world that he can control rain or fertility and other aspects of life. So long as his magic proves effective, his power is absolute, but when his powers fail he is sent back to the supernatural world by being put to death. The ancient collection of rituals and myths called the Pyramid Texts, from about 2400 BC in their extant form but incorporating beliefs from prehistoric times, shows behind the Egyptian king of historical times a magician of this category. That this person was originally put to death when his powers failed is hinted at by traces of cannibalism and human sacrifice in the Pyramid Texts, but the clearest indication is in a ceremony called the Sed festival. This was a ceremony to rejuvenate the king's failing powers after thirty years of rule. It began with the ritual burial of the king, which surely indicates that originally, when the powers of the king or his magician predecessor failed, he was put to death and there was a real burial.

From the beginning, these prehistoric antecedents invested the living king in Egypt with the aura of a divine being. Because the king was an incarnate god, with Egypt's welfare in his care, it was in everyone's interest to conform to his will. His religious sanction was everywhere evident, for he was nominally the chief priest in every temple. The very circumstances of the unification of Egypt may have served to reinforce belief in the divine nature of the pharaoh. If Menes did indeed divert the sacred life-giving Nile and drain a huge area to build a great capital where formerly there had been swamps, his divine powers could not be doubted. Also, since he controlled the whole Nile valley, he unquestionably had power over the water-supply to every part of the land, an aspect of royalty graphically illustrated in one of the earliest representations of a pharaoh, which shows him cutting the dyke of an irrigation canal with a hoe. From very early times the king of united Egypt had measurements taken of the height of the Nile as it was rising in the south, so that he could accurately predict the area which could be irrigated further north. All these factors meant that, from the point of view of an ancient Egyptian, the king was, quite literally, a fertility giver and controller of the Nile and all the life of the land; from the Egyptians' point of view he was, without question, a god upon whom the life of the land depended. Moreover, because of the ease of navigation from one end of the country to the other by means of the gentle Nile, it was relatively easy to produce a unified system of government (even if administered in duplicate for north and south separately). . . .

The definiteness of the tradition makes it likely that Menes was a real king, but which? The name does not occur in native Egyptian records. Three kings, known to egyptologists as Scorpion, Narmer, and Hor-aha, have left monuments from about the time attributed to Menes. If one of these kings has to be picked as Menes, the most probable seems to be Narmer, but quite possibly more than one of them contributed to the tradition. This would accord with the probability that the unification was not an innovation abruptly introduced after conquest, but came about gradually over several reigns.

With Menes we enter the Dynastic Period. This terminology derives from an Egyptian priest, Manetho, who at about 300 BC compiled in Greek a list of all Egyptian kings from the beginning, divided into thirty dynasties (later extended to thirty-one), with, of course, Menes as the first king of the First Dynasty. . . .

STATE OFFICERS

There are more theories than evidence about the running of the early Egyptian state. There are virtually no administrative records, and the text called the Palermo Stone provides less than it seems to promise, for whilst it gives us a record of one or more outstanding events for each year down to the Fifth Dynasty, these are mainly about festivals, divine statues, building works or expeditions abroad, with few details directly bearing on administration.

There is one type of evidence which is plentiful in this area: the titles of officials. Some scholars have used these in an attempt to build up a picture of the administrative network. Ancient Egyptians who could afford it delighted in arranging for their autobiographies to be written on their tombs, and [scholar] Klaus Baer has analysed tomb inscriptions of over 600 notables, who between them recorded nearly 2000 titles in use during the Old Kingdom. But in fact this mass of titles—legal, scribal, fiscal, religious, organizational, linked to the king or the royal court, or purely honorific—tells us less about the details of the administrative system than we might expect. Some titles which obviously began as marks of function quickly became at first markers of rank within a hierarchy and then merely honorific. . . .

What this mass of titles gives us, therefore, is not an outline of the administrative system but a picture of a society obsessed with considerations of rank. Paradoxically, this nonfunctional use of titles performed a useful function. An evolving society creates new offices and ceases to need old ones. But without a mechanism for sweeping away obsolete offices, there grows up an enormous amount of unproductive dead wood. Conversion of old functional offices, no longer required, into honorific titles discharged this burden.

Although official titles do not give us an adequate picture of how the early Egyptian state was run, the material does enable us to extract information about a few of the greatest offices in the state, sufficient to give us a rough sketch of the administrative framework, mainly in the time of the Fifth Dynasty. At that period all senior functions in the state were shared amongst six classes of officials; these bore the titles, the Overseer of the Great Mansions, the Overseer of the Scribes of the Royal Records, the Overseer of Works, the Overseer of Granaries, the Overseer of the Treasuries, and what we usually translate as the Vizier.

The 'Great Mansions' of the first title were the courts of justice. There are indications that there were originally six such courts, but their location is unknown.

The 'Overseer of the Scribes of the Royal Records' was the head of the scribal administration, responsible for the preparation and filing of all state documents. There was at least one occasion during the Fifth Dynasty when two persons held this title simultaneously; since one of the two was the vizier, the greatest officer of state, he presumably had overall control, leaving the other holder of the title to supervise details.

The Overseer of Works was responsible for organizing workforces for such operations as building, agriculture, expeditions to distant places to obtain materials, and probably (although there is no specific Old Kingdom evidence) digging and maintaining canals. Several holders may have shared this title, each responsible for a particular sector of public works.

The general area of the duties of the 'Overseer of the Granaries' is obvious, but the details are not clear. Sometimes there were simultaneous holders of the title. Little is known of the location of state granaries, but these officials presumably used them to stockpile corn against future shortages. . . . Since the state could not survive unless it kept its peasantry fed, this was a vital need. There were also granaries on private estates, where the Overseers of Granaries may have been responsible for assessment for taxation. This would explain their close connection with the Overseer of the Treasuries.

A major part of the duties of Overseer of Treasuries in the Old Kingdom was recording and collecting dues from private estates. Mention of a 'treasury of the residence' in the late Fifth and early Sixth Dynasties suggests there was a central treasury at the capital Memphis, for which this official would have been responsible. There were apparently also provincial treasuries. Later the collection of taxes came into the orbit of the vizier.

THE VIZIER

The most important officer in the state administrative system was undoubtedly the vizier. His office must already have existed by the beginning of the Third Dynasty, since the title occurs on stone vessels found beneath the Step Pyramid, built by the first king of that Dynasty. The earliest viziers were all royal princes, a relic from the original situation in which the king kept all authority within the circle of his kinsmen. The people nearest to the pharaoh in life were also those nearest in death, and the grouping of tombs associated with pyramids in Saqqara and Giza indicates that down to the Fourth Dynasty his immediate executives were mainly his close male relatives—sons, uncles, cousins, nephews. In the Fifth Dynasty this ceased to be the case, and high officials, including viziers, were no longer necessarily princes by birth. But even when no longer royal by birth, the men appointed as viziers, and sometimes other officials, were given the rank of prince by the honorific title King's Son.

The vizier needed to be a man of considerable ability, since his task was to oversee the whole administration, judiciary and economy of the country: second only to the king in status, in some circumstances he was of greater importance in practice. By the time of the Middle Kingdoms, this office had become divided into two, with separate viziers for Upper and Lower Egypt; there is the possibility that this division went back to the Old Kingdom.

The third millennium provides no detailed account of the duties of a vizier, but texts and reliefs from the tomb of Rekhmire, who held that office in the fifteenth century, tell us what they had become.

Rekhmire ranked second only to the king, and all the royal courtiers did obeisance to him. The king, who was ultimately responsible for justice, appointed Rekhmire to act on his behalf, with no one able to override his decision. Rekhmire prided himself on his administration of justice. He claimed to be 'smiter of the smiter', to judge rich and poor impartially, to rescue the weak from the strong, to defend the widow and relieve the aged, to establish a son in his paternal inheritance, to give food and drink to the hungry and thirsty and clothing to the destitute. He gave judgement daily in his audience hall, seated upon a cushion on a chair, with a rug on the floor and a cushion beneath his feet. . . .

At some point every day Rekhmire conferred with the king. He also received reports from the chief treasurer, from the officers responsible for military security, and from all other senior officials, since all functions of the state—judiciary, treasury, army and navy, police, and agriculture—were under the supervision of the vizier. To communicate with various departments, the vizier had a staff of messengers, who had the right of immediate admission to any official. Wills had to be brought before the vizier to be sealed.

Reliefs in his tomb show Rekhmire accepting tribute from foreigners, and receiving the taxes from representatives of various cities. Much of the latter was in gold or silver, but it also included commodities in such forms as hides, bows, cedar wood, apes, cloth, oxen, corn, honey.

THE BEGINNINGS OF A NATIONAL SYSTEM

The various high offices of the Old Kingdom, little as we know in detail about their functions, show that already by the middle of the third millennium there was considerable departmentalization in the running of the Egyptian state. The directives of the great officers of state at the top were implemented by lower ranking officials, in a departmental system which probably went back in origin to the organization of servants in the royal household.

The administrators had the efficient running of Egypt in their hands, and good government was threatened if those administrators sank to the level of bureaucrats. It could happen. Instead of concentrating upon getting necessary work done, officials might act as though what mattered was to adhere at all costs to established procedures, whether or not it was the most efficient way of performing the task in hand. A letter found at Saqqara shows a case of bureaucratic palsy as early as 2200 BC. The writer was an officer in charge of quarry workers, and obviously a man who took a pride in doing his job well. He expostulated at having been ordered to take his men across the river to government headquarters to receive their clothing, an unwarranted interruption in his duties. In the past, he pointed out, this procedure had wasted up to six days, as a result of delays at the issuing office. Why, he asked, should not the clothes be sent to him by barge, when the whole business could be settled within a single day?

The king himself was not a mere figurehead. Since the earliest viziers were royal princes, there is the possibility that some of those who succeeded as kings may earlier have served in that role. Certainly kings undertook specific functions in the administration of the kingdom. From very early in the Dynastic Period, the king made periodic tours by river to inspect the whole land, and from the reign of the Fourth Dynasty ruler Sneferu, this became a census of all the cattle, normally biennially, occasionally in successive years. This was in effect a periodic assessment of wealth, and must imply the beginning of a national system of taxation. It was this that brought the king the economic power which eventually made possible such huge public works as the building of the Giza pyramids.

From prehistoric times the hydrology of the Nile had subdivided Egypt into a number of flood basins. These may have been the basis of the territorial divisions called nomes (totalling about forty, with variations from time to time), which formed the later units of provincial administration. They were already assuming that function by the Third Dynasty, and from soon after that time the administrators in charge of the nomes began to acquire a degree of independence of the capital. In addition, local officials received grants of land for their maintenance, which, in consequence of customarily being regranted to heirs, gradually became treated as private property; with their own estates, such officials became less subject to control from the capital.

THE MYSTERIOUS PEOPLE OF THE INDUS VALLEY

A.L. BASHAM

This comprehensive overview of India's Harappan culture, which flourished from about 2500 to 1600 B.C., is by A.L. Basham, a former professor of Asian civilization at Canberra's Australian National University. He describes the two main Harappan cities (Harappa and Mohenjo-Daro), comments on various aspects of Harappan culture, and concludes with speculation about the fall of these cities, which may have been caused by the arrival of the Aryans, a nomadic people from the steppes of central Asia.

I n the early part of the 3rd millennium, civilization, in the sense of an organized system of government over a comparatively large area, developed nearly simultaneously in the river valleys of the Nile, Euphrates, and Indus. We know a great deal about the civilizations of Egypt and Mesopotamia, for they have left us written material which has been satisfactorily deciphered. The Indus people, on the other hand, did not engrave long inscriptions on stone or place papyrus scrolls in the tombs of their dead; all that we know of their writing is derived from the brief inscriptions of their seals, and there is no Indian counterpart of the Rosetta Stone [the stone found in Egypt on which a message was written in three languages, including hieroglyphics, enabling scholars to decipher the latter]. Several brilliant efforts have been made to read the Indus seals, but none so far has succeeded. Hence our knowledge of the Indus civilization is inadequate in many respects, and it must be classed as prehistoric, for it has no history in the strict sense of the term.

ORIGINS OF HARAPPĀ CULTURE

The civilization of the Indus is known to the archaeologist as the Harappā Culture, from the modern name of the site of one of its two great cities, on the left bank of the Rāvī, in the Panjāb. Mohenjo Daro, the second city, is on the right bank of the Indus, some 250 miles from its mouth. Recently, excavations have been carried out on the site of Kālībanga, in the valley of the old River Sarasvatī, now almost dried up, near the border of India and West Pākistān. These have revealed a third city, almost as large as the two earlier known, and designed on the same plan. As well as these cities a few smaller towns are known, and a large number of village sites, from Rūpar on the upper Satlaj to Lothal in Gujarāt. The area covered by the Harappā Culture therefore extended for some 950 miles from north to south, and the pattern of its civilization was so uniform that even the bricks were usually of the same size and shape from one end of it to the other. . . .

This great civilization owed little to the Middle East, and there is no reason to believe that it was formed by recent immigrants; the cities were built by people who had probably been in the Indus Valley for several centuries. The Harappā people were already Indians when they planned their cities, which hardly altered for about a thousand years. We cannot fix a precise date for the beginning of this civilization, but certain indications synchronize it roughly with the village cultures of Balūchistān [the southwestern region of Pākistān]. The site of Rānā Ghundāī produced a stratification which showed, in the third phase of the village's history, a type of pottery with bold designs in black on a red background. From evidence discovered by Sir R. Mortimer Wheeler in 1946 it seems that the city of Harappā was built on a site occupied by people using similar pottery. There is no evidence of the date of the foundation of the other great city of Mohenjo Daro, for its lowest strata are now below the level of the Indus, whose bed has slowly risen with the centuries; though diggings have reached 30 feet below the surface, flooding has prevented the excavation of the earliest levels of the city. Important fresh light on the origins of the Harappā culture has recently been thrown by the excavations at Kot Dijī, opposite Mohenjo Daro a few miles from the left bank of the Indus. Here, below the level of the Harappā Culture, have been found remains of an earlier culture, with pottery and tools of cruder workmanship. This Kot Dijī culture seems to have been the prototype of the developed city civilization which grew out of it.

Thus the Harappā Culture, at least in the Panjāb, was later in its beginnings than the village cultures, but it was certainly in part contemporary with them, for traces of mutual contact have been found; and some of the village cultures survived the great civilization to the east of them. From the faint indications which are all the evidence we have, it would seem that the Indus cities began in the first half, perhaps towards the middle, of the 3rd millennium B.C.; it is almost certain that they continued well into the 2nd millennium.

A Conservative, Traditional People

When these cities were first excavated no fortifications and few weapons were found, and no building could be certainly identified as a temple or a palace. The hypothesis was then put forward that the cities were oligarchic commercial republics, without sharp extremes of wealth and poverty, and with only a weak repressive organization; but the excavations at Harappā in 1946 and further discoveries at Mohenjo Daro have shown that this idyllic picture is incorrect. Each city had a well-fortified citadel, which seems to have been used for both religious and governmental purposes. The regular planning of the streets, and the strict uniformity throughout the area of the Harappā Culture in such features as weights and measures, the size of bricks, and even the layout of the great cities, suggest rather a single centralized state than a number of free communities.

Probably the most striking feature of the culture was its intense conservatism. At Mohenjo Daro nine strata of buildings have been revealed. As the level of the earth rose from the periodic flooding of the Indus new houses would be built almost exactly on the sites of the old, with only minor variations in ground plan; for nearly a millennium at least, the street plan of the cities remained the same. The script of the Indus people was totally unchanged throughout their history. There is no doubt that they had contact with Mesopotamia, but they showed no inclination to adopt the technical advances of the more progressive culture. We must assume that there was continuity of government throughout the life of the civilization. This unparalleled continuity suggests, in the words of Professor Piggott, "the unchanging traditions of the temple" rather than "the secular instability of the court". It seems in fact that the civilization of Harappā, like those of Egypt and Mesopotamia, was theocratic in character.

The Layout of Streets and Houses

The two cities were built on a similar plan. To the west of each was a "citadel", an oblong artificial platform some 30–50 feet high and about 400×200 yards in area. This was defended by crenelated walls [i.e., having defensive bastions with spaces between, as in medieval castles], and on it were erected the public buildings. Below it was the town proper, in each case at least a square mile in area. The main streets, some as much as 30 feet wide, were quite straight, and divided the city into large blocks, within which were networks of narrow unplanned lanes. In neither of the great cities has any stone building been found; standardized burnt brick of good quality was the usual building material for dwelling houses and public buildings alike. The houses, often of two or more stories, though they varied in size, were all based on much the same plan—a square courtyard, round which were a number of rooms. The entrances were usually in side alleys, and no windows faced on the streets, which must have presented a monotonous vista of dull brick walls. The houses had bathrooms, the design of which shows that the Harappan, like the modern Indian, preferred to take his bath standing, by pouring pitchers of water over his head. The bathrooms were provided with drains, which flowed into sewers under the main streets, leading to soak-pits. The sewers were covered throughout their length by large brick slabs. The unique sewerage system of the Indus people must have been maintained by some municipal organization, and is one of the most impressive of their achievements. No other ancient civilization until that of the Romans had so efficient a system of drains.

The average size of the ground floor of a house was about 30 feet square, but there were many bigger ones: obviously there were numerous well-to-do families in the Indus cities, which perhaps had a middle class larger and more important in the social scale than those of the contemporary civilizations of Sumer and Egypt. Remains of workmen's dwellings have also been discovered at both sites—parallel rows of two-roomed cottages, at Mohenjo Daro with a superficial area of 20×12 feet each, but at Harappā considerably larger; they bear a striking resemblance to the "coolie lines" of modern Indian tea and other estates. At Harappā rows of such buildings have been found near the circular brick floors on which grain was pounded, and they were probably the dwellings of the workmen whose task was to grind corn for the priests and dignitaries who lived in the citadel. Drab and tiny as they were, these cottages were better dwellings than those in which many Indian coolies live at the present day.

The most striking of the few large buildings is the great bath in the citadel area of Mohenjo Daro. This is an oblong bathing pool 39×23 feet in area and 8 feet deep, constructed of beautiful brickwork made watertight with bitumen. It could be drained by an opening in one corner and was surrounded by a cloister, on to which opened a number of small rooms. Like the "tank" of a Hindu temple, it probably had a religious purpose, and the cells may have been the homes of priests. The special attention paid by the people of the Harappā Culture to cleanliness is hardly due to the fact that they had notions of hygiene in advance of those of other civilizations of their time, but indicates that, like the later Hindus, they had a strong belief in the purificatory effects of water from a ritual point of view.

A THRIVING ECONOMY

The largest building so far excavated is one at Mohenjo Daro with a superficial area of 230×78 feet, which may have been a palace. At Harappā a great granary has been discovered to the north of the citadel; this was raised on a platform of some 150×200 feet in area to protect it from floods, and was divided into storage blocks of 50×20 feet each. It was doubtless used for storing the corn which was collected from the peasants as land tax, and we may assume that it had its counterpart at Mohenjo Daro. The main food crops were wheat, barley, peas, and sesamum, the latter still an important crop in India for its seeds, which provide edible oil. There is no clear evidence of the cultivation of rice, but the Harappā people grew and used cotton. It is not certain that irrigation was known, although this is possible. The main domestic animals known to modern India had already been tamed— humped and humpless cattle, buffaloes, goats, sheep, pigs, asses, dogs, and the domestic fowl. The elephant was well known, and may also have been tamed. The Harappā people may have known of the horse, since a few horse's teeth have been found in the lowest stratum of the Balūchistān site of Rānā Ghundāī, probably dating from several centuries earlier than the foundation of Harappā. This would indicate that horse-riding nomads found their way to N.-W. India in small numbers long before the Āryan invasion; but it is very doubtful whether the Harappā people possessed domestic horses themselves and if they did they must have been very rare animals. The bullock was probably the usual beast of burden.

On the basis of this thriving agricultural economy the Harappā people built their rather unimaginative but comfortable civilization. Their bourgeoisie had pleasant houses, and even their workmen, who may have been bondmen or slaves, had the comparative luxury of two-roomed brick-built cottages. Evidently a well organized commerce made these things possible. The cities undoubtedly traded with the village cultures of Balūchistān, where outposts of the Harappā Culture have been traced, but many of their metals and semi-precious stones came from much longer distances. From Saurāshtra and the Deccan they obtained conch shell, which they used freely in decoration, and several types of stone. Silver, turquoise and lapis lazuli were imported from Persia and Afghānistān. Their copper came either from Rājasthān or from Persia, while jadeite was probably obtained from Tibet or Central Asia.

TRADE AND WRITING

Whether by sea or land, the products of the Indus reached Mesopotamia, for a number of typical Indus seals and a few other objects from the Indus Valley have been found in Sumer at levels dating between about 2300 and 2000 B.C., and some authorities believe that the land of *Melukka,* reached by sea from Sumer, and referred to in Sumerian documents, was the Indus Valley. Evidence of Sumerian exports to India is very scant and uncertain, and we must assume that they were mainly precious metals and raw materials. The finding of Indus seals suggests that merchants from India actually resided in Mesopotamia; their chief merchandise was probably cotton, which has always been one of India's staple exports, and which is known to have been used in later Babylonia. The recently excavated site at Lothal in Gujarāt has revealed harbour works, and the Harappā people may have been more nautically inclined than was formerly supposed. No doubt from their port of Lothal they were in touch with places farther south, and it is possibly thus that certain distinctive features of the Harappā Culture penetrated to South India.

It seems that every merchant or mercantile family had a seal, bearing an emblem, often of a religious character, and a name or brief inscription in the tantalizingly indecipherable script. The standard Harappā seal was a square or oblong plaque, usually made of the soft stone called steatite, which was delicately engraved and hardened by heating. The Mesopotamian civilizations employed cylinder seals, which were rolled on clay tablets, leaving an impressed band bearing the device and inscription of the seal; one or two such seals have been found in Mohenjo Daro, but with devices of the Harappā type. Over 2,000 seals have been discovered in the Indus cities, and it would seem that every important citizen possessed one. Their primary purpose was probably to mark the ownership of property, but they doubtless also served as amulets, and were regularly carried on the persons of their owners. Generally they depict animals, such as the bull, buffalo, goat, tiger and elephant, or what appear to be scenes from religious legend. Their brief inscriptions, never of more than twenty symbols and usually of not more than ten, are the only significant examples of the Harappā script to have survived.

This script had some 270 characters, which were evidently pictographic in origin, but which had an ideographic or syllabic character. It may have been inspired by the earliest Sumerian script, which probably antedates it slightly, but it bears little resemblance to any of the scripts of the ancient Middle East, though attempts have been made to connect it with one or other of them. The most striking similarities are with the symbols used until comparatively recent times by the natives of Easter Island, in the eastern Pacific, but the distance in space and time between the two cultures is so great that there is scarcely any possibility of contact or influence. We do not know what writing media were used, though it has been suggested that a small pot found at the lesser site of Chanhu Daro is an inkwell. Certainly the Harappans did not inscribe their documents on clay tablets, or some of these would have been found in the remains of their cities.

ARTISTIC EFFORTS

They were not on the whole an artistic people. No doubt they had a literature, with religious epics similar to those of Sumer and Babylon, but these are forever lost to us. The inner walls of their houses were coated with mud plaster, but if any paintings were made on these walls all trace of them has vanished. The outer walls, facing the streets, were apparently of plain brick. Architecture was austerely utilitarian, a few examples of simple decorative brickwork being the only ornamentation so far discovered. No trace of monumental sculpture has been found anywhere in the remains, and if any of the larger buildings were temples they contained no large icons, unless these were made of wood or other perishable material.

But if the Harappā folk could not produce works of art on a large scale they excelled in those of small compass. Their most notable artistic achievement was perhaps in their seal engravings, especially those of animals, which they delineated with powerful realism and evident affection. The great urus bull with its many dewlaps, the rhinoceros with knobbly armoured hide, the tiger roaring fiercely, and the many other animals are the work of craftsmen who studied their subjects and loved them.

Equally interesting are some of the human figurines. The red sandstone torso of a man is particularly impressive for its realism. The modelling of the rather heavy abdomen seems to look forward to the style of later Indian sculpture, and it has even been suggested that this figurine is a product of much later times, which by some strange accident found its way into the lower stratum; but this is very unlikely, for the figure has certain features, notably the strange indentations on the shoulders, which cannot be explained on this hypothesis. The bust of another male figure, in steatite, seems to show an attempt at portraiture. It has been suggested that the head is that of a priest, with his eyes half closed in meditation, but it is possible that he is a man of Mongolian type, for the presence of this type in the Indus Valley, at least sporadically, has been proved by the discovery of a single skull at Mohenjo Daro.

Most striking of the figurines is perhaps the bronze "dancing girl". Naked but for a necklace and a series of bangles almost covering one arm, her hair dressed in a complicated coiffure, standing in a provocative posture, with one arm on her hip and one lanky leg half bent, this young woman has an air of lively pertness, quite unlike anything in the work of other ancient civilizations. Her thin boyish figure, and those of the uninspiring mother goddesses, indicate, incidentally, that the canons of female beauty among the Harappā people were very different from those of later India. It has been suggested that this "dancing girl" is a representative of a class of temple dancers and prostitutes, such as existed in contemporary Middle Eastern civilizations and were an important feature of later Hindu culture, but this cannot be proved. It is not certain that the girl is a dancer, much less a temple dancer.

The Harappā people made brilliantly naturalistic models of animals, specially charming being the tiny monkeys and squirrels used as pinheads and beads. For their children they made cattle with movable heads, model monkeys which would slide down a string, little toy carts, and whistles shaped like birds, all of terracotta. They also made rough terracotta statuettes of women, usually naked or nearly naked, but with elaborate head-dresses. These are certainly icons of the Mother Goddess, and are so numerous that they seem to have been kept in nearly every home. They are very crudely fashioned, so we must assume that the goddess was not favoured by the upper classes, who commanded the services of the best craftsmen, but that her effigies were mass produced by humble potters to meet popular demand. . . .

THE END OF THE INDUS CITIES

When Harappā was first built the citadel was defended by a great turreted wall, 40 feet wide at the base and 35 feet high. In the course of the centuries this wall was refaced more strongly than before, though there is no evidence that the city was dangerously threatened by enemies. But towards the end of Harappā's existence its defences were further strengthened, and one gateway was wholly blocked. Danger threatened from the west. . . .

After the barbarians had conquered the outlying villages the ancient laws and rigid organization of the Indus cities must have suffered great strain. At Mohenjo Daro large rooms were divided into smaller ones, and mansions became tenements; potters' kilns were built within the city boundaries, and one even in the middle of a street. The street plan was no longer maintained. Hoards of jewellery were buried. Evidently the city was overpopulated and law and order were less well kept, perhaps because the barbarians were already ranging the provinces and the city was full of newcomers, whom the city fathers could not force into the age-old pattern of its culture.

When the end came it would seem that most of the citizens of Mohenjo Daro had fled; but a group of huddled skeletons in one of the houses and one skeleton of a woman lying on the steps of a well suggest that a few stragglers were overtaken by the invaders. . . . From Harappā comes evidence of a different kind. Here, near the older cemetery of interments, is another cemetery on a higher level, containing fractional burials in pots of men with short-headed Armenoid skulls. A skull of similar type was buried in the citadel itself. At Chanhu Daro, on the lower Indus, the Harappā people were replaced by squatters, living in small huts with fireplaces, innovations which suggest that they came from a colder climate. These people, though unsophisticated in many respects, had superior tools and weapons. Similar settlements were made in Balūchistān at about the same time. Among the scanty remains of these invaders there is clear evidence of the presence of the horse. The Indus cities fell to barbarians who triumphed not only through greater military prowess, but also because they were equipped with better weapons, and had learnt to make full use of the swift and terror-striking beast of the steppes. In other parts of India, however, the impact of the invaders was not immediately felt, and it appears that the Harappā city of Lothal, in Gujarāt, survived long after its parent cities had fallen, and its culture seems to have developed gradually, merging into that of the later period with no sharp break in continuity.

The date of these great events can only be fixed very approximately from synchronisms with the Middle East. Sporadic traces of contact can be found between the Indus cities and Sumeria, and there is some reason to believe that this contact continued under the First Dynasty of Babylon, which produced the great lawgiver Hammurabi. This dynasty was also overwhelmed by barbarians, the Kassites, who came from the hills of Iran and conquered by virtue of their horse-drawn chariots. After the Kassite invasion no trace of contact with the Indus can be found in Mesopotamia, and it is therefore likely that the Indus cities fell at about the same time as the dynasty of Hammurabi. Earlier authorities placed the latter event in the first centuries of the 2nd millennium B.C., but . . . the fall of the First Babylonian Dynasty is now thought to have taken place about 1600 B.C.

The earliest Indian literary source we possess is the *Ṛg Veda*, most of which was composed in the second half of the 2nd millennium. It is evidently the work of an invading people, who have not yet fully subjugated the original inhabitants of N.-W. India. . . . Many competent authorities . . . now believe that Harappā was overthrown by the Āryans. It is suggested that the interments in the later cemetery at Harappā are those of "true Vedic Āryans", and that the forts or citadels which the Vedic war-god Indra is said to have destroyed included Harappā in their number.

There is not enough evidence to say with certainty that the destroyers of the Indus cities were members of the group of related tribes whose priests composed the *Ṛg Veda*, but it is probable that the fall of this great civilization was an episode in the widespread migratory movements of charioteering peoples which altered the face of the whole civilized world in the 2nd millennium B.C.

THE RISE OF ASSYRIA AND BABYLONIA

GEORGES ROUX

By about 2000 B.C., the Sumerian civilization that had dominated Mesopotamia for over a thousand years had declined, making way for the rise of other peoples. As the distinguished Near Eastern scholar Georges Roux explains in this concise viewpoint, the early second millennium B.C. saw the rise of several small kingdoms in the region, among them Assyria (in the Mesopotamian highlands), Mari (on the Euphrates River, southwest of Assyria), Larsa (northwest of the Persian Gulf), Ekallatum (probably not far to the southeast of Assyria), and Babylonia, consisting of the lands immediately surrounding the city of Babylon. Eventually, most of these states fell under the sway of either the short-lived first Assyrian Empire, which rose in the early eighteenth century B.C., or the first Babylonian Empire, led by the vigorous Hammurabi (author of the most famous Mesopotamian law code). Though their power and influence would frequently and variously increase and decrease, over the course of the next thousand years the Assyrians and Babylonians would remain the major players in international Mesopotamian affairs.

The foundation of the Assyrian kingdom and its promotion to the rank of a great political and military power are capital events in a period particularly rich in new developments. The city which gave its name to this kingdom, Assur . . . lay in a strong strategic position: built on a hill overlooking the Tigris . . . , protected on one side by the great river, on the other by a canal, and strongly fortified, it commanded the road which, from Sumer or Akkad, went up the Tigris valley either to Kurdistan or to Upper Jazirah. . . .

After the fall of the Sumerian Empire Assur, like many other cities, became independent. Puzur-Ashur I, who must have reigned about 2000 B.C., opens a new line of kings bearing such genuine Akkadian names as Sargon or Narâm-Sin. . . . It was probably during this period that the new kingdom was enlarged to include Nineveh, sixty miles to the north of Assur. But the true founders of Assyrian might were the Western Semites, who during the first centuries of the second millennium flooded northern Iraq as they flooded the southern regions. Halê, the chief of an Amorite tribe, pitched his tent somewhere between the Khabur and the Tigris, and his successors ruled in the orbit of the 'Akkadian' kings of Assur until one of them called Ilâkabkabû succeeded in taking the city and ascended the throne. About the same time another Amorite became King of Mari on the Euphrates, and from then on the destinies of the two great northern kingdoms were intimately blended. . . .

SHAMSHI-ADAD I AND HIS SONS

The man who annexed Mari and built up what is often referred to as 'the first Assyrian Empire', Shamshi-Adad or -Addu (1813–1781 B.C.), began his career as an outlaw. When his brother Amînu [ascended the throne] . . . Shamshi-Adad fled to the south, gathered a troop of mercenaries, took Ekallâtum—an as yet unidentified city on the Middle Tigris . . . marched against Assur and snatched the sceptre from Amînu's hands. Once enthroned he led his armies to the west, to the forest-covered mountains of Lebanon and to that sea which marked the boundaries of the world and fascinated all Mesopotamian conquerors, the Mediterranean:

> A stele inscribed with my great name I set up in the country of Labân (Lebanon), on the shore of the Great Sea.

Then . . . Shamshi-Adad occupied Mari, put it in the hands of his son Iasmah-Adad and appointed another of his sons, Ishme-Dagan, viceroy of Ekallâtum. The Assyrians now held both the Tigris and the Euphrates and governed nearly all northern Mesopotamia.

In the whole history of ancient Iraq few periods are as well documented as the reign of Shamshi-Adad and his sons. Moreover, our information is derived not from the usual official inscriptions, but from the most accurate and reliable documents that an historian can expect: the letters exchanged between the three princes and between Iasmah-Adad and other rulers, and the reports from various officials to their masters; in all, more than three hundred tablets forming part of the royal archives found in the palace of Mari. While these letters are generally undated and therefore difficult to arrange in chronological order, they throw an invaluable light on the daily routine of the court and on the relationship between the governments of Assur, Mari and Ekallâtum and the various peoples, kingdoms and tribes surrounding them. Besides—and this is not the least of their interest—they offer a first-hand moral portrait of the three rulers. For the first time we are in the presence not of mere names but of living persons with their qualities and defects: Ishme-Dagan, a born warrior like his father, always ready to go to battle and proud to announce his victories to his brother—'At Shimanahe we fought and I have taken the entire country. Be glad!'— but on occasion taking him under his wing:

> Do not write to the king. The country where I stay is nearer the capital city. The things you want to write to the king, write them to me, so that I can advise you . . .

Iasmah-Adad of Mari, on the contrary, docile, obedient, but lazy, negligent, cowardly:

> You remain a child, writes his father, there is no beard on your chin, and even now, in the ripeness of age, you have not built up a 'house' . . .

Or again:

> While your brother here is inflicting defeats, you, over there, you lie about amidst women. So now, when you go to Qatanum with the army, be a man! As your brother is making a great name for himself, you too, in your country, make a great name for yourself!

And finally, Shamshi-Adad the father, wise, cunning, meticulous, sometimes humorous, who advises, reprimands or congratulates his sons and keeps Mari under very close control, a control which would have been found unbearable by a more mature prince.

ASSYRIA'S ENEMIES

A constant source of worry for the three rulers were the nomads, particularly numerous in the region of Mari. In and around that kingdom were three large groups of tribes: the Hanaeans, the Bene-Iamina and the Sutaeans. . . . Extremely numerous and mobile, always on the move along the Khabur or across the Euphrates . . . they escaped control, dodged royal census and recruitment, and eventually lent assistance to the King of Eshnunna

and other enemies of the Assyrians. Iasmah-Adad, however, handled them gently, gave them land and ploughs and grain in time
of famine, and remained on fairly good terms with them. . . .

The relations between the Assyrian kingdom and the small
kingdoms around it varied from place to place and often, we
may say, from day to day. With the west (Syria) they were as a
rule excellent. We learn, for instance, that Aplahanda, King of
Karkemish (Jerablus), sent 'excellent wine', food, ornaments and
fine clothing to his 'brother' Iasmah-Adad, granted him the monopoly over certain copper mines in his territory and offered to
give him 'whatever he desired'. We also read that Iasmah-Adad
gave boats for the sheep-rearing nomads from Iamhad (Aleppo)
to cross the Euphrates, married the daughter of the ruler of
Qatanum (or Qatna) and sent troops to his aid. In return, the
ruler of Qatna put his pastures at the disposal of Iasmah-Adad's
shepherds and proposed to pay him a visit. But the peoples and
tribes to the north and east of Assyria proper were far less
friendly. Throughout the twenty odd years covered by the royal
correspondence we see Shamshi-Adad intervening in the 'Upper
Country' (Balikh and Khabur valleys) and leading campaign after campaign along the Zab and around Kirkuk. . . .

Finally, we come to Babylon, the second powerful neighbour
of Assyria. With Babylon relations were cold but polite, since neither Sin-muballit (1812–1793 B.C.) nor Hammurabi (1792–1750
B.C.)—both contemporaries of Shamshi-Adad—had yet turned
their ambition towards the north. Thus Shamshi-Adad dis-
patched to Hammurabi tablets copied at his request, and Iasmah-
Adad returned to Babylon a caravan which had been delayed in
Mari and a Turruku captive who had escaped and sought refuge
in that city. In only one letter do we feel a shadow of anxiety: apparently, Iasmah-Adad had been informed of certain unfriendly
projects of 'the man of Babylon', but after inquiry one of his officials reassures him:

> Now, may my lord's heart be at ease, for the man of
> Babylon will never do harm to my lord.

Some thirty years later, however, Hammurabi was to take and
destroy Mari. . . .

THE RISE OF HAMMURABI AND BABYLON

The victory over four powerful princes and the unification of Mesopotamia are in themselves remarkable achievements sufficient
to single out Hammurabi as one of the greatest Mesopotamian
monarchs. But the King of Babylon was not merely a successful
war-leader: his handling of his opponents reveals the qualities of

a skilful diplomat; his Code of Law displays a passion for justice which, to a great extent, balances the repulsive cruelty of punishments; his inscriptions show a genuine concern for the welfare of his subjects and a deep respect for the traditions of a country which was, after all, foreign to his race; his letters prove that the descendant of an Amorite sheikh could administer a vast kingdom with the same care and attention to detail as the ruler of a Sumerian city-state. Hammurabi's long and glorious reign brought, once again, peace and unity to the country [and] raised Babylon to the rank of a major capital-city. . . . These forty-three years (1792–1750 B.C.) [were] a decisive period in the history of ancient Iraq. Without any doubt, the great figure of King Hammurabi, statesman and lawgiver, deserves special attention.

When Hammurabi ascended the throne he inherited from his father Sin-muballit a comparatively small kingdom, some eighty miles long and twenty miles wide. . . . All around were larger states and more powerful kings: the south was entirely dominated by Rîm-Sin of Larsa who two years before had taken Isin and put an end to the rival dynasty (1794 B.C.); to the north the horizon was barred by the three kingdoms of Mari, Ekallâtum and Assur in the hands of Shamshi-Adad and his sons; and to the east, just across the Tigris, Dadusha, allied to the Elamites, still reigned in Eshnunna. The new King of Babylon was no less determined than his ancestors to enlarge his domain, but he patiently waited for five years before making the first move. Then, when he felt secure enough on the throne, he attacked in three directions: he captured Isin and advanced along the Euphrates as far south as Uruk (sixth year), campaigned in Emutbal, between the Tigris and the Zagros range and occupied the key to that district, Malgum (tenth year), and finally took Rapiqum, upstream of Sippar (eleventh year). Thereafter, it would seem from his date-formulae that for twenty successive years he devoted his time solely to the embellishment of temples and the fortification of towns.

ASSYRIA IN DECLINE

This short series of military operations infringed on the territories of Larsa and Eshnunna and no doubt aroused considerable hostility. . . . As for the Assyrians, they would have rejoiced at the humiliation of 'the man of Eshnunna' had they not been occupied with more serious problems. In the eleventh year of Hammurabi (1781) Shamshi-Adad had died, leaving the sceptre to the more energetic of his two sons, Ishme-Dagan. The weak Iasmah-Adad was still viceroy of Mari, and we possess a letter from the new king to his brother assuring him that his position would not be altered and that he, Ishme-Dagan, would protect him:

> Have no fear. Your throne is definitely your throne and
> I hold in my hand (the gods) Adad and Shamash. The
> people of Elam and the man of Eshnunna, I have them
> on a leash. Have no fear. As long as we live, I and you,
> for ever you will sit on your throne. Let us swear to-
> gether a solemn oath of the gods, then I and you, let us
> meet and establish fraternity between us for ever.

But a few months later Iasmah-Adad was overthrown by a
prince of the 'national' dynasty of Mari, Zimri-Lim . . . who, with
the help of the powerful King of Aleppo, succeeded in 'ascending the throne of his father's house.'. . . .

While we can hardly expect friendly relations between Mari
and Assur, there is no evidence that Ishme-Dagan attempted to
overthrow Zimri-Lim. Hostilities were limited to attacks on one
or two cities on the border between the two kingdoms. . . .

Since Babylon and Mari commanded the entire course of the
Euphrates, the two rulers [of these kingdoms—Hammurabi and
Zimri-Lim] had everything to gain in joining hands together.
Zimri-Lim's ambassador at the court of Babylon kept him fully
posted on 'all the important affairs' of that kingdom, and reciprocally Babylonian messengers reported to Hammurabi all the news
they heard in Mari, this bilateral 'intelligence service' functioning,
it seems, with the full knowledge and approbation of the two sov-
ereigns. The two kings lent each other troops—even soldiers from
Aleppo were once called to the rescue of Babylon by Zimri-Lim—
and rendered each other the minor or major services expected of
good neighbours. But in the light of later events the attitude of
Hammurabi was perhaps less disinterested than it appears, and
he may have used his ally merely to consolidate his power. Piece
by piece emerges from these undated and therefore unclassifiable
archives the figure of a patient and cunning politician. . . .

HAMMURABI TRIUMPHANT

At long last . . . [in the year 1763 B.C.] Hammurabi took the offensive and . . . attacked Larsa. Rîm-Sin . . . was overthrown after a reign of sixty years, the longest in Mesopotamian annals. . . .

Now the master of southern and central Mesopotamia, Hammurabi was not a man to stop there. The great empires of Akkad
and Ur must have been in his mind when he decided to attack
his old friend Zimri-Lim. . . . Zimri-Lim did not lose his throne
but was made a vassal of Hammurabi. Two years later, however,
the Babylonian troops were again sent to Mari, perhaps to quell
a rebellion. This time the city wall was dismantled, the beauti-

ful palace of Zimri-Lim was sacked and burnt down, and the great metropolis of the middle Euphrates turned into ruins for ever (1759 B.C.).

Finally, in the thirty-sixth and thirty-eighth years of his reign Hammurabi 'overthrew the army of the country Subartu (Assyria)' and 'defeated all his enemies as far as the country of Subartu'. What treatment was reserved for Assur we do not know. Somehow the Assyrian dynasty managed to survive, but the Assyrian domination in northern Iraq had come to an end.

Thus in ten years all but one of the five Mesopotamian kingdoms had successively disappeared, and Mesopotamia now formed one single nation under Babylonian rule. How far Hammurabi's power extended is difficult to say. A stele with his inscription is said to have been found near Diarbakr, at the foot of the Taurus, but Elam and Syria remained independent. . . . To subdue them would have required more time and forces than were at Hammurabi's disposal. The Babylonian monarch called himself 'mighty King, King of Babylon, King of the whole country of Amurru, King of Sumer and Akkad, King of the Four Quarters of the World' but, wisely no doubt, he did not attempt to gain effective control over 'the Universe'.

AN EYEWITNESS TO MIGHTY ANCIENT BABYLON

HERODOTUS

The famous Greek historian Herodotus, often called the "Father" of history, visited the great city of Babylon in the mid–fifth century B.C. Well more than a thousand years following the glory days of the lawgiver Hammurabi, at this time Babylon was one of the capitals of the Persian Empire, which had risen and taken control of most of the Near East in the mid–sixth century B.C. In this excerpt from his *Histories*, Herodotus describes the city, then the largest and most splendid in the world, including its famous stepped ziggurat, which may have been the inspiration for the biblical Tower of Babel.

B abylon lies in a wide plain, a vast city in the form of a square with sides nearly fourteen miles long and a circuit of some fifty-six miles, and in addition to its enormous size it surpasses in splendour any city of the known world. It is surrounded by a broad deep moat full of water, and within the moat there is a wall fifty cubits wide and two hundred high (the royal cubit is three inches longer than the ordinary cubit). And now I must describe how the soil dug out to make the moat was used, and the method of building the wall. While the digging was going on, the earth that was shovelled out was formed into bricks, which were baked in ovens as soon as a sufficient number were made; then using hot bitumen for mortar the workmen began by revetting with brick each side of the moat, and then went on to erect the actual wall. In both cases they laid rush-mats between every thirty courses of brick. On the top of the wall they constructed, along each edge, a row of one-roomed buildings facing inwards with enough space between for a four-horse chariot to pass. There are a hundred gates in the circuit of the wall, all of bronze with bronze uprights and lintels.

Eight days' journey from Babylon there is a city called Is on a smallish river of the same name, a tributary of the Euphrates, and in this river lumps of bitumen are found in great quantity. This was the source of supply for the bitumen used in building the wall of Babylon. The Euphrates, a broad, deep, swift river which rises in Armenia and flows into the Persian Gulf, runs through the middle of the city and divides it in two. The wall is brought right down to the water on both sides, and at an angle to it there is another wall on each bank, built of baked bricks without mortar, running through the town. There are a great many houses of three and four storeys. The main streets and the side streets which lead to the river are all dead straight, and for every one of the side streets or alleys there was a bronze gate in the river wall by which the water could be reached.

THE GREAT TEMPLE OF BEL

The great wall I have described is the chief armour of the city; but there is a second one within it, hardly less strong though smaller. There is a fortress in the middle of each half of the city: in one the royal palace surrounded by a wall of great strength, in the other the temple of Bel, the Babylonian Zeus. The temple is a square building, two furlongs each way, with bronze gates, and was still in existence in my time; it has a solid central tower, one furlong square, with a second erected on top of it and then a third, and so on up to eight. All eight towers can be climbed by a spiral way running round the outside, and about half-way up there are seats for those who make the ascent to rest on. On the summit of the topmost tower stands a great temple with a fine large couch in it, richly covered, and a golden table beside it. The shrine contains no image and no one spends the night there except . . . one Assyrian woman, all alone, whoever it may be that the god has chosen. The Chaldaeans [Babylonians] also say—though I do not believe them—that the god enters the temple in person and takes his rest upon the bed. . . .

In the temple of Babylon there is a second shrine lower down, in which is a great sitting figure of Bel, all of gold on a golden throne, supported on a base of gold, with a golden table standing beside it. I was told by the Chaldaeans that, to make all this, more than twenty-two tons of gold were used. Outside the temple is a golden altar, and there is another one, not of gold, but of great size, on which full-grown sheep are sacrificed. (The golden altar is reserved for the sacrifice of sucklings only.) On the larger altar the Chaldaeans also offer something like two and a half tons of frankincense every year at the festival of Bel. In the time of [the Persian ruler] Cyrus there was also in this sacred building a solid golden statue of a man some fifteen feet high—I have this on the authority of the Chaldaeans, though I never saw it myself. . . . In addition to the adornments I have described there are also many private offerings in the temple.

BRIDGING THE RIVER

There have been many kings of Babylon who helped to fortify the city and adorn its temples. . . . There were also two queens, the earlier, Semiramis, preceding the later by five generations. It was Semiramis who was responsible for certain remarkable embankments in the plain outside the city, built to control the river which until then used to flood the whole countryside. The later of the two queens, Nitocris, was a woman of greater intelligence than Semiramis, and not only left as a memorial of her reign the works which I will presently describe, but also, having her eye on the great and expanding power of the Medes and the many cities, including Nineveh itself, which had fallen before them, took every possible measure to increase her security. For instance, she changed the course of the Euphrates, which flows through Babylon. . . .

She was responsible for another undertaking of a less important kind: the city, as I have said, being divided in two by the river, it was necessary under its previous rulers for anyone who wanted to get from one half to the other to cross over by boat and no doubt this was a tiresome business. Nitocris, however, when she was having the basin dug for the lake [which she created near the city], had the foresight to make that work a means of getting rid of the inconvenience as well as of leaving yet another monument of her reign. She ordered long stone blocks to be cut, and when they were ready and the excavation complete, she diverted the river into the basin; and while the basin was filling and the original bed of the stream was drying up, she built with burnt brick, on the same pattern as the wall, an embankment on each side of the river where it flowed through the city, and also along the descent to the water's edge from the gates at the end of the side streets; then, as near as possible to the centre of the city, she built a bridge over the river with the blocks of stone which she had had prepared, using iron and lead to bind the blocks together. Between the piers of the bridge she had squared baulks of timber laid down for the inhabitants to cross by—but only during daylight, for every night the timber was removed to prevent people from going over in the dark and robbing each other. Finally when the basin had been filled and the bridge finished, the river was brought back into its original bed, with the result that the basin had been made to serve the queen's purpose, and the people of the town had their bridge into the bargain. . . .

A WEALTHY CITY

I will give several indications of the wealth and resources of Babylon, but the following is a specially striking one. Apart from normal tribute, the whole Persian empire is divided into regions for the purpose of furnishing supplies for the king and his army, and for four months out of the twelve the supplies come from Babylonian territory, the whole of the rest of Asia being responsible for the remaining eight. This shows that the resources of Assyria are a third part of the resources of Asia as a whole. It will be seen that the governorship (or satrapy, as the Persians call it) of Assyria is by far the most coveted of all their provincial posts, when one realizes that Tritantaechmes the son of Artabazus, who held it from the king, received an *artaba* of silver every day—the artaba is a Persian dry measure of about five bushels. . . . He also had as his personal property, in addition to war horses, eight hundred stallions and sixteen thousand mares, twenty for each stallion, and so many Indian dogs that four large villages in the plain were exempted from other charges on condition of supplying them with food. This will give an idea of the wealth of the governor of Babylon.

CHINA'S FIRST DYNASTIES

L. CARRINGTON GOODRICH

Far to the east of the Near Eastern realms of Egypt and Mesopotamia lay China, which also developed a high civilization along a mighty river, in this case the Yellow River (Huang Ho). The first important dynastic rulers of China were the Shang. Their domain was centered on the lower and middle reaches of the Yellow River in what is now eastern China. The Shang dynasty flourished from the sixteenth to eleventh centuries B.C., the period in which the Mycenaeans rose and fell in Greece, the second Assyrian Empire rose in Mesopotamia, and the first kingdom of Israel rose in Palestine. L. Carrington Goodrich, a former professor of Chinese at Columbia University, here describes the Shang achievement, including the mastery of writing, government by the king and his officials, the invention of a workable calendar, warfare and weapons, and local arts and crafts.

The beginning of history in China coincides, more or less, with the latter half of the second millennium before the Christian era. . . .

The Chinese call this period Shang (a later name is Yin), after the royal house that ruled over the region near its capital . . . [dated] approximately from 1523 to 1028 B.C. The origins of the Shang dynasty can only be guessed at; however, we must certainly assume developments of fundamental significance that could produce a governing group which could command many lesser chiefs who in turn dominated the peasants, could make war with wheeled vehicles and sizable bodies of troops, could initiate and carry on the construction of public works, and could perform religious rites apparently on behalf of the people as a whole. These developments must have included a population increase that required some centralization of authority; the storing of millet, wheat, and possibly rice against times of drought, flood, and siege; the collection of metals from a wide area for the casting of tools and weapons; and increased specialization in skills on the part of the people.

According to traditional history, the first Shang princes succeeded in subduing eighteen hundred city-states; that they had periodic difficulties with the more powerful aggregations of these city-states is clear. On several occasions they were forced to shift their capital, possibly because of raids or the difficulty of defending it, or because of some calamity like a flood. The exact location of the capital cities is unknown; possibilities are near modern Chengchou (Honan), Tsinan (Shantung), and Sian (Shensi), where archeologists have recently found extensive remains of early and middle Shang culture. Around 1300 B.C. one ruler and his court arrived near modern Anyang and slowly erected a city that contained government buildings, palaces, temples, and mausoleums.

SURVIVING WRITTEN EVIDENCE

The discovery of this capital city has thrown light on what was hitherto only dimly known, for the remains of its buildings and their contents have withstood the dampness and man's destructive hand better than less complex structures and furnishings. In addition to the exact knowledge about architecture, defensive weapons, and ritual vessels thus made possible, a great body of information has been acquired through the recovery of tens of thousands of inscriptions, most of them fragmentary and unquestionably representing only a small portion of the written documents of the period. There are a few laconic inscriptions on bronze, such as blades of dagger axes or the bowls of altar pieces, and on pieces of pottery and jade; but most of them are found on the bones of animals or the shells of a tortoise now extinct which derived from the valley of the Yangtze or farther south. . . . Some of these inscriptions indicate that there was a special group of men in the government whose duty was to keep records. In addition to writing on metal, shell, and bone, the inscriptions suggest that the Shang Chinese also wrote on wood, bamboo, and possibly silk. Depending on the writing surface, their tools included a knife or burin and a primitive brush; ink, probably made from soot, was used on wood and pottery; and the scratched lines were often filled in with cinnabar.

The non-primitive writing and the number of written words—

around 3000 (about 1400 can be read)—argue a considerable history before the thirteenth century B.C.; but where writing originated is as yet unknown. Some scholars suggest connections with western Asia on the basis of the similarity between the pictographic forms of certain words used by both eastern and western scribes. It may be, but there is a gap of some two thousand years between the pictographs of, say, Egypt and those of China, and it is entirely possible that these early Chinese devised their signs for such words as they had for sun and rain independently, as did the Sioux and Ojibways in North America. Moreover, the arguments for an independent origin are reinforced by the fact that certain written signs, such as those for the numerals 5, 6, 7, 8, 9, 10 and for the twenty-two characters indicating the Chinese cycle, have no parallels elsewhere. Obviously there was some extended development within the Yellow River valley itself, for many of the signs have a purely Chinese connotation. As one of the principal English investigators has remarked, even in the Shang period these signs were "so greatly stylized and disguised as to presuppose the passage of a long, a very long past.". . .

Although recent discoveries have given us a great deal of knowledge about the written language, we have far less information regarding the spoken. The inscriptions show that the order of words was not unlike our own, that there were—to give Chinese parts of speech the same names as our own—pronouns and prepositions, that the nouns were not inflected to show number or gender, and that the verbs were not conjugated. The pronunciation, however, can only be guessed at from the study of groups of words of a much later date. Probably far more words were used in speech than have been preserved on bones and shells. There also must have been many dialects; intercommunication was slow and hazardous because of the many variations in the writing of certain words. The writing problem was solved by fiat ten centuries later when one dominant group forced the adoption of a single form, but the dialects have continued with modifications until our own day.

THE KING AND HIS GOVERNMENT

The scribes at the royal court and elsewhere were only one of several groups who provided for the functioning of the government. At the head was the king, with whom was associated one or more queens. (The inscriptions contain the names of twenty-three of the thirty-one kings named in later documents.) There is a remote possibility that eunuchs officiated in his household. The king led in battle, in the hunt, and in special sacrifices as an intermediary between his people and nature—the latter to such an extent that he came to have a kind of priestly function. On questions that perplexed him he consulted his ancestors—the possible beginning of ancestor worship. The rule of succession was mixed, some being from father to son, some from elder to younger brother, with five deviations from both practices.

City government was well developed, for the titles of a number of functionaries in the capital city have been found. Their duties concerned the collection and expenditure of tribute, the construction of public buildings and defenses, and the care of irrigation works. The priests were important associates; they probably presided over all ceremonies and advised the king on everything to prevent him from offending the unseen world. They made sacrifices to the royal ancestors in the temples, and to the shên, or gods, both indoors and out. The sacrifices included sheep, pigs, dogs, cattle, and at times horses and humans, the latter probably captured on raids into enemy lands.

The determination of the calendar, which was then and has been throughout history a major function of the Chinese government as it is for any people who depend largely on farming, was also doubtless in the hands of the priests. The Shang calendar, though clumsy, was fairly stable and was frequently adjusted to make it agree with the seasons. The shortest period was ten days; three such periods (sometimes shortened by one day) made a month, the character for which was a moon. Six ten-day periods made a sixty-day cycle; this was a fundamental unit and each day in it had a two-character designation. Six cycles made a year. (The character for a year, says one scholar, represents a man carrying a sheaf of grain on his back—in other words, the annual harvest in the one-crop country of northern China.) When necessary, the offices of the celendrical bureau added to the six-cycle year one, two, or more commonly three ten-day units; there is one instance of the addition of a whole cycle, making fourteen months in all. This practice, which is called intercalation, was continued until modern times.

The men who managed the calendar must have been both knowledgeable and responsible, for on them in considerable measure depended the favor the king received from the people. Among a credulous people, the king was presumed to commune with the spirits; if he failed to perceive their signs, he had obviously lost their favor. Hence his hold on his court and his subjects had to be maintained by calendrical accuracy as well as military success abroad and political adroitness at home. This accounts for the attention paid to this branch of science throughout thirty-odd centuries, and for the eagerness with which Chinese rulers welcomed astronomers from India, central Asia, Persia, and Europe, when they excelled the Chinese in these calculations. The men responsible for the calendar in the Shang period were probably less advanced than the Babylonians in their knowledge of the stars, but their performance was good and as a result they may have been entrusted with other recordkeeping duties. In the second century B.C., the Grand Astrologer and his son who succeeded to this title were both official archivists and historians as well. This combination of offices in one man helps to explain why the earliest Chinese historical documents (down to 200 B.C.) include so many data on eclipses and other celestial phenomena.

Warfare during the Shang period, both offensive and defensive, was apparently frequent, for there are references to such struggles in the inscriptions. To collect tribute and supply the court with all its needs and luxuries—cattle, horses, slaves, copper, tin, furs, ivory, plumes—must have necessitated a great deal of "power politics" and foraging in regions far away from the capital. Similarly, outside tribes must often have looked with envy and longing at the growing wealth of the central plain and reached out in force to seize it. The people fought with the composite bow (a powerful weapon, widely used in northern Asia but not in Europe) and feathered arrows tipped with ribbed or barbed bronze or clay points. Other bows "shot" pellets of bone points or stone. Bronze spears, halberds, and battle-axes were used in close fighting. The common soldier or slave fought on foot; the noble, from a chariot drawn by two horses. Certain soldiers were protected by bronze helmets and possibly by armor and shields made of leather, wood, or bone.

A HIGH DEGREE OF MATERIAL CULTURE

Life in the country districts probably did not change materially from the Stone Age to the Bronze, although agriculture may have increased in importance. Hoes and mattocks were still bladed with stone, and the ground was still tilled with a foot plow. Some of the people tended cattle; others made coarse unpainted pottery. Everyone lived—at least in winter—in subterranean dwellings or loess caves. According to a poem of a slightly later date:

> Of old Tan-fu the duke
> Scraped shelters, scraped holes;
> As yet they had no houses.

Life in the capital city, however, and doubtless in other urban centers became complex, and specialization appeared. Some of the city dwellers must have handled the sale and distribution of products coming in from the country districts and elsewhere. Others made clothes, cord, and pennants from silk and hemp.

There were basket weavers, craftsmen in bone and wood and stone, potters who made incised white vessels, bronze casters, and builders of houses, temples, and mausoleums. Men will probably marvel for all time at the handiwork of this period that has survived—the great royal tombs furnished with ceremonial bronze and pottery vessels and pieces of sculptured marble; the wrought ivory, and the bone inlaid with turquoise; the small figures cast in bronze; the various musical instruments, such as triangular stones, bells, and ocarinas; the dagger axes, chariot fittings, harness ornaments, and box covers. They indicate a high degree of material culture. Some of them, like the *li* tripod and certain decorative motifs, are obviously descended from Late Stone Age prototypes. . . .

The collapse of the Shang dynasty in the eleventh century B.C. has been ascribed to the advent of the Chou, a new power that developed to the west. In all probability the members of the old ruling house had become effete and were unable to carry on the hard fighting with frontiersmen born to war and welded into an effective unit by an able leader. At all events, their capital was ruthlessly destroyed by the invader and those who escaped had to flee for their lives. This was an important moment in the history of civilization in eastern Asia, for the defeat of the Shang suddenly widened the range of Chinese civilization. Korean history traditionally begins with the overthrow of the Shang. For over ten centuries the Fu-yü, a people of Manchuria, celebrated annually a religious rite based on the Shang calendar. Some of the fleeing Shang adherents too may have reached the Yangtze state of Ch'u.

Mesopotamia: Cradle of Human Culture?

CHAPTER 2

WHEN AND WHERE WAS THE GREAT FLOOD?

PETER JAMES AND NICK THORPE

One of the most enduring cultural legacies of ancient Mesopotamia, the so-called cradle of civilization, is the story of the "great flood," which appears in the folk legends of many ancient peoples. Until recently, modern scholars were not certain that such a catastrophe actually occurred; and many believed that if it did take place, it was a local event that affected only a small part of the Near East. But could the flood have been a much more pivotal event, one that actually set in motion the original settlement of the Mesopotamian plains? In fact, historians have long disagreed about how and when large numbers of people first settled the region. It is still not clear, for example, whether the Sumerians came from the east or north; and the location of their original homeland remains a mystery. Nor is it certain where the stone-age farmers who preceded them in the area originated. A provocative new theory suggests that the great flood took place in the Black Sea region and that large masses of refugees from the disaster (or those displaced by them) moved southward and settled the Tigris-Euphrates valley in the sixth millennium B.C. The following essay by historian Peter James and archaeologist Nick Thorpe provides an overview of the various modern theories about the great flood (and in general the idea of large catastrophes influencing human history) and concludes with the Black Sea scenario.

O n July 16, 1994, a small fragmenting comet known as Shoemaker-Levy began ripping through the atmosphere of the planet Jupiter, causing explosions of almost unimaginable intensity. As the second fragment fell there was a blast equivalent to 250 million tons of TNT—several times more powerful than all the world's nuclear arsenals put together. When the third chunk of the comet struck it created a hole in Jupiter's atmosphere the size of the Earth. The full extent of the damage that Shoemaker-Levy inflicted on Jupiter is still being assessed, though one thing is already perfectly clear: the long-cherished scientific belief that comets are harmless and cannot crash into planets has been dispelled forever.

The question immediately arises—could a comet, or cometary fragment, crash into the Earth? Or has it already done so? In the seventeenth and eighteenth centuries, in the days before Darwin, scientists freely speculated about such matters, wondering whether a comet might have been responsible for the Great Flood described in the Bible. While theologians were happy to accept that the Flood was caused by God directly, scientists were busy researching possible physical mechanisms. Some, including the great Edmond Halley (who gave his name to the famous comet), looked beyond the Earth for a trigger. In 1694 he proposed, in a paper to the Royal Society, that Noah's Flood was caused by the collision between the Earth and a comet, which landed in the Caspian Sea and drenched the surrounding lands with water. Others speculated that a watery comet was responsible.

From the standpoint of pre-Darwinian science, belief in a Great Flood was entirely reasonable, as such an event seemed to explain many of the world's greatest historical enigmas. The rocks that scientists were beginning to examine were full of the fossilized remains of millions of extinct plants and creatures, and a catastrophic flood could account for why these life-forms no longer existed and why their remains had been trapped and preserved in sedimentary rock. It seemed natural, then, to borrow an explanation from the Bible, which told of the deluge in the time of Noah. Assuming that there had been a real Flood also provided an economical explanation for why there are so many similar legends around the world.

CATASTROPHISM GOES OUT OF FASHION

Such quaint ideas went completely out of fashion in the early nineteenth century. The relatively new science of geology was maturing, and the naive view that all the world's rock strata had been laid down in a single event was seen to be unworkable. It was becoming clear that there was a whole sequence of layers from different ages, laid one upon the other, each containing its own life-forms. The question now was what had created these strata and how long they took to form. One school of geology was the catastrophists, who expanded the idea of a Great Flood into a whole series of cataclysms—sometimes of water, sometimes of fire (from volcanic activity). Their opponents represented a new school of thought—the uniformitarians. Founded in the 1830s by lawyer Charles Lyell, they set new ground rules for the debate. Geologists generally agreed that special causes—such as direct divine intervention—should be excluded from scientific discussion, and Lyell now introduced his principles of "uniformity," which attempted to rule out special events as well.

The law of uniformity states that the "present is the key to the past": only the same forces that are visible today were responsible for shaping the world. . . .

Here there was another force at work besides the desire to develop a rationalist view of the Earth's history free from biblical influence. This was the straightforward desire—shared by scientists with the rest of us—to view the Earth as a safe place to live. This desire was the root cause of a fierce and protracted philosophical debate that had been raging for over two thousand years. On the one side was Plato, who used the evidence of myth and legend (as well as his own gleanings from geology and archaeology) to argue that the Earth had been subject to periodic catastrophes brought about by causes outside our world. On the other side was his pupil Aristotle, who insisted that as the heavens were made of perfect matter they could present no dangers to the Earth. . . .

WOOLLEY'S SUMERIAN FLOOD

And what of the greatest catastrophe legend of all, the worldwide story of a Great Flood? The Flood story still remains one of the most baffling, unsolved mysteries of our distant past. Only biblical fundamentalists accept the story in the completely literal sense that the entire world was covered by a single deluge, from which Noah and his family were the sole survivors. Despite the best efforts of creationist scientists, they have never been able to agree among themselves on a model that can explain the Earth's strata in terms of the Flood, let alone produce one that is convincing to secular scientists.

Atlantologists, of course, have tried to explain the origin of the Flood legends by the sinking of Atlantis—survivors fled to different parts of the globe, bringing with them similar versions of the same events. But the theory is only credible if we accept the existence of a lost Atlantic continent.

The longest-standing explanation of the Flood legends is that the story spread from the ancient Near East, having grown from a real but localized event, which struck some of the earliest cities of southern Mesopotamia. In 1928 British archaeologist Sir Leonard Woolley was excavating the Sumerian city of Ur when, underneath a city dating to c. 3500 B.C., he came across a thick layer of "clean water-laid mud." Somewhat puzzled, he continued digging and eight feet farther down he found flint implements and pottery again—remains of an earlier phase of the city *before* the mud was laid down. It was Woolley's wife who voiced their suspicions about the cause of the mysterious sediment layer: "Well, of course, it's the Flood."

It seemed easy enough to deduce that a great flood had swept across southern Mesopotamia, and that from there the story had spread, giving rise to different but closely related versions around the Near East and Eastern Mediterranean. Small details changed, such as the name of the hero who survived the Flood, known in Mesopotamia as Utnapishtim—the Hebrews called him Noah, while the Greeks remembered the Flood of Deucalion. Woolley's "Flood level" at Ur is still frequently cited as if the mystery were completely solved. Yet matters are not quite so simple. The flood discovered by Woolley doesn't seem to have been that important, as it caused no real break in culture at Ur. Nor was it that extensive. There is no trace of the same mud level at other cities, even at Ubaid, a mere twenty miles away. Other cities have evidence of equally great floods. For example, another British archaeologist, Sir Max Mallowan (the husband of Agatha Christie), identified a slightly later sediment layer at another Sumerian city, Kish, as traces of the Flood. Yet Mallowan's candidate suffers from the same problems as Woolley's—it was extremely localized and not that disastrous. In fact, flood levels are common at Mesopotamian sites. The twin rivers, Tigris and Euphrates, around which Mesopotamian civilization grew, were an ever-present danger, as well as a blessing, and there are many textual references to massive local floods. Yet the ancient Mesopotamians, rather like the people who live today in the tornado belt of Texas, Oklahoma, Kansas and Nebraska, seem to have taken such disasters in their stride. It is hard to believe that such local floods could have inspired the myth of a universal deluge.

THE BLACK SEA FLOOD

Unconvinced by the Mesopotamian theory, biblical scholar John Bright argued in 1942 that the Flood legend must date much earlier than the fourth millennium B.C., possibly reflecting a real catastrophe of much greater dimensions "taking place far back in the Stone Age." In the last couple of years a fascinating new theory proposed by two American geologists would seem to fit the bill. Ever since the end of the Ice Age the world's sea levels have been rising, usually gradually, but sometimes in fits and starts. Bill Ryan and Walt Pitman, marine geologists at the Lamont-Doherty Earth Observatory in New York, have proposed that a catastrophic episode around 7000 B.C. completely transformed the Black Sea. During the Ice Age it seems that sea levels were so low that the Black Sea, surrounded as it is by the Balkans, southern Russia, and Turkey, was like a gigantic freshwater lake, unconnected with the salty Mediterranean. Separating the two seas was a plug of sediment where the Bosphorus Straits now lie. Ryan and Pitman argue that as the level of the Mediterranean rose, the pressure of the water on this plug would have reached a critical point, with the sea bursting through about 7000 B.C. With this sudden onrush, all the coasts of the Black Sea would have been swamped and their inhabitants driven farther afield. If some migrated southward to Mesopotamia, they could have preserved memories of this catastrophe as the legend of the Great Flood.

Ryan and Pitman's new theory has much to recommend it. Both the biblical and Babylonian traditions locate the place of refuge of the Flood survivors in the mountains to the north of Mesopotamia (Ararat), the high ground just to the south of the Black Sea coast.

THE INVENTION OF
WRITING

WOLFRAM VON SODEN

In this informative essay, Wolfram von Soden, a distinguished Assyriologist of Germany's University of Münster, summarizes the beginnings of writing in the Near East and its subsequent spread to other regions. He begins with the invention of cuneiform, the wedge-shaped writing used first by the Sumerians and then by other peoples in the Near East. The people of Ebla, in northern Syria, for instance, learned to record their own language in cuneiform symbols. The Hurrians, Hittites, Luwians, and Paleans, all ancient inhabitants of mountainous Asia Minor, also employed versions of this form of writing. Von Soden then explains how alphabetic writing rose among Canaanites (who inhabited Palestine), including the Phoenicians; and how, through the Greeks, alphabetic writing later spread across Europe and eventually most of the world.

T he invention of writing was one of the most consequential innovations in human history. Millennia had already passed in which quite different technologies had been developed. Then an expanding economy and the agglomeration of a large mass of people within a confined space in Western Asia created a situation which could no longer be managed merely by the spoken word and improvised notes recording quantities of animals and objects. We have learned only recently that the earliest writing had precursors. Clay counting stones had already been used throughout Southwest Asia and Egypt for many hundreds of years. These had symbols for animals and certain objects scratched into them and were placed in the appropriate number in a pouch or clay holder. The use of plates with numerical points or marks followed. After the middle of the fourth millennium, clay tablets with distinctly differentiated numerical marks were introduced, as well as individual numerical stones, and, later on, cylinder seals. Nevertheless, these improvisations became less and less sufficient for the increasingly complex demands which were being made on the marking system. Thus around 3000, the Sumerians in Uruk came upon the idea of creating hundreds of somewhat abbreviated pictograms and many signs for numbers and measures. These pictograms were pressed into clay tablets with a reed stylus, making possible records not only for immediate use but for archival purposes as well. A few signs for certain adjectives, verbs, and abstract terms soon followed this initial development. It is impossible to say whether the transition to a genuine system of writing, representing audible words by means of visible signs, came about swiftly or demanded a longer amount of time. In any case, desperate administrators at that time gave impetus to a new creation, the possibilities and consequences of which no one in contemporary Sumer could have foreseen.

Writing "Captures" Languages

The further development of writing can be sketched here only with a few brief strokes. The pictograms were increasingly simplified, and the forms of the signs generally became abstract and geometric. Curved lines, which could be written in clay only with difficulty, were replaced by straight ones. Above all, deeper impressions were produced at the beginning of the lines through the pressure of the stylus. These impressions became increasingly broader until the middle of the third millennium, when distinctive, wedge-shaped signs became characteristic, and cuneiform became a distinctive writing system that could even be used on metal and stone. The particular writing traditions in Babylonia, Assyria, Syria, Asia Minor, and so forth led to variant forms for most signs. At first, writing was from top to bottom, but after about 2400 it was from left to right, whereby the signs were turned 90 degrees.

The signs for Sumerian words had already been used at a very early stage for other homonyms as well; thus, for example, *ti*, "arrow," was also used for *ti(l)*, "life." Later, most signs became simultaneously word and syllabic signs and, in rare cases, bisyllabic signs. Signs existed for single sounds only in the cases of the vowels *a, e, i, u*, and perhaps *o*. Partially as a result of the coinciding of originally variant signs—their number was greatly reduced in the course of time to about six hundred—many signs had multiple word and phonetic values quite early on. Since a series of signs could also stand for a word (e.g., A.TU.GAB.LIŠ for *asal*, "Euphrates poplar"), some signs even took on multiple meanings. With the aid of graphic determinatives for materials such as wood or copper, places, rivers, classes of persons, deities, and other things, the scribes sought to reduce the ambiguity of the polyphony of signs to a bearable mass, but they achieved thereby only limited success. Aids to our own reading very often are provided by variations in the writing, as when one could write a syllable such as *tar* as *ta-ar*, and when two or more signs could be used for many syllables in certain periods or in specific groups of texts.

The idea that it was possible to capture a language by means of writing soon traveled along the trade routes to the west and east. The Egyptians learned from the new art and soon created their own writing system—Egyptian hieroglyphics—which indicated vowels only in rare instances. In the East, neighboring Elam was the first to adopt the new writing with some modifications. . . . The idea of writing then migrated further eastward to India, where sometime later the Indus script developed, and still further, to China.

CUNEIFORM WRITING SPREADS TO OTHER REGIONS

In Babylonia itself, the most important event in the history of cuneiform was the adoption of the Sumerian writing system by the Semitic Akkadians at a still unknown time in the third millennium. This process was completed over a long period of time. Indeed, the absence of any systematic means for solving the problems inherent in this adoption shows that the Akkadians adapted the Sumerian writing system to a language with a completely different structure. . . .

From this it can be seen that cuneiform, despite its difficulty and the absence of any other form of writing besides Egyptian hieroglyphics, was used in many countries in Western Asia, far beyond the region in which the Babylonian-Assyrian language was established. Only recently have we discovered that the earliest adoption of writing in the West was of cuneiform, in which the Eblaite language was written from about 2400 or even somewhat earlier. . . .

According to our knowledge, Assyrian merchants brought cuneiform to Asia Minor about 1900. They wrote their Old Assyrian letters and documents, in cuneiform, in a style which deviated considerably from the Old Babylonian. After about 1500 the writing customs in Assyria changed sharply.

When the Hittites, Luwians, and Paleans came to Asia Minor they were not writing their languages, so far as we know, nor did they even adopt the writing style of the Assyrian merchants. After about 1600, however, some royal inscriptions allow us to recognize the influence of the scribal school in Old Babylonian Mari. The typical Old, Middle, and Neo-Hittite writing style of the capital of Hattusas must have had still other models which we are yet unable to identify. . . .

THE PHOENICIAN ALPHABET

Certainly the desire to write in their own language and, especially, to loose themselves from the complicated writing systems of cuneiform in the north and Egyptian hieroglyphics in the south emerged among the western Canaanites early in the second millennium. The oldest witnesses to this are some stone and bronze inscriptions from Byblos. Here we can identify 114 writing signs, a few of which were still pictograms, but most of which were syllabic signs. . . .

Numerous lesser remains of early writing systems have been discovered at primitive mining sites in the Sinai peninsula and southern Palestine. However, attempts to decipher the Sinai inscriptions, which have long been known, have not progressed beyond conjecture.

After the idea of writing was conceived, probably in Sumerian Uruk . . . , the second great achievement in this field was the transition from ideograms and syllabic writing to the isolation of individual phonetic sounds in the form of alphabetic writing. For this, too, we must assume a monogenetic origin, since all later alphabets were either derived from the Phoenician or were created under the influence of its derivatives. Sadly, we still do not know where and when the oldest alphabet came into existence. The oldest Phoenician inscription of significance, found on the sarcophagus of Ahiram of Byblos, is to be dated around 1000. Smaller inscriptions with a similar orthography may be some centuries older. The discovery of Ugaritic cuneiform proves that the Phoenician alphabetic script cannot have come into existence much later than 1500, since the scribes at Ugarit adopted the principle of alphabetic writing and took over the Phoenician alphabet with certain alterations; even in the forms of the signs Ugaritic depended heavily on the Phoenician alphabet. The ancient port city of Byblos (Gebal) could have been the place where alphabetic writing was invented. . . .

The Phoenicians were able to indicate their consonantal phonemes much more exactly than had been possible with cuneiform. Still, as in Egyptian, the Phoenicians initially had to leave undetermined almost all vowels and, later, all short vowels. It has frequently been argued that the letters were initially syllabic signs; so, for example, *m* had originally been a *ma*. Even should that proposal be correct, the fact remains that *m* and *m* + a vowel were written with the same letters. The writing is from right to left.

As early as 1000 alphabetic writing was adopted in South Arabia. There the forms of the signs became more starkly geometric, and writing was either from right to left or from left to right, often with a change of direction in each line (the so-called bustrophedon-style). For the ancient Semitic consonants, which were particularly well preserved in Old South Arabic, seven further signs were added to the twenty-two Phoenician letters. From South Arabia alphabetic writing further migrated to India, where it was considerably transformed by the introduction of vowel signs. Much later it came to Ethiopia, where it was written from left to right, as in India.

Alphabetic writing for Aramaic spread quickly after 1000 in Syria-Palestine and in Mesopotamia. After 900 the Aramaeans began to introduce letters for initial *aleph* and the half-vowels *w* and *y*, as well as *h* instead of *aleph*, as designations for the long vowels *a, i/e,* and *u/o*. Additional signs for short vowels were first introduced in different systems after 500. Nevertheless, (North) Arabic and the other languages employing the Arabic script (e.g., Neo-Persian, Osmanic-Turkish until the time of Ataturk) have been written right down to the present without vowel signs.

We do not know when Israel adopted the Phoenician script with its ancient alphabet, which is still in use today. It must be assumed, however, that this took place under David at the latest. Moab and other neighboring states may have followed quickly. The script migrated westward with the Phoenician-Punic language, but it was not until a thousand years later that the Arabic script was developed out of the script of the Nabateans of southern Palestine, who wrote Aramaic; this script then became a worldwide script.

Even more significant was the adoption of the alphabetic script by the Greeks, which took place around 800 at the latest. Since these people were accustomed to writing with vowels, they made vowel letters out of six consonant signs which they found to be unnecessary; to these were added four letters, among them the *omega*. The Phoenician-Hebraic alphabet was only slightly altered, and all European alphabets were subsequently derived from the Greek script.

THE SUMERIANS
CREATE THE WORLD'S
FIRST LITERATURE

JACQUETTA HAWKES

Once they had fashioned a usable mode of writing, the Sumerians were able to create actual literature, including epic and other poetry, letters, proverbs, and other literary forms. This discussion of Sumerian literature is by the distinguished historian and archaeologist Jacquetta Hawkes, author of numerous widely read books about ancient history. Here, she summarizes the different kinds of Sumerian literature and speculates about Mesopotamian bards (wandering poets) and how they may have performed the epics after they had been committed to writing. She also compares the most famous of these early epics—a collection of poems about the hero Gilgamesh—to the later epic poems (the *Iliad* and *Odyssey*) attributed to the Greek bard Homer.

I n the Sumeria of the third millennium B.C. the art of written literature was born. No doubt for very long before that man's image-making mind had been creating stories of the gods or god-like heroes and perhaps also of more local chiefs and war leaders. As time went by the bards who must have been mainly responsible for passing on such tales probably gave greater formality alike to the episodes and to their use of rhythm, word music and poetic imagery. But while all had depended on memory, tongue, ear and vibrations in the intervening air, creative shaping could not go far and much might be lost through the destruction of communities and the deaths of individuals. Now at last there were letters to pin down the sound of words, and oral tradition could become literature.

TRANSMISSION BY BARDS?

The question . . . is how far the *nar*, the Sumerian bard or minstrel, contributed to this literature, and in particular whether he provided elements that were incorporated in the Gilgamesh and other epic works. Professor [Samuel] Kramer [a highly noted Near Eastern scholar], who has taken so heavy a share in the immense labour of identifying, assembling, and translating the precious tablets by which the world's first great literature survives, has no doubt that the *nar* was 'a key figure in the growth and development' of the literary tradition of Sumeria.

Although there has been some opposition to this idea, it seems inherently probable. Several Sumerian Gilgamesh episodes were certainly woven into the long and magnificent poem written in Akkadian and preserved at Nineveh which is what people generally have in mind when they refer to the *Epic of Gilgamesh*. . . .

It seems probable that the Sumerian rulers, like the Greek, loved to have their deeds and those of their half-forgotten ancestors celebrated by bards who sang or recited to the lyre while they themselves ate and drank at leisure.

In style the Sumerian epics have much in common with the Greek: fixed epithets, long repetitions, detailed descriptions and reported speeches. In content there is the same concentration on the fortunes of individual heroes, but there are also fundamental differences. Not only do they have far less individual characterization, but they lack the essential rationality and humanity of the Homeric tradition, the heroes seem not quite human and their adventures are more profoundly affected by mythical forms—descents to a weird underworld, symbolic dreams, battles with monsters. . . . To put it another way, it could be said that the Sumerian epics are far more deeply permeated by elements rising from the unconscious mind and therefore closer to the myths where these elements are supreme.

EARLIEST LITERARY ORIGINS

One of the greatest difficulties in the way of studying the literature of Mesopotamia is that so much of it comes to us from late copies and redactions. . . . The greater part of the five thousand or so literary tablets so far discovered either date from the opening centuries of the second millennium or had been copied for [the Assyrian king] Assurbanipal's library. It is impossible to know when many of the works were first composed or written down, or how much they had been modified in the course of time. On the whole, however, research has tended to push back their origins and to emphasize the remarkable conservatism of a tradition that persisted through all the upheavals of Mesopotamian history. Although fluency and style might be improved in the second millennium, an astonishing proportion of the forms and content of the literature sprang from the creative energy of the Sumerians. . . .

There is every reason to suppose that there was an increased output of Sumerian literary works during the last centuries of the third millennium when the *edubbas* [schools for scribes] were many and flourishing. At present the only substantial literary text surviving from this period is the long hymnal poem celebrating Gudea's building of the Eninnu temple of Lagash. It was probably composed by an Eninnu poet during the Third Dynasty of Ur. We can hope that more tablets inscribed at this time will one day be unearthed. We know that after the fall of the Third Dynasty the scribal schools were zealous in copying and revising the old texts, a scholarly activity that continued in Old Babylonian times. Although by now, of course, Akkadian had become the spoken language of the country, the scribes not only copied the old compositions in Sumerian but wrote more of their own. At the same time Akkadian literature was being created. The *Epic of Gilgamesh,* which, in spite of its incorporation of Sumerian episodes, was virtually a new and far finer creation, was probably first composed quite early in the second millennium. Among other major works the creation epic, *Enuma elish,* may not have been very much later. Indeed it seems that the Mesopotamians had already written most of their outstanding literature by the end of the Old Babylonian period. . . .

LITERARY TYPES AND OCCASIONS

The main groupings of Sumerian and Akkadian literature were the myths of the gods; the epic tales where kings and other heroes mingled with their divinities; hymns, mostly addressed to gods and their temples but also to kings during the divinizing Third Dynasty of Ur and the succeeding period of Isin; lamentations and elegies of a more or less historical kind; the wisdom literature consisting mainly of collections of precepts and proverbs but also including the disputations and the 'job' type compositions. Most of these works were composed in poetic form. Rhyme, alliteration and regular metre were not used, but the rhythmic structure of the line . . . was carefully controlled and sometimes, as in the *Gilgamesh* epic, there was a division into stanzas. The poetic effect was heightened by such devices as the balance of opposites—say that of heaven against earth—

refrains, and by a use of similes that were sometimes of brilliance and beauty. . . .

Enough has already been quoted from almost all these literary categories to give as much idea of their character as the obstacles of decipherment and translation allow. It is unfortunately far more difficult to relate them to the societies among which they were composed, written down, read, recited and listened to. Extraordinarily little is known about their authorship or how or where they were enjoyed.

Of one thing we can be reasonably sure: this was not a private literature. Although it would be rash to say that such a scene was impossible, we need hardly picture professional men or others adept in the scribal art reclining on their couches with tablets from their own libraries piled on the table beside them silently reading some work of national literature. Both in its composition and its reception Sumerian and Akkadian literature was a social undertaking. . . .

On the question of the occasions when any of the more important works were to be heard, the only certain information we have is that in later times at least the creation epic was recited during the New Year festival. It is not implausible that some of the other myths were similarly related to the religious calendar. Hymns must, of course, have been intended for temple services and perhaps the lamentations also. What one would most like to know was whether a predominantly secular masterpiece such as the Akkadian *Gilgamesh* was ever recited to popular audiences in the cities or whether it was heard only in courts and princely houses. The Gilgamesh story certainly had a wide appeal, for copies taken from it have been found as far apart as Hattusas, Ugarit and Megiddo.

A REVERENCE FOR TRADITION

Many authorities speak of the *reading* of the myths and epics, yet is it not unlikely that any performer actually read aloud from cuneiform tablets? It seems far more reasonable to think that even if they had a text before them, priests, court poets and entertainers had really memorized their lines and were reciting them after the manner of actors who perform 'readings' today. It is tempting to guess that the *Dispute,* that peculiar Sumerian device that was maintained, though with less enthusiasm, by the Akkadian writers, may have been dramatically performed by two individuals representing the protagonists—silver and copper, pick axe and plough, cattle and grain, the two graduates and the rest.

Obviously of popular origin as well as popular appeal were the proverbs, of which there were at least a thousand already extant in Sumerian times. The scribes collected them and made them into anthologies—and they provided a favourite exercise for pupils to copy. Yet like our own proverbial sayings they certainly came from the 'wisdom' of ordinary experience. In addition to those quoted there are many with this flavour:

> Let what's mine stay unused, but let me use what is yours—this will not endear a man to his friend's household.

> Into an open mouth, a fly enters.

> The traveller from distant places is an everlasting liar.

> A loving heart builds the home; a hating heart destroys the home.

> Has she become pregnant without intercourse? Has she become fat without eating?

We can be grateful to the scribes who saved these sayings to remind us of some of the unchanging commonplaces of human affairs. No doubt there were all kinds of fables and stories of the *Poor Man* kind, as well as the songs, mostly love songs, that never got into the scribal canon.

The scribes and scholars of the Sumerian *edubbas* and the schools that followed them were marvellous conservationists, keeping a dead language and its literature current through two millennia. This long-drawn effort represents an exceptional reverence for ancient traditions which is manifest also in most aspects of Mesopotamian culture.

GILGAMESH: THE EARLIEST HERO

TRADITIONAL

The greatest and most influential single piece of Mesopotamian literature was the epic tale of the hero Gilgamesh. It originated with the Sumerians; the Babylonians, Assyrians, and others subsequently adopted and perpetuated it; and some of its events and themes became part of the Hebrew Old Testament and other basic Western writings. The following excerpts from the epic, translated by E.A. Speiser, deal with the hero's relationship with his "other self" and his quest for the secrets of life. The gods, who had fashioned Gilgamesh two-thirds divine and one-third human, decide to create his wild-man double, Enkidu. At first, Gilgamesh and Enkidu fight each other; but then they become friends and take part in several heroic adventures together. Eventually, however, Enkidu dies and the grieving Gilgamesh sets out to discover the secret of immortality, only to find in the end that death is inevitable for all humans.

G ilgamesh's despotic behavior leads to the creation of Enkidu.
The nobles of Uruk are gloomy in their chambers:
"Gilgamesh leaves not the son to his father;
Day and night is unbridled his arrogance.
Yet this is Gilgamesh, the shepherd of Uruk.
He should be our shepherd: strong, stately, and wise!
Gilgamesh leaves not the maid to her mother,
The warrior's daughter, the noble's spouse!"
The gods hearkened to their plaint,
The gods of heaven, Uruk's lords . . .

Excerpted from *The Epic of Gilgamesh*, translated by E.A. Speiser, in *Ancient Near Eastern Texts Relating to the Old Testament*, edited by James B. Pritchard. Copyright © 1969 by Princeton University Press. Reprinted by permission of Princeton University Press.

The great Aruru they called:
"Thou, Aruru, didst create Gilgamesh;
Create now his double;
His stormy heart let him match.
Let them contend, that Uruk may have peace!". . .
Aruru washed her hands,
Pinched off clay and cast it on the steppe.
On the steppe she created valiant Enkidu, . . .
Shaggy with hair is his whole body,
He is endowed with head hair like a woman. . . .
He knows neither people nor land; . . .
With the gazelles he feeds on grass,
With the wild beasts he jostles at the watering-place,
With the teeming creatures his heart delights in water. . . .

Having heard of the animal-like Enkidu, Gilgamesh sends a harlot to civilize him and bring him to Uruk.

The lass beheld him, the savage-man,
The barbarous fellow from the depths of the steppe: . . .
The lass freed her breasts, bared her bosom,
And he possessed her ripeness.
She was not bashful as she welcomed his ardor.
She laid aside her cloth and he rested upon her.
She treated him, the savage, to a woman's task,
As his love was drawn unto her.
For six days and seven nights Enkidu comes forth,
Mating with the lass.
After he had had his fill of her charms,
He set his face toward his wild beasts.
On seeing him, Enkidu, the gazelles ran off,
The wild beasts of the steppe drew away from his body.
Startled was Enkidu, as his body became taut,
His knees were motionless—for his wild beasts had gone.
Enkidu had to slacken his pace—it was not as before;
But he now had wisdom, broader understanding.
Returning, he sat at the feet of the harlot.
He looks up at the face of the harlot,
His ears attentive, as the harlot speaks;
The harlot says to him, to Enkidu:
"Thou art wise, Enkidu, art become like a god!
Why with the wild creatures dost thou roam over the steppe?
Come, let me lead thee to ramparted Uruk,
To the holy temple, abode of Anu and Ishtar,
Where lives Gilgamesh, accomplished in strength,
And like a wild ox lords it over the folk."
As she speaks to him, her words find favor,

His heart enlightened, he yearns for a friend. . . .
Enkidu says to her, to the harlot:
"Up, lass, escort thou me,
To the pure sacred temple, abode of Anu and Ishtar,
Where lives Gilgamesh, accomplished in strength,
And like a wild ox lords it over the folk.
I will challenge him and will boldly address him,
I will shout in Uruk: 'I am he who is mighty! . . .' "
The nobles rejoiced:
"A hero has appeared
For the man of proper mien!
For Gilgamesh, the godlike,
His equal has come forth." . . .

Enkidu and Gilgamesh meet and battle to a draw.

They met in the Market-of-the-Land.
Enkidu barred the gate with his foot,
Not allowing Gilgamesh to enter.
They grappled each other, butting like bulls,
They shattered the doorpost, as the wall shook.
As Gilgamesh bent the knee—his foot on the ground—
His fury abated and he turned away. . . .
They kissed each other
And formed a friendship. . . .

*Enkidu quails at the prospect of fighting the monstrous Huwawa,
guardian of the Cedar Forest, and Gilgamesh reassures him with a re-
minder of the heroic meaning of life.*

Gilgamesh opened his mouth, saying to Enkidu:
"In the forest resides fierce Huwawa.
Let us, me and thee, slay him,
That all evil from the land we may banish! [. . .]
Enkidu opened his mouth, saying to Gilgamesh:
"I found it out, my friend, in the hills,
As I was roaming with the wild beasts.
For ten thousand leagues extends the forest.
Who is there that would go down into it?
Huwawa—his roaring is the flood-storm,
His mouth is fire, his breath is death!
Why dost thou desire to do this thing?
An unequal struggle is tangling with Huwawa." . . .
Gilgamesh opened his mouth, saying to Enkidu:
"Who, my friend, is superior to death?
Only the gods live forever in the sun.
As for mankind, numbered are their days;
Whatever they achieve is but the wind!

Even here thou art afraid of death.
What of thy heroic might?
Let me go then before thee,
Let thy voice call to me, 'Advance, fear not!'
Should I fall, I shall have made me a name:
'Gilgamesh'—they will say—'against fierce Huwawa
Has fallen!' Long after
My offspring has been born in my house, [. . .]
Thus calling to me, thou hast grieved my heart.
My hand I will poise and will fell the cedars.
A name that endures I will make for me! . . ."

Having slain Huwawa, Gilgamesh next scornfully rejects the goddess Ishtar's offer of love, and she forces the gods to create the Bull of Heaven to punish his insolence. . . .

The heroes slay the Bull of Heaven and again insult Ishtar.

Up leaped Enkidu, seizing the Bull of Heaven by the horns,
The Bull of Heaven hurled his foam in his face,
Brushed him with the back of his tail. . . .
Between neck and horns he thrust his sword.
When they had slain the Bull, they tore out his heart,
Placing it before Shamash.
They drew back and did homage before Shamash.
The two brothers sat down.
Then Ishtar mounted the wall of ramparted Uruk,
Sprang on the battlements, uttering a curse:
"Woe unto Gilgamesh because he insulted me
By slaying the Bull of Heaven!"
When Enkidu heard this speech of Ishtar,
He tore loose the right thigh of the Bull of Heaven
And tossed it in her face:
"Could I but get thee, like unto him I would do unto thee.
His entrails I would hang at thy side!" . . .
In the Euphrates they washed their hands,
They embraced each other as they went on,
Riding through the market street of Uruk.
The people of Uruk are gathered to gaze upon them.
Gilgamesh to the lyre maidens of Uruk
Says these words:
"Who is most splendid among the heroes?
Who is most glorious among men?"
"Gilgamesh is most splendid among the heroes,
Gilgamesh is most glorious among men."

By means of a dream, Enkidu learns two things: that the gods have de-

cided he must die as punishment for the insolent behavior of the two heroes, and that the land of the dead is a most dismal place. . . .

Enkidu dies, and the reality of death as the common lot of all mankind—even fearless heroes—strikes home to Gilgamesh. The remainder of the epic deals with his attempt to find everlasting life, a quest that all tell him is hopeless. In the following selection, Gilgamesh is talking to a barmaid who gives him sage advice.

> "He who with me underwent all hardships—
> Enkidu, whom I loved dearly,
> Who with me underwent all hardships—
> Has now gone to the fate of mankind!
> Day and night I have wept over him.
> I would not give him up for burial—
> In case my friend should rise at my plaint—
> Seven days and seven nights,
> Until a worm fell out of his nose.
> Since his passing I have not found life,
> I have roamed like a hunter in the midst of the steppe.
> O ale-wife, now that I have seen thy face,
> Let me not see the death which I ever dread."
> The ale-wife said to him, to Gilgamesh:
> "Gilgamesh, whither rovest thou?
> The life thou pursueth, thou shalt not find.
> When the gods created mankind,
> Death for mankind they set aside,
> Life in their own hands retaining.
> Thou, Gilgamesh, let full be thy belly,
> Make thou merry by day and by night.
> Of each day make thou a feast of rejoicing,
> Day and night dance thou and play!
> Let thy garments be sparkling fresh,
> Thy head be washed; bathe thou in water.
> Pay heed to the little one that holds on to thy hand,
> Let thy spouse delight in thy bosom!
> For this is the task of mankind!" . . .

Gilgamesh next searches out Utnapishtim, the immortal hero of the Flood, who also cannot help him. The dejected Gilgamesh is about to depart when he is told of the Plant of Life—his last and most disappointing hope.

> His spouse says to him, to Utnapishtim the Faraway:
> "Gilgamesh has come hither, toiling and straining.
> What wilt thou give him that he may return to his land?"
> At that he, Gilgamesh, raised up his pole,

To bring the boat nigh to the shore.
Utnapishtim says to him, to Gilgamesh:
"Gilgamesh, thou hast come hither, toiling and straining.
What shall I give thee that thou mayest return to thy land?
I will disclose, O Gilgamesh, a hidden thing,
And about a plant I will tell thee:
This plant, like the buckthorn is [. . .].
Its thorns will prick thy hands just as does the rose.
If thy hands obtain the plant, thou wilt attain life."
No sooner had Gilgamesh heard this, . . .
He tied heavy stones to his feet.
They pulled him down into the deep and he saw the plant.
He took the plant, though it pricked his hands.
He cut the heavy stones from his feet.
The sea cast him up upon its shore.
Gilgamesh says to him, to Urshanabi, the boatman:
"Urshanabi, this plant is a plant apart,
Whereby a man may regain his life's breath.
I will take it to ramparted Uruk . . . .
Its name shall be 'Man Becomes Young in Old Age.'
I myself shall eat it
And thus return to the state of my youth."
After twenty leagues they broke off a morsel,
After thirty more leagues they prepared for the night.
Gilgamesh saw a well whose water was cool.
He went down into it to bathe in the water.
A serpent snuffed the fragrance of the plant;
It came up from the water and carried off the plant,
Going back to shed its slough [skin].
Thereupon Gilgamesh sits down and weeps,
His tears running down over his face.
He took the hand of Urshanabi, the boatman:
"For whom, Urshanabi, have my hands toiled?
For whom is being spent the blood of my heart?
I have not obtained a boon for myself.
For the serpent have I effected a boon!"

THE WORLD'S FIRST EMPIRE

JEAN BOTTÉRO

In addition to creative and constructive endeavors, human cultures often build large political states, and some of these eventually become empires. This aspect of culture, which many see as negative and exploitative, began in ancient Mesopotamia along with more constructive achievements, such as the invention of writing and literature. Noted Near Eastern scholar Jean Bottéro here tells the story of the world's first known empire, established by the monarch Sargon of Agade (or Akkad). As Bottéro explains, Sargon was a Semite (the Semites being immigrants who entered Mesopotamia in waves from the deserts of eastern Syria and Palestine) who rose to power in Kish, a city lying not far east of Babylon. He eventually managed to conquer most of the cities of what became Babylonia and Assyria; but like all empires that followed across the globe and through the centuries, his realm was eventually plagued by discontent and rebellion, which brought about its downfall.

T he Empire of Agade (ca. 2340–2198) was the work of a *dynasty* in the true sense of the word, in that the five kings who built and sustained it succeeded one another in a direct line from fathers to sons for nearly a century and a half; this continuity was both a cause and a sign of the long stability of their state. This, to be sure, does not seem to have been entirely free of difficulty, for the literary tradition refers to the violent deaths of at least Rimush and Manishtushu in palace revolutions; the same is true for Shar-kali-sharri, but then the monarchy never recovered from his fall.

Their names (at least the first is a "throne name," Sargon= Sharru-kin, "True King"; perhaps also Shar-kali-sharri, meaning "King of all Kings") are nearly all that we know for certain as far as the personalities of these monarchs is concerned; except for a few facts about their immediate families and their courts, their original inscriptions have preserved to us not a single "biographical" detail.

SARGON'S OBSCURE ORIGINS

Even with Sargon (2340–2284 B.C.), the first and greatest of the line, we know precious little about his origins or the manner in which he reached his throne. By the end of the third millennium men still knew only that he had appeared, as it were, full-grown on the historical scene. Later on, he was given a nomad for a father and a temple votary for a mother, the latter having cast him adrift on the river in a basket of rushes, which bore him to a peasant who adopted him. . . .

The legend of Sargon's origins, then, highlights his Semitic background: He was one of that long line of immigrants whose lives had left no mark on history until himself. So much does he represent them all that, after the sensational rise in status that he and his successors brought them, the Babylonian Semites have no other national name than Akkadians, from the name of the capital he founded: Agade. This name, too, in the form of "Akkad," was applied to all the northern part of Lower Mesopotamia, the south alone retaining the name of Sumer. With Sargon, the Semites emerge from the shadows: He and his successors glory in Semitic names; their language, "Akkadian," begins to replace the Sumerian tongue; longhaired, bearded faces replace the generally round, shaven Sumerian heads on the reliefs. In the history of Babylonia, shot through with the coexistence, to a certain extent even the cultural rivalry, of Sumerians and Semites, this is a prime development. . . .

If we follow the same legend, Sargon was born into one of the already settled Semitic groups, although his ancestors would still have been seminomadic at some earlier point in time. He entered political life, we have no idea how, in the great Semitic center of Kish; the *King List* figures him as "cupbearer" to the second king of the Third Dynasty of Kish, Ur-Zababa. No doubt he later on led a revolt against his sovereign, perhaps on the occasion of the king's defeat in a war that had destroyed the power of Kish. Favored by extraordinary luck (the literary tradition attributes it to a special fondness toward him on the part of the great Semitic goddess Ishtar), Sargon succeeded in carving out a personal domain around the site of Agade, where he either constructed a new or expanded an existing city as his capital—a sin of pride, as men said later on. We do not know the exact location of Agade (its ruins have never been found), but a contemporary document situates it near Kish, and the literary tradition places it not far from Babylon, so we can infer that it must have been somewhere in the territory of the ancient city of Sippar (to give one possibility), and probably on the banks of the Euphrates.

HOW EXTENSIVE WERE HIS CONQUESTS?

We are deplorably short of details on the great work of Sargon, namely the creation of an empire ruled from Agade. Or, better put, we do not have the guiding thread that would tie known events together to give us a chronologically ordered picture of the growth of that empire. We can attempt to supply this by following the order in which the scribes of Nippur arranged their copies of his inscriptions, or we might, where this fails us, fall back on "historical logic"—if only history behaved logically.

What we do know is that his empire began with Agade, which remained its center; "King of Agade" was always the first in line of his titles. He adds "King of Kish." The old Semitic capital, that is, even in its fallen state, still had all of its prestige, and the new king's first task was to assure himself of the primacy of all northern Babylonia by conquering it. Perhaps he carried this out under the color of "liberating" it from Uruk, and "restoring" it to its former glory.

Now master of the north and confident of his power, Sargon could hardly have resisted the temptation to strike at the greatest conqueror of the time in his own lands. . . . There are allusions in the inscriptions to a threefold invasion and to Sargon's "thirty-four battles"; having finally vanquished the king of Uruk, having cast him down with a stock around his neck before the national sanctuary of Sumer (the Enlil temple at Nippur), Sargon, at the end of these wars, found himself master of Uruk, Ur, Eninmar, Lagash and Umma—in a word of all the Sumerian states "up to the shores of the sea." From now on, the king of Agade and Kish could add, to his titles, "King of the Land."

What had his motive been? . . . The need, at first, to respond to threats from the surrounding states, made uneasy by the rise of a new power so near their borders? We simply have no idea. In any case his next steps took him westward, once the land was united under his rule. The chronicles claim to know that his conquest of the northwest, Sargon's most extraordinary exploit, was carried out in two great campaigns: the first in the year one, the second in the year eleven of his reign. Perhaps he restricted himself, in the first, to the conquest of Tuttul (the present-day Hit) on the Euphrates, the gateway to the "Upper Land," and of Mari. By the end of his second campaign, in any case, the king had led his armies as far as northern Syria (Ebla), the shores of the Mediterranean (Iarmuti?), the Lebanon or Amanus mountains ("The Cedar Forest") and the Taurus range, or at least its eastern foothills ("The Silver Mountains"?). Legend early set to work to embroider this great adventure, so that we are now unable to tell where it retains and where it invents historical fact. . . . What we can know with assurance, then, is this: Sargon had brought together under his control territories stretching from the "Lower Sea" (the Persian Gulf) to the "Upper Sea" (the Mediterranean), a distance slightly under 900 miles.

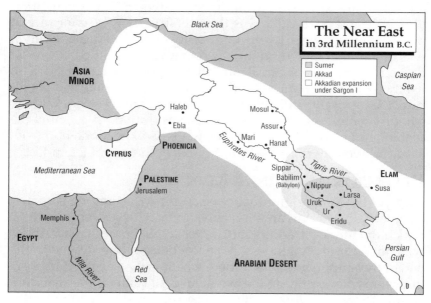

THE ENORMITY OF HIS ACCOMPLISHMENTS

Nor was this all: The king may have taken offense at an alliance between his eastern neighbors, Elam and Warahshe, whose object was surely the hope of discouraging the conqueror. In a double inscription (representing a twofold campaign?) Sargon boasts of having defeated the two allies together, proudly listing their kings, governors and great officers of state, and the cities from which he had taken rich booty.

The omen literature [among surviving Assyrian writings] contains a reference to Sargon's conquest of the "Land of Subartu," a place we have difficulty locating—perhaps Upper Mesopotamia from the Zagros mountains to the Khabur or the Balikh

River, perhaps something farther west. We cannot be entirely sure that this project was ever more than planned by the great Akkadian. Yet one of the date formulae of his reign names a year by a campaign in Simurru, toward the Zagros range; his immediate successors controlled both the region around the modern Kirkuk and Assyria proper; which leads us to think that, in the course of his endless reign, Sargon had himself brought northern Mesopotamia under his rule.

Even if the "fifty-six" years that the *King List* grants him include, which is possible, the early and more insignificant stages of his career . . . his time on earth was long enough to allow for countless prodigies of action, of which we would have no trace. He called himself "He Who Keeps Traveling [?] the Four Lands," an Akkadian expression meaning the universe. The imagination of people and poets alike was thunderstruck by the enormity of his accomplishments, by the immensity of his conquest. Surely it was of him that men thought when they came, a little later, to set down the great deeds of Gilgamesh. Someone took the trouble to list the sixty-five countries and great cities of his unbounded empire, the thousand-mile distances that separated its four corners from its center. A mythological map was drawn up, to show the distant and miraculous countries whose soil he alone had trod, save for two others only—both figures of the age of legend.

REBELLION AND FINAL RUIN

And yet his long reign must have seen revolts among so many peoples subjected to an alien rule, and defeats, even disasters, which the literary tradition attributes to his immoderacy. And it was not an untroubled legacy he left behind him. Down to the end of the empire he had founded, rebellion never ceased to break out everywhere, putting the extent and cohesion of the state constantly to the test, forcing his successors constantly to recapitulate, in a sense, the astonishing conquests of Sargon the Great.

Rimush (2284–2275 B.C.), to begin with, immediately on his accession had to put down a chain reaction of revolts in the Land of Sumer (Ur, Lagash, Umma, Adab, Uruk and Kazallu). Then, in the year three of his reign, in a pitiless war marked by bloodbaths, by cities shorn of their walls or razed to the ground, he faced his father's old enemies to the east: Elam and Warahshe had allied again, trying to shake off the overlordship of Agade. Rimush's presence to the north of Nineveh is also attested, by his foundation of a city to which he gave his own name.

Manishtushu (2275–2260 B.C.) had, it seems, other preoccupations to start out with, i.e. a revolt by his eastern vassals, Anshan and Sheriku, in which he had to take "thirty-two cities" by force to retain his suzerainty over Elam; then, on the western shore of the Persian Gulf, the conquest (reconquest?) of the quarries of "black stone." An inscription of his found at Assur, and the memory persisting, half a millennium later, of his founding of the temple of Ishtar at Nineveh, show him active in the northern part of his inheritance.

An Akkadian poem of the beginning of the second millennium B.C. lists the Mesopotamian cities in revolt against Naram-Sin (2260–2223) at the beginning of his reign: Kish, Kutha, Kazallu, Marad, Umma, Nippur, Uruk, Sippar, to which it adds the countries of Magan, to the south, of Elam, Warahshe, Mardaman and Simurru to the east and northeast, of Mamar and Apishal to the north and Mari to the west. So many rebellions, breaking out all at once at the very outset of his reign—the hand of the poet is apparent. But we have not the least reason to doubt that each of these cities and countries broke into revolt at *some* time during the thirty-seven-year reign of Sargon's grandson; his own inscriptions corroborate it. . . . More than Sargon, he felt himself to be the conqueror and master of the universe: He it was who took unto himself a truly "imperial" title, never employed in all the ages before him: "King of the Four Quarters." His royal inscriptions reveal an unbroken succession of victories—royal inscriptions always do. But we must read between the lines, and then we cannot escape the impression, in the midst of all these triumphs, of total disaster to come. . . . Everywhere, appearances of imperial glory: beneath them, so many signs of the way in which the real weaknesses of the Akkadian Empire were growing more pronounced with time, even under the leadership of a sovereign so energetic as Naram-Sin. It may well be that the dismemberment of the empire begins in his reign.

For his son and successor, Shar-kali-sharri (2223–2198 B.C.), no longer bears the title of "King of the Four Quarters." He has returned to the more modest style of "King of Agade," and we must suppose he has good reason for it. Uruk, in his reign, seeks to throw off the rule of Agade, this time perhaps successfully; Elam wins its independence at last. . . . Finally, and above all, a new threat from the northeast becomes clearly discernible: the Gutians, to whom coming ages will attribute the final ruin of all that Sargon has created.

ASSYRIA'S MAGNIFICENT RELIEF SCULPTURES

SETON LLOYD

The highly distinguished archaeologist Seton Lloyd, who also taught at London's Institute of Archaeology, penned this informative tract about Assyrian relief sculpture. While the Sumerians gave the world writing and literature, the Assyrians set high standards of artistic achievement. Of those Assyrian arts that survive, without doubt the most striking and original were the magnificent carved stone bas-reliefs that adorned the walls of the royal palaces. Especially numerous and striking were those created in the reigns of the Sargonids, making the seventh century B.C. a golden age of wall sculpture. In room after room, corridor after corridor, many thousands of feet of reliefs bore detailed scenes of the lives and exploits of the reigning monarchs. Lloyd, who studied all of these reliefs up close and in detail, here covers their themes, styles, and techniques and comments on the extraordinary skill of the artists.

T he Assyrians first began to adorn the walls of their palaces with reliefs early in the ninth century, when Assurnasirpal II moved the capital from Assur itself to Nimrud (Caleh) on the left bank of the Tigris. It seems possible that this was a genuine innovation, for till then the only comparable form of ornament in Mesopotamia had been the processions of rather squat figures painted along the base of the walls in Kassite palaces, as for instance at Dur Kurigalzu. The earliest group of reliefs then, is derived from excavations at Nimrud and date from the reigns of Assurnasirpal II and his son Shalmaneser III in the first quarter of the ninth century B.C. Another group comes from Khorsabad (Dur Sharrukim) where Sargon II established a short-lived capital . . . in the second half of the eighth century. The third group comes from the palaces of Nineveh which, after Sargon's venture at Khorsabad had been abandoned, was largely rebuilt by [the Assyrian kings] Sennacherib and Assurbanipal.

THEMES OF WAR AND CONQUEST

The reliefs are used exclusively to decorate the interior of buildings, and are designed to form a continuous frieze around the walls of halls and chambers. In the early days they were usually about seven feet high, with the design occasionally arranged in two superimposed registers with a band of cuneiform inscription between. But in later buildings, as for instance in Sargon's palace at Khorsabad, the individual sculptured figures reached a height of nine feet. The subjects generally chosen for the designs show little interest in religious matters. This has given place to a straightforward glorification of the King himself, either by scenes of ceremonial homage or by prolonged pictorial narratives of his achievements. In the more heraldic groups, miscellaneous monsters with a protective purpose do occasionally appear, as well as benevolent winged beings, usually referred to as 'genii'. But the form of an actual god rarely appears unless it be the ever-present figure of Assur himself, enshrined with his bow in a winged sun-disk.

The most oft-repeated, though never quite monotonous, subjects of the reliefs are detailed scenes of military conquest and the ruthless suppression of revolt in disaffected provinces or dependencies. The Assyrian army prepares for war; led by the King it crosses difficult country on the way to attack a walled city, probably among mountains: the city is taken, burnt, and demolished; the enemy leaders are punished with ingenious brutality; a victory is then celebrated. In the inscriptions the outcome of a minor campaign of this sort is recorded by the laconic comment, 'So I came upon them and destroyed them utterly and turned their cities into forgotten mounds.' It has been suggested that Assyrian sculptors learnt something from the reliefs of the Egyptian New Kingdom. Probable as this may seem (since the latter had for the most part already been in existence for five centuries), differences of approach to the actual purpose of the designs are no less conspicuous than contrasting qualities of style. There is no question of the Assyrian sculptures being dedicated to any magic or religious function: they are mere records of profane events directed to a temporal end. For this reason the figure of the King, for instance, is never distinguished by disproportionate size. His stature is no more than human. Nor does one find in the battle scenes that which in the Egyptian reliefs has been called 'the timeless assertion of inevitable royal victory'. The scenes themselves are often arranged episodically—that is, they represent successive developments in the progress of a single action—and if one examines them in detail one sees that at no time is the overall outcome anticipated. The King himself in his chariot is in obvious danger from enemy archers, from whom at times he appears most inadequately protected.

DETAIL AND REALISM

But what above all distinguishes the Assyrian sculptures is their stylistic vitality and fanciful detail. Horses in particular are drawn with great understanding and expression. Even their movements in swimming seem the result of close observation. Those drawing chariots are not thrown upwards diagonally in a stylized prance but conform realistically to the horizontal limitations of the frieze. Interest, too, in the relationship in space of figures composing a scene had much increased. Already in the Nimrud reliefs one sees the stereoscopic effect obtained when a river-bank is given vertical depth, or how the placing of figures in a void without ground-lines can suggest the idea of relative distance.

Some of these qualities are again in evidence during the reign of Shalmaneser III [reigned 858–824 B.C.], which saw a new and very striking development in architectural ornament, namely relief-modelling in metal. The huge wooden gates of a palace at Balawat, near Nimrud, were decorated with horizontal bands of bronze, eleven inches deep, each modelled by a *repoussé* process with a double register of narrative scenes. The artistic quality of the designs shows no particular distinction, but they give an impression of great animation and the modelling is technically excellent. Like the relief-sculptors, these metal-workers were concerned with the episodic rendering of historical subjects, and the limitations imposed on them by the narrow dimensions of the registers naturally made them prefer those most easily treated as a procession. Less frequently static scenes do occur, and great ingenuity has then to be used in giving reality to a landscape. The artist has in this case been compelled to fall back on traditional formulae for suggesting features such as a river and a range of mountains. . . .

COMPLICATED ACTION AND HUNTING SCENES

There remain two more notable groups of Assyrian reliefs—both from buildings on the major palace-mound, Küyünjik, at Nineveh. One comes from the palace of Sennacherib and dates from the time when he rebuilt the city after Sargon's death. . . . The other belongs to the time of his son, Assurbanipal. The sculptors of Sennacherib's time returned with unmistakable zest to the narrative and documentary subjects of the pre-Sargonid period. They brought a new ingenuity to bear on the rendering of complicated action and the characteristic details of the landscapes in which it took place. Sometimes their efforts were remarkably successful, particularly when attention was paid to the studied composition of contrasting sculptural textures. This is best seen in the narrative of a campaign fought by Sennacherib in the famous marsh-country at the junction of the Tigris and Euphrates . . . and it is most interesting to compare with the Egyptian rendering of events in a similar setting where the textural patterns used for instance to signify water, have the same meaning. Sometimes, however, the results were less satisfying. The full height of the slabs had once more been brought into use in order to obtain space for larger and more elaborate pictures; and one sees successive attempts, each more misguided than the last, to convey essential impressions of distance and space-relationship, which a few centuries later would have presented little difficulty. The attempt to use diagonal lines for this purpose ended in a form of frustration which can also be seen in Assurbanipal's palace.

Among the sculptures of Assurbanipal's time there is evidence of greater restraint in the struggle for pictorial expression. In the narrative scenes, the use of multiple registers is once more in order, and when diagonals occur they are used with so much subtlety that some critics are inclined to detect in them the first elements of true perspective. But the most remarkable contribution to the perfection of contemporary design made during this reign, was in another milieu. Even in the life of an Assyrian king, there must have been occasional periods of military inactivity, and during these, the hunting of wild animals was substituted as a suitably masculine occupation. And here the Assyrian relief-sculptors found a subject entirely to their liking. The 'Lion Hunt' carvings from Assurbanipal's palace are perhaps the best known of all their works. They reveal many remarkable qualities—dramatic composition—close, and even affectionate observation of characteristic form or gesture—vivid rendering of violent action—and so forth. But to anyone familiar with the desert background against which these episodes are enacted, the central accomplishment amounting to an artistic *tour de force* is the rendering of a featureless landscape by no other means than the studied spacing of the figures. The expression of more abstract situations as for instance the poignant quandary of a mare whose flight is impeded by the presence of her foal—a general understanding of animal suffering, capable of 'raising these scenes to the stature of a tragedy', suggests a degree of sensibility with which one almost hesitates to credit Assyrian artists [since the Assyrians were universally known for their warlike qualities and cruelty].

Egypt: Land of Pharaohs and Pyramids

CHAPTER 3

THE MAJESTIC NILE SUSTAINS AND REGULATES LIFE

FEKRI HASSAN

This well-written essay by Fekri Hassan, a professor of Egyptology at the Institute of Archaeology, University College London, describes the importance of the Nile River to the development of almost all aspects of civilized life in ancient Egypt. Hassan describes the river's source, delta, annual floods, and so on. Then he explains how the ancient Egyptians grew abundant quantities of crops in the rich soil laid down by the river's floods; how the Nile was used as a highway to link the various cities in the kingdom; and how the river's seasonal cycles helped to regulate everyday life.

E gypt lies at the northern end of the longest river in the world: the Nile, which rises in the East African highlands and flows into the Mediterranean more than four thousand miles (6,500km) away. The rhythm of the river was the most important feature of life in ancient Egypt. Until this century, when huge dams have been built to control the Nile's flow, monsoon rains in Ethiopia caused it to swell along its lower reaches and inundate the surrounding countryside every year from June to October. Most of Egypt's population were farmers, who stood idle during the inundation, unless they were called up to work on public monuments such as the king's tomb. When the Nile receded, it deposited rich silt, ensuring that the farmers always planted in fertile soil. Except for those years when the flood was disastrously high or low, Egyptians were secure in their knowledge that the river would guarantee them enough to eat.

GEOGRAPHY OF THE NILE VALLEY

The Nile in Egypt has two main parts: the Valley and the Delta, corresponding to the ancient divisions of the country into Upper and Lower Egypt. The Valley, some 660 miles (1,060km) long, is a remarkable canyon that is an offshoot of the African Great Rift Valley. The floodplain occupies 4,250 square miles (11,000km²) and ranges in width from just one and a quarter miles (2km) at Aswan to eleven miles (17km) at el-Amarna.

At present, the Nile splits near Cairo into two branches that flow into the sea at Rosetta (Rashid) and Damietta (Dumyat). These are all that remain of several branches that existed until medieval times. The silt left by the branches formed a broad triangle of fertile land that covers some 8,500 square miles (22,000km²). The Greeks called this land the "Delta" because its shape reminded them of the inverted fourth letter of their alphabet (Δ). The Delta is fifty-seven feet (17m) above sea level near Cairo and is fringed in the coastal regions by lagoons, wetlands, lakes and sand dunes. In parts of the eastern Delta there are conspicuous low hills known as "turtle backs". These sandy "islands" in the surrounding silty plain were rarely submerged by the annual inundation and in Predynastic times (to ca. 4000BCE) villages and burial grounds became established on their slopes. From the Old Kingdom (ca. 2625–2130BCE) onward, the apex of the Delta was close to Memphis, the ancient capital. It is now fifteen miles (25km) north of Cairo.

The Nile divides the eastern margin of the Sahara into the Western Desert (also known as the Eastern Sahara and the Libyan Desert) and the Eastern Desert. The Western Desert covers about two-thirds of Egypt, and its most striking features are a series of rocky desert plateaux and sandy depressions in which nestle lush oases. The Eastern Desert, characterized by the prominent Red Sea Hills, was important in pharaonic times for its minerals. The Sinai, essentially an extension of the Eastern Desert across the Gulf of Suez, was also a major source of minerals, especially copper. Wheat, barley, sheep and goats were domesticated in the Near East at least two thousand years before they appeared in the Nile Valley. Herders in the deserts of Palestine and the Sinai were probably driven to seek refuge in the Delta by great droughts seven thousand years ago. . . .

The civilization of Egypt and its spectacular achievements were based throughout its history on the prosperity of a mainly agrarian economy. The country's verdant green fields and boun-

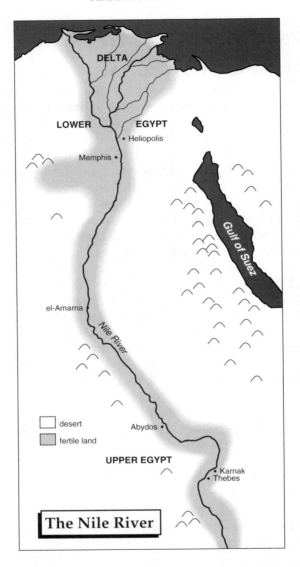

DELTA

LOWER   EGYPT
                    • Heliopolis

Memphis •

Gulf of Suez

el-Amarna

Nile River

desert
fertile land

Abydos •

UPPER EGYPT

• Karnak
• Thebes

The Nile River

tiful food resources depended on the fertile soil of the Nile flood-plain and the annual summer flood, which commenced in mid-June and lasted until mid-October. As soon as the waters began to recede, the farmers returned to their sodden fields to sow their seeds. The crops were ready for harvest from February to early June, when the Nile was at its lowest level.

Egyptian agriculture involved the cultivation of a wide range of plants, the most common being emmer-wheat and barley, staples from which Egyptians made bread, cakes and a nutritious type of beer that was frequently flavoured with spices, honey or dates. The predominantly cereal diet was supplemented by fava beans, lentils and peas (good sources of protein); and other vegetables grown included lettuces, cucumbers, leeks, onions and radishes. Among the most popular fruits, grown in orchards, were melons, dates, sycamore figs and pomegranates. Grapes were also cultivated and were used to make both red and white wines. Oils were extracted from flax and the castor-oil plant *(Ricinus communis)*, as well as from sesame in Ptolemaic times. The Egyptians also grew a wide variety of herbs for medicinal purposes.

Poultry and livestock had an important place in the economy. Geese were a common sight along the canals and villages that lined the Nile, and at the time of the annual inundation, migratory water birds flocked to Egypt from afar. Pintail ducks, in particular, were caught in nets and snared in traps. Farmers also kept sheep, goats, cattle and pigs. Donkeys were Egypt's main beasts of burden and chief mode of transport on land. Horses were introduced only during the New Kingdom (after ca. 1539BCE); camels and buffaloes did not appear in the Egyptian landscape until a thousand years later, during the Persian occupation.

The Nile itself was a source of an abundance of fish such as tilapia and catfish, both of which were found close to the banks of the river in the muddy waters between the reeds. Nile perch *(Lates nilotica)* was a favoured catch in the irrigation ditches that were dug to channel water from the Nile to the fields.

A LIQUID HIGHWAY

The Nile was at once Egypt's richest source of sustenance and its main communications artery. It flowed from south to north at an average speed of four knots (7.4kph) during the season of inundation, which meant that the voyage from Thebes to Memphis, a distance of around 550 miles (885km), would have taken approximately two weeks. Navigation was faster during the inundation because the water was on average about twenty-five to thirty-three feet (7.5–10m) deep. In contrast, during the season of drought, when the water level was low, the speed of the current was much slower, about one knot (1.8kph), and the same trip would have taken at least two months. At the Nile's lowest point, in June, the water was no more than seven feet (2m) at Aswan compared with just under eighteen feet (5.5m) near Memphis.

The trip from north to south would have been extremely slow before the invention of sails (probably ca. 3350 BCE or a little later) to take advantage of the northerly and northwesterly winds blowing off the Mediterranean. At all times of the year the great bend near Qena, where the Nile flows from west to east and then back from east to west, slows down river travel considerably. Night sailing was generally avoided because of the danger of running aground on one of the many sandbanks and low sandy islands.

In the late Predynastic or Naqada II period (ca. 3500–3100 BCE), Egyptian boats developed from craft made of reed bundles into big ships constructed from wood planks. Early rock art suggests that some boats were over fifty feet (15m) long and could carry a crew of thirty-two. Multi-oared boats existed before this time, in the early fourth millennium BCE. Clay models of boats found at Merimde Beni Salama in the Delta date back to the fifth millennium BCE.

By the Early Dynastic Period, Egyptian boatbuilding had attained high standards. At Abydos, boat pits associated with a First-Dynasty funerary complex of ca. 3000 BCE have revealed a fleet of twelve boats between fifty and sixty feet (15–18m) long. But perhaps the greatest discovery from this period is that of a barque of the pharaoh Khufu, builder of the Great Pyramid. Buried in pieces next to the pyramid, it was recently reassembled and measured an impressive 144 feet (43.8m) in length.

From the earliest times, boats were used to transport people between villages during the inundations, to ferry them across the river, and to transport cattle, grain and other commodities. They were also deployed in military campaigns. From the Fifth Dynasty [which began in 2494 BCE] onward, Egyptian shipwrights were making sailing boats capable of ocean navigation.

Together with the donkey—the principal overland transport—boats made possible the economic and political integration of the country. The capitals of the nomes, or provinces, were linked with the national capital by boats and barges that carried local revenues to the royal storehouses. The emergence of a royal state in Egypt may have been linked with the coordination of grain collection and other relief activities developed as part of a strategy to deal with unexpected crop failures in a particular district. In pharaonic times, grain from several districts stored in a central granary would be sent by river to an area hit by famine.

Artificial harbours and ports to accommodate large cargo boats were an essential feature of the riverine landscape. Towns took advantage of the deeper side of the Nile channel close to the shore to establish ports. They also built rock jetties that extended a short way into the river, perhaps in response to changes in the course of the Nile. The site of a huge harbour at Medinet Habu in Western Thebes, built during the reign of Amenhotep III (ca. 1390–1353 BCE), is marked by huge elongated mounds created by the earth from the harbour's excavation.

Other large harbours are known from Memphis and the Delta city of Tanis. The port at Tanis was used by Thutmose III (ca. 1479–1425 BCE) to connect Memphis with the eastern Delta.

CREATING ORDER FROM CHAOS

The unpredictability of the Nile floods exercised a powerful hold on the Egyptian imagination. The period just before the inundation, when the river was so low that in places a person could cross on foot, was a time of apprehension: when the flood came it was frequently wild and dangerous. The Egyptians could not tame the river, but they sought to prevent its worst effects by managing the landscape to take advantage of natural conditions—for example, by strengthening natural levees to form embankments. At times of low floods, artificial canals carried water to the thirsty uplands of the floodplain. Flood basins were managed so that water could flow from one basin to another, enabling areas up and down the valley to have sufficient water in time for planting. The desire for order which permeated the Egyptians' world-view was surely derived in no small measure from the chaotic presence of the river in their midst.

To the Egyptians, every being, including Pharaoh and the gods, had to abide by the fundamental cosmic principle of *ma'at*, personified as Ma'at, the goddess of order, justice and goodness. The cosmic order was also embodied in the movement of the god Re, the sun, the other prominent natural element whose rhythms regulated Egyptian lives. The sun god was believed to be ferried daily across the sky in a boat, and to return through the underworld on a barque to a point below the eastern horizon. Such mythological vessels recalled the ferryboats that plied between the banks of the Nile.

On earth, order was maintained by the pharaoh, the manifestation of the god Horus, son of Osiris and Isis. According to allusions in early religious texts, and later literary and artistic references, Osiris taught the people how to take advantage of the Nile by giving them the arts of cultivation and civilization. He was slain by his brother, Seth, who was identified with the forces of evil and chaos. After death, Osiris returned to life as king of the underworld, where he ordained the life-giving waters of the annual inundation.

Egyptian concepts of time were based on the daily rising and setting of the sun and the three-part cycle of the Nile: drought; the season in between; and the season of inundation. Cosmic space was delimited by the four corners: the south (the source of the Nile), the north (where the pole star shone), the east (where the sun rose) and the west (where it set). Time and space were thus linked to the two most important elements in Egyptian cosmology; and these elements, in turn, were linked in the cosmic order with life, death and rebirth.

Preparation for the Afterlife

Nicolas Grimal

Some of the richest and most unique elements of ancient Egyptian culture were its funerary beliefs and customs, which culminated in preparing the deceased for the afterlife and providing a proper resting place for the body. From his widely acclaimed study of ancient Egypt, Nicolas Grimal, a professor of Egyptology at the Sorbonne University in Paris, provides this useful synopsis of these beliefs and customs. He begins with an explanation of the various non-corporeal (having no material form) manifestations taken by a dead person, according to Egyptian beliefs. Then he discusses the funerary stele, a stone slab or marker that bore the deceased person's name and listed the grave offerings left for him or her; the tombs, including mastabas (oblong stone or brick structures with flat roofs) and the more familiar pyramids; funerary inscriptions and decorations and their meanings; and the complex process of mummification.

To the Egyptians, each human individual was made up of five elements: the shadow (the non-corporeal double of each of the forms assumed in a lifetime), the *akh*, the *ka*, the *ba* and the name.

The *akh* was an aspect of the sun, the luminous clement that permitted the dead to join the stars when they passed into the hereafter; it was the form in which the power—the spirit—of the gods or the dead manifested itself.

The *ka* was the vital force possessed by every being; it multiplied according to the power of the being in question—Ra, for example, had fourteen *kas*—and it had to be provided with food supplies in order to maintain its efficiency. Once the body had been suitably prepared for its triumph over death, it was the *ka* that allowed it to resume a life similar to the one it had enjoyed on earth. The *ka* not only needed nutrition in order to exist, it also needed a medium. From an early date therefore the Egyptians provided substitutes for the body, which was prone to decay, in the form of effigies of the deceased. They adopted the custom of incorporating a special chamber in the royal tomb: the *serdab.* This was a subterranean gallery inside the *mastaba* or the funerary infrastructure in general, which was connected with the cult rooms [where worship took place] by means of an eye-level slit so that the statues placed there could gain access to the offerings. This practice was at first restricted to the king, but before very long it began to be adopted by private individuals. A deliberate gap left at the side of the tomb chamber played the role of the *serdab,* thus allowing the dead person to gain access to offerings left at the bottom of the shaft during the funeral.

The *ba* was also a non-corporeal entity which possessed the power of its owner, whether a god, corpse or living being. It was a kind of double of the deceased, existing independently of the body. The *ba* (usually incorrectly translated as 'spirit') was represented in the form of a bird with a human head which left the mortal remains at the moment of death, only returning after the process of mummification had taken place. It was an *alter ego* which could actually converse with its owner.

Finally, the Egyptians believed that the process of naming an individual was an act of creation, not only when the baby was named at the moment of birth—when the mother gave it a name which described its appearance and predicted its fate in life—but also on every occasion that the name was uttered. This belief in the creative power of the word determined all behaviour regarding death: the act of naming a person or thing corresponded to the act of endowing it with life even after it had physically disappeared. It was therefore essential to provide numerous different means of recognizing the individual. This was why the funerary chapel, or the general cult-place, brought together as many explicit references as possible to the means by which the *ka* could enjoy the offerings due to it. . . .

The [funerary] stele . . . was a response to the *ka*'s needs, and during the Old Kingdom it went through a long process of development. The stele was the focal point of the tomb chapel, and the mural decorations were arranged so as to converge on it. . . .

The stele was placed between the upper and lower lintels of the door. The lower lintel listed the titles of the deceased, which were repeated and augmented on the jambs at either side of the door; occasionally these also bore a raised relief representation of the *ka* of the deceased. The first was generally inscribed with the beginning of the 'offering formula', by which the king dedicated offerings to a divinity who would, in his turn, supply benefits to the deceased. This principle theoretically ensured the continued observance of the funerary cult, even after the disappearance of the estate normally intended for the maintenance of the conces- sion and the supplying of provisions for the tomb, which was en- trusted to a specialized priesthood. . . . The continued flow of of- ferings was guaranteed by the perpetuation of the cult of the god which then passed on some of its offerings to the deceased. This 'transferral' of offerings was a means of keeping the dead within the fabric of the universe. By ensuring that the deceased re- mained united with the organized world, his survival was ren- dered as certain as that of the rest of the cosmos. . . .

THE PYRAMID TEXTS AND COFFIN TEXTS

[Among the most important elements of funerary belief and cus- tom were the structure and layout of the tomb itself. The most impressive tombs, of course, were those of the pharaohs. Origi- nally they were large *mastabas*, but beginning in the 2600s B.C. these were often converted to or replaced by pyramids of vari- ous sizes. The pyramids were surrounded by complexes con- taining courtyards, chapels, and other buildings dedicated to fu- nerary rituals and celebrations. As for the interiors of these structures, the twenty-fifth-century B.C. pharaoh] Wenis estab- lished the typical plan of the internal chambers of the pyramid according to a scheme that was to remain in use until the end of the Old Kingdom [2686–2181 B.C.]. The entrance was in the north, leading down first to a vestibule and then, past three granite portcullises [gateways] . . . to an antechamber. This antechamber was served by a *serdab* to the east (the side of the living) where the statues of the deceased were placed. To the west of the an- techamber (towards the world of the dead) was the room con- taining the sarcophagus. This design was abandoned in the Twelfth Dynasty [1985–1795 B.C.], when attempts were made to resist the onslaughts of tomb-robbers.

The pyramid of Wenis is also important for another reason: it is the first in which the internal corridors were decorated with funerary texts. These Pyramid Texts are found not only in the royal tombs at Saqqara (those of [the pharaohs] Wenis, Teti, Pepy I, Merenre, Pepy II and Qakare Iby) but also in the tombs of the queens of Pepy II (Neith, Wedjebten and Ipuit) and perhaps in the queens' pyramids discovered in the funerary complex of

Pepy I by the French Archaeological Mission at Saqqara. . . .

The texts consist of a succession of formulae, some of which only appear in Wenis' tomb, while the majority were passed on until the time of Qakare Iby [about 2150 B.C.]. These formulae also appear in another aspect of the funerary corpus: the Coffin Texts, the earliest examples of which have been found on Sixth Dynasty sarcophagi [dated to about 2300 B.C.] at the Dakhla Oasis. The Coffin Texts were not restricted to kings' tombs, and they superseded the Pyramid Texts in the Middle Kingdom. In the mortuary temple of Pepy I traces have even been found of the literary transition from the Pyramid Texts to the Coffin Texts. Later, the Coffin Texts in their turn provided the basis for the *Book of the Dead* of the New Kingdom [1550–1069 B.C.] and the Late Period [747–332 B.C.].

These funerary formulae recount a ritual which was intended to ensure that the deceased passed through into the afterworld and an existence among the blessed. They describe his ascension into the sky, his establishment among the stars, his transformation into the sun and his metamorphosis into Osiris. They also provided him with the necessary texts for his purification and the magic incantations that enabled him to overcome the obstacles blocking his path. The formulae probably derived from a set of archaic rituals that have not survived, either because the documents themselves have been destroyed or more probably because they were at first oral traditions.

The Pyramid Texts supply certain pieces of information that allow the development of the royal tomb in the Old Kingdom to be better understood. The *mastaba* reproduced, within the home of the dead, the primeval mound from which Atum created the world—and so stood as a symbol of creation. The texts also suggest why Imhotep decided to turn the *mastaba* into a square and to cover it with a pyramid. According to the Pyramid Texts the aim of the king was to rise up to the sky, where he would undergo transformation into both the sun and a star. To achieve this aim, he had several means at his disposal: the desert whirlwinds . . . the assistance of the god Shu who could lift him up in his arms, transformation into a bird (most often the falcon, which flew highest) or, most poetically, he could drift up into the sky with the smoke from the censers. On the other hand, the king could choose the more prosaic method of ascending a stairway or a ladder formed by the rays of the sun. This stairway was provided by the step pyramid, the hieroglyphic symbol for which was also the determinative sign of the word *r* ('to climb'). The step pyramid method of ascension was, however, superseded after just over a century by the smooth-sided pyramid of the Fourth Dynasty [2613–2494 B.C.]. From the Fourth Dynasty onwards the pyramid, like the *benben* stone, appears to have symbolized the petrified rays of the sun by means of which the king could climb up to heaven. . . .

The texts first describe the march to the tomb: the entrance hall of the pyramid corresponds to the valley temple, the corridor is the equivalent of the causeway and the antechamber is the mortuary temple. The chamber containing the sarcophagus serves as the inner sanctum, and the *serdab*—both here and in the mortuary temple itself—contains the images of the king. This sense of being able to read the texts from the entrance of the tomb to the sarcophagus is clearly apparent in Pepy I's pyramid. Once the deceased has been placed in his sarcophagus the texts can be read again but in the opposite direction, from the tomb chamber towards the entrance; this time the meaning relates to resurrection, in the course of which the rooms acquire symbolic roles. When the king leaves the sarcophagus, he is leaving Dwat, the underworld. When he finds himself in the antechamber—the horizon—he is Atum. From there he embarks on his ascension by climbing back up the corridor to the granite portcullises, which now symbolize the gates of heaven closed. . . . Once the doors have been broken, the king finds himself back in the tomb, which has become Dwat, night, domain of the stars in the midst of which he achieves immortality.

PRIVATE TOMBS

At the time of his ascension to the heavens, the king was not content with gaining eternal life only for himself. He himself became one of the companions of Ra, but he was also responsible for his subjects, whom he took with him into the hereafter. For their part, his subjects welcomed his guardianship as they sought to ensure their own survival. They obtained life after death not by being buried in the same tomb as the king, as they had been in earlier times, but by placing their tombs in close proximity to his. Complete cities of the dead grew up in this way, with tombs arranged like houses into roads and quarters, and the hierarchical position of each occupant was measured by his distance from the pyramid. In this way the social hierarchy was perpetuated after death, with the nobles, courtiers and officials guaranteed their eternal reward alongside the king.

The tombs of private individuals were built in the form of *mastabas* until the end of the Old Kingdom. The term 'private individuals' is here understood to cover the whole of the population except the king, including members of the royal family. Princes tended to assume political roles and therefore saw themselves primarily as officials, even though their titles stressed their royal origins or connections with the ruling family. It is more difficult to make this kind of distinction between the tombs of kings and queens, for not all queens had a small pyramid attached to their husbands' tombs. In general, queens' tombs are treated as private monuments which are more or less similar to the king's, depending on their importance and the role they had played as a wife or mother of a ruler. . . .

The development of the *mastaba* gradually caught up with the pyramid, changing at the end of the Third Dynasty [2686–2613 B.C.] from mud-brick to marly limestone, and then, in the Fourth Dynasty, to siliceous limestone, which was particularly impressive when furnished with an outer casing of fine limestone. It was the superstructure rather than the substructure that underwent the most development. The tomb chamber itself went through hardly any process of evolution; it was essentially the container for the corpse, sometimes square, sometimes rectangular and sometimes even circular. In the Fourth Dynasty tombs were still most frequently built of mud-brick with a stone roof in the form of a 'corbelled' vault. Each contained a rectangular sarcophagus made of either limestone or granite according to the generosity of the king who granted it to the official, since the man himself would have been unable to afford the expense of a quarrying expedition to Tura, Hatnub or Aswan.

It is difficult to be sure whether bodies were mummified at this date. Theoretically, there is evidence for mummification as early as the First Dynasty and remains of a mummy were found in the tomb of Djoser [ca. 2600 B.C.]. The remains of the dead buried in the great necropolises of the Old Kingdom are very poorly preserved however, and there is no scene in any of the chapels to confirm the practice of mummification, which is only described in later periods, at least as far as private individuals are concerned. Moreover, no royal mummy has survived from the earlier Old Kingdom. It is likely that most of the population continued to rely on the natural dessication of the body, which was greatly facilitated by the arid desert environment. . . .

THE MUMMIFICATION PROCESS

The Egyptians themselves produced no detailed description of the process of embalming, or at any rate no such document has survived. Existing pictorial representations of embalming are never totally explicit, consisting more of religious than technical allusions. Written descriptions of Egyptian mummification therefore derive mainly from the Greek authors: Herodotus, Diodorus, Plutarch or Porphyrus. From these sources it is possible to reconstruct the principal methods and aims of the process and the symbolic value which the Egyptians ascribed to mummification. But sometimes it is only the 'unwrapping' of mummies and their analysis with modern technology that can definitively refute the received ideas on mummification. . . .

After death the body was taken to a special 'house of purification', where the treatment began. It was stretched out on a table and the brains were removed. One of the dissectors—the surgically-trained priests who specialized in the preparation of cadavers—made an incision in the left side, using a knife which, for ritual purposes, was made of flint. Through the wound the priest broke through the diaphragm and eviscerated [disemboweled] the corpse. The internal organs were removed and treated separately; once they had been embalmed and wrapped in bandages they were usually placed in vessels, a practice continued until the beginning of the Third Intermediate Period. The first known jars for viscera were found among the funerary furniture of Queen Hetepheres, the mother of Cheops. . . . These vessels became known erroneously as 'canopic jars'. The jars were placed alongside the sarcophagus in the tomb chamber, under the protection of the Four Sons of Horus—Imsety, Hapy, Duamutef and Qebehsenuef—who looked after the liver, the lungs, the stomach and the intestines respectively. In later times the viscera were simply placed in their correct place on the body in the form of 'canopic packets' which had been properly treated. Only the heart and kidneys were left in the body, since their location made them difficult to extract.

Once the corpse had been emptied of its internal organs, the embalmer began the task of 'salting' the body by placing it in natron for about thirty-five days. Since this treatment had the side-effect of darkening the flesh, some of the limbs were dyed with henna or coated with ochre (red for the men and yellow for the women, as in the painting of statues and reliefs) in an attempt to counteract this process. Then the abdomen and chest were stuffed with pieces of material usually provided by the family of the deceased; the wads of material were soaked in gums, herbs and various unguents so that the body could be preserved and restored to its original shape. The opening made by the surgeon in the abdomen was covered up with a plaque which was also placed under the protection of the four sons of Horus.

The body, having been restored in this way, was cleaned and purified. It was then wrapped in bandages, in a process consisting of several stages. First of all, linen strips were used to wrap each individual part of the body, including the fingers and the phallus; then the body was covered with a large piece of material acting as a shroud and the whole of the torso was bandaged.

This process was carried out according to a very precise ritual, which took the same form whether the body was that of a king or a private individual. The only difference was in the value of the amulets which were slid under certain parts of the body and among the bandages. From the New Kingdom onwards funerary texts were also included in the bandages, fulfilling the same purpose as the amulets and jewels; a *Book of the Dead*, for instance, was often inserted between the legs of the mummy. Finally, the face was covered with a mask. . . . The mask gradually developed from the New Kingdom onwards until it became a 'board' covering the whole of the body and reproducing the appearance of a coffin lid. The final stage in its development was reached with the Faiyum 'mummy portraits' painted on wood in encaustic (a mixture of pigment and wax).

The coffin in which the mummy was placed also went through a long process of evolution. At first it acted primarily as a kind of house for the deceased, judging from its rectangular appearance and 'palace façade' decoration. But from the Sixth Dynasty onwards, although it still maintained its role as a false door, the coffin began to be decorated with texts. . . .

THE MEANING OF TOMB DECORATIONS

The funerary furniture continued to be made up of the same basic elements: headrests, pottery vessels, toiletries and the remains of the funeral feast. The entrance to the tomb chamber was at first blocked by a stone slab as in the royal tombs, and the shaft, which might include a stairway or a corridor emerging into the courtyard in front of the superstructure, was blocked at the time of the funeral ceremony.

It was the chapel, always located in the superstructure of the monument, which went through the most complicated process of development. The chapel was at first cruciform, and located in the eastern part of the *mastaba;* at this stage it was simply the logical development of the original niche acting as a false door. But after the reign of Snofru [or Seneferu, about 2600 B.C.] the plan of the chapel changed and a complex typology began to evolve, varying in such aspects as the general plan, the presence of niches and the number of rooms. The most radical developments took place at Giza, where more systematic use of stone brought about a drastic change in the appearance of private funerary monuments: stone chapels could be built with a more accentuated batter than mud-brick, and they tended to have more extensive surfaces available for internal decoration. The development of the chapel in the Fifth and Sixth Dynasties involved the addition of more and more rooms, which gradually altered the general layout and produced the richest and most beautiful examples of this type of tomb. . . .

The basic scheme of decoration in the tomb chapel was virtually always identical. The deceased welcomed the visitor at the doorway to the tomb, which was decorated with his own image and titles. Inside the chapel, on the western wall opposite the entrance door, were one or more false doors which allowed the deceased and his family to enjoy their offerings. The northern false door was usually reserved for the owner of the tomb and the southern one was usually his wife's, while the wall between tended to be decorated with plant forms or imitation tapestries. On the wall opposite the false doors were scenes of the funerary pilgrimage by boat to the holy cities of Busiris and Abydos, at the northern and southern ends of the wall respectively (corresponding to their geographical locations). The northern and southern walls were decorated with scenes of daily life on the estates: agriculture, animal husbandry, games, arts and crafts. The southern wall usually bore depictions of the censing of the statues which were placed in the *serdab* behind it. . . .

The scenes in Old Kingdom tombs are a crucial source of information on the economic and, to some extent, the social aspects of life during this period. They also provide information on funerary traditions and practices themselves. It is apparent above all, that whereas the king was thought to ascend to the heavens, the deceased private individual remained in his tomb, where he enjoyed a continued existence based on his earthly life. It was the proximity of the god, and therefore of the king (expressed in the layout of the necropolis), that guaranteed the incorporation of the deceased into the divine world. This explains the omnipresence of the king inside private tombs: first, through the actual patch of land allotted to a private funerary monument; second, through the concession of key architectonic elements such as the sarcophagus, the false door and the offering table; and third, in the autobiography of the tomb's owner. The deceased was totally dependent on the king. . . . The imprisonment of the deceased in the interior of his tomb, accompanied by an extraordinary wealth of precautions taken to multiply the chances of the soul's survival . . . , reduced the image of the universe to a set of earthly realities.

Decorative themes developed in detail as time went by, but continued to focus on the essential realities of the life of the deceased. All the various phases of human existence can be followed in these themes: from life itself, through the scenes of daily activities, to the final acts in which the deceased was conveyed from the funereal house to eternity.

BUILDING THE GREAT PYRAMIDS

DESMOND STEWART

Of all the impressive achievements of ancient Egypt, the great stone pyramids are the most famous, and deservedly so, for they remain among the true wonders of the world—ancient or modern. Popular opinion, shaped by periodical articles, books, and TV programs by amateurs and sensationalists, often holds that no one knows how the pyramids were built or that the ancient Egyptians did not have the skill or tools to erect such huge and mathematically precise structures; and therefore that aliens or perhaps some kind of mystical or supernatural forces must have played a part in their construction. This line of thinking is misguided and completely without foundation. Reputable scholars have long had a relatively clear general idea of how the Egyptians built these monuments, even if they are unsure of some of the details. The fact is that what they lacked in the way of modern measuring and lifting devices, the builders amply made up for in their access to nearly unlimited amounts of labor, time, patience, and native ingenuity. The following concise overview of the steps in pyramid construction is by Desmond Stewart, a noted authority on Near Eastern history and culture. He cites the evidence provided by the ancient Greek historians Herodotus (fifth century B.C.) and Diodorus Siculus (first century B.C.) in describing the building of the pyramid tombs, including the largest of all, that of the pharaoh Khufu (whom the Greeks called Cheops).

Fortunately the pyramids . . . embody clues as to how they were built. Patient excavation by modern archaeologists has made the pyramids' construction less mysterious than the origins of the kings who built them. The pyramid builders had certain limited assets. For one thing they could call on considerable reserves of labor. The figure mentioned by Herodotus—100,000 men—is not impossible, and the Greek historian's remark that they were rotated in three-month shifts may be nothing more than a distorted recollection of the probable case that work on the pyramids proceeded in stages during the three summer months when the flooding Nile turned the valley into one huge lake. At that season agricultural work became impossible and the fellahin [agricultural peasants] might well have been glad to work on any project that brought them rations of food, quite apart from the fact that such labor was a sacred task connected with the well-being of Egypt. The flooded Nile also made it possible to ferry to the western escarpment stone brought from the quarries of upriver Aswan as well as limestone from the quarries across the Nile Valley.

The greatest asset of the pyramid builders was an unsurpassed organizing talent. Two Western experts on ancient Egyptian building methods, architect Somers Clarke and engineer R. Engelbach, have flatly stated that the rulers of the Old Kingdom [2686–2181 B.C.] were "the best organizers of human labor the world has ever seen." This compliment does not seem excessive when the same experts further inform us that "the only mechanical appliances they knew were the lever, the roller, and the use of vast embankments." The split-second skill of the ancient overseers, a modern Egyptian authority on the pyramids has wryly remarked, seems the one talent that has disappeared.

CHOOSING THE SITE AND LEVELING THE BASE

The first task of the royal architects—which they probably shouldered early in each king's reign—was to select a site that met certain basic requirements. It had to be on the western edge of the valley, since the evening ridge was the particular realm of the dead. It had to stand above the level of the highest floods, but not so high as to inhibit the ferrying of stone to within a convenient distance. It needed to be reasonably flat, and large enough to accommodate its suburb of courtiers' tombs. The rock must be solid and flawless in view of the giant burden it would have to bear. The local stone should be adequate for the hidden parts of the core.

The Giza plateau met these requirements perfectly.

The next stage was to peg out a base, which in the case of the Great Pyramid covered an area of just over thirteen acres. A knoll of projecting rock inside this area was incorporated into the bulk of added stone. The sides of the giant square, each roughly 755 feet long, faced the four cardinal points; the future entrance would look directly north to the Pole Star.

The next stage, the leveling of the base, was facilitated by techniques derived from Egyptian agriculture. Mud retaining walls such as those used in the valley fields were built around the pegged-out area and the space so formed filled with water. When the water covered all but the central knoll, a grid of trenches was excavated in the rock until the bottom of each trench was at the same distance from the surface of the water. This done, the mud walls were breached and the water allowed to escape. It was then possible to chip away the intervening rock between the trenches and so secure a level square with a protruding knoll around which the Great Pyramid would rise. This method of using water as a gigantic spirit level was so successful that the southeast corner of the pyramid stands only half an inch higher than the northwest corner. Other dimensions were only slightly less precise, there being a difference of 7.9 inches between the longest side—the south—and the shortest side—the north.

VARIOUS PLANS FOR THE INTERIOR

If these dimensions reveal the calm confidence of men who had already achieved an effective calendar, the pyramid's internal design shows men still experimenting. Analysis of the pyramid has revealed their changes of plan. None of these changes affected the external appearance of the Great Pyramid (which retained the pure pyramidal form first achieved by Snofru, the father of Cheops, in his second pyramid at Dahshur) or altered the entrance site, which remained some fifty-five feet above ground level on the north.

The changes concerned the pyramid's main function: the storage of the royal cadaver. Imhotep had constructed Zoser's burial chamber deep in the solid rock beneath the Step Pyramid, and a similar mortuary plan was first devised for Cheops. An entrance corridor was designed to slant downward for almost 350 feet, first through the pyramid itself, then through the rock on which it stood. Finally a short horizontal passage led to a modest chamber, now choked with the rubble left by nineteenth-century explorers.

Only when the pyramid had advanced by several courses was a second plan made: to construct the chamber in the exact center of the pyramid, but not very high above ground level. It was now too late to plan for a corridor leading straight from the pyramid entrance to the pyramid's heart. Instead, the roof of the descending corridor was pierced and a new ascending corridor (the one in which you bend your back today) was constructed. This culminated, under the second plan, in a horizontal passage leading to the misnamed Queen's Chamber, intended for Cheops. (His queens were in fact buried under the three smaller pyramids that still survive to the east of the Great Pyramid.) This second attempt was next abandoned for a third, more ambitious design—one that involved the construction of the Grand Gallery with its corbeled roof and King's Chamber of granite.

No improvisation such as had modified the corridor system for the second plan was involved in the third. The Gallery and King's Chamber were built from plans as the pyramid nudged skyward, layer by layer. Wooden scaffolding, erected inside the Grand Gallery, supported great stone plugs that could be lowered immediately after the funeral so as to block forever the ascending corridor. The workmen responsible for closing off the Gallery arranged for their own future: a well-like shaft was bored down to meet the original descending corridor in the rock; having sealed the access route they could then escape, pulling a trapdoor after them.

MOVING THE STONES

It was long a puzzle how more than two million stones—the nine granite slabs roofing the King's Chamber average forty-four tons—were raised on the ascending layers. Most historians reached the conclusion that a Greek contemporary of Julius Caesar, Diodorus Siculus, was on the right track when he wrote that the pyramid had been constructed by the use of "mounds," or ramps. His view was theoretically endorsed by Somers Clarke and Engelbach, since they knew that the Old Kingdom Egyptians, who lacked practical knowledge of the wheel, capstan, and pulley, had relied on manpower for most of their haulage. This view found practical confirmation when the unfinished step pyramid of a successor to Zoser was excavated at Sakkara. Ramps made of rubble and builders' waste were found still in place. The remains of one such ramp almost certainly underlie the road by which the modern visitor approaches the Giza plateau.

These ramps were probably of two kinds. Long, broad supply mounds gave an easy incline for the blocks of cut stone, which were edged forward on rollers whose only lubricants were milk or water. Shorter, more sharply pitched ramps probably raised workmen and lighter materials close to the working face. The outer casing, which filled the triangular gap between each layer and the next, was probably laid stage by stage as the work rose higher. When the apex had been reached and the granite capstone placed in position, the ramp would have been removed and the limestone casing smoothed and polished till a seamless sheet reflected the sun by day and the moon by night.

THE NEW KINGDOM AND EGYPT'S AGE OF EMPIRE

CHARLES FREEMAN

Ancient Egypt reached its height of size, power, and splendor during the period that modern historians call the New Kingdom, encompassing the Eighteenth, Nineteenth, and Twentieth Dynasties, and usually dated from 1550 to 1069 B.C. (It followed a series of other major eras, including the Middle Kingdom, dated 2055–1650, and Second Intermediary Period, dated 1650–1550 B.C. During the latter, the Hyksos, foreign invaders from Palestine, ruled much of Egypt.) This informative synopsis of the New Kingdom, during which Egypt acquired an empire and became in a sense a world power, is by Charles Freeman, author of several recent widely read books about ancient societies. He describes the major rulers of Egypt in these years, among them the famous Akhenaton (the religious heretic depicted in the novel and movie *The Egyptian*), Tutankhamen ("King Tut"), and Ramses II (the pharaoh who enslaved the Hebrews in the Old Testament). He also recounts the expansion of the empire into Palestine and Nubia (the region lying directly south of Egypt) and explains religious developments (especially the rivalry between the sun god Aton and the traditional gods, headed by the Theban deity Amon, sometimes referred to as the "king of the gods").

W ith the triumph of Ahmose I of the Eighteenth Dynasty over the Hyksos, unity and stability returned to Egypt. There was a very different atmosphere to the New

Excerpted from *Egypt, Greece, and Rome: Civilizations of the Ancient Mediterranean*, by Charles Freeman. Copyright © 1996 by Charles Freeman. Reprinted with permission from Oxford University Press.

Kingdom (*c.* 1550–1070 BC). The shock of the Hyksos incursions had been a profound one for a society as isolated and ordered as Egypt and, in retaliation, the rulers of the New Kingdom became warrior kings, building an empire in Asia which at its height reached as far as the Euphrates. The forces of Seth [god of chaos and confusion], normally seen as undermining the power of the kings, were now considered to have been subdued by them and redirected at Egypt's enemies. It was Thutmose I (1504–1492 BC) who reached the Euphrates and defeated the state of Mitanni in Syria. With control established over the cities of Palestine, local princes, with Egyptian troops to oversee them, were used to maintain the new empire intact.

As in previous dynasties, the kings of the New Kingdom also established firm control over Nubia. Egyptian rule was imposed further south than ever before, down to the Fourth Cataract [a rocky area with river rapids located south of present-day Aswan] and probably beyond. A frontier post was established at Napata, under the shadow of a table mountain, Gebel Barkal, which acted as a landmark for traders coming across the desert. For the first time the Egyptians could now directly control the trade routes with their rich harvest of exotic goods coming from central Africa. The Nubian gold mines were also worked so intensively that by the end of the New Kingdom they had become exhausted.

Recently it has been suggested by Martin Bernal in his *Black Athena* that the Egyptian empire also extended into the Mediterranean, with Egypt exercising what he called 'suzerainty' over the Aegean between 1475 and 1375 BC (with contact also at earlier periods). So far little evidence has been found to support the argument. Some Egyptian artefacts have been found in the Mediterranean, but hardly enough to support the claim of 'suzerainty'. A survey made in 1987 found a total of only twenty-one artefacts carrying Egyptian royal cartouches, most of these discovered in Crete, the nearest part of the Aegean to Egypt. It seems that many of these may have been traded through the Levantine ports. Egypt had no city on the Mediterranean coast until Alexandria was founded by Alexander the Great in 332 BC, and no seagoing navy is recorded before the seventh century. It is hard, therefore, to see how Egypt could have maintained any form of control over the Aegean, and Bernal's thesis has received little scholarly support.

It took some time for the New Kingdom to build up its strength. Despite his military successes, Ahmose of the Eighteenth Dynasty did not reopen the limestone quarries at Tura until late in his reign. His own buildings were all in mudbrick. His successor, Amenhotep I (1525–1504 BC), portrayed himself as an aggressive warrior king (his Horus name was 'Bull who conquers the lands'), but the evidence is of twenty years of peace and stability. All the usual signs of Egyptian prosperity now returned. New temples were built in Thebes and Nubia, and raw materials started to flow in to support a resurgence of artistic activity.

A RULING QUEEN

Shortly afterwards the Dynasty produced a rarity in Egyptian history, a ruling queen. There had been signs of the growing power of the queens early in the Eighteenth Dynasty. Both Ahmose's mother and wife seem to have been formidable women who had cults dedicated to them at Thebes. Hatshepsut, the niece of Amenhotep I and daughter of his successor Thutmose I, went further. Hatshepsut had married her half-brother, King Thutmose II. She had no sons, but Thutmose II had one by a concubine who, although still only a boy, succeeded as Thutmose III on the death of his father in 1479 BC. Hatshepsut was accepted a coregent, but soon took absolute power for herself, claiming that she was ruler by right as the heir of Thutmose I.

Every successful Egyptian ruler had to establish himself within a well-established ideology of kingship. For a woman this presented an almost insurmountable problem and Hatshepsut had to define her image carefully. In some representations—sculptures, for instance—Hatshepsut was happy to present herself as female, and she took a female Horus name, 'The She-Horus of fine gold'. In more conventional settings, however, such as temple reliefs, she is shown as male. She also made great play of her divine ancestry, spelling out the details of her conception by Amun in the temple she built at Deir el-Bahri. Here she referred to herself as the son of Amun. It is a fascinating example of the ways in which Egyptian rulers, particularly those who were outsiders, moulded their image to fit within the patterns established in earlier centuries.

Hatshepsut ruled for over twenty years. It was a successful and stable reign. For the first time in the New Kingdom a ruler had effective control over Middle Egypt, and a mass of new temples were built there. Hatshepsut was blessed with an outstanding chief official, Senemnut, a man of humble family who worked his way up to a position of far-reaching power. (Inevitably there have been suggestions that he was the queen's lover. The intimacy of his relationship with the royal family is confirmed by a charming statue, now in the British Museum, of him nursing the queen's only child, her daughter by Thutmose II.)

Senemnut's talents and interests were wide-ranging, as was typical for leading officials of the court. His tomb was decorated with astronomical symbols and contained the classics of Middle Kingdom religious literature. One of his greatest achievements, in his role of chief architect, was the mortuary temple he built for his queen at Deir el-Bahri, running along the northern side of the imposing tomb of Mentuhotep, founder of the Middle Kingdom. A succession of terraces supported by colonnades led up into the natural amphitheatre of the hillside with side chapels commemorating Thutmose I, Amun, and the goddess Hathor, the most popular of the Egyptian goddesses. Finally, a passage cut in the rock face contained an inner sanctuary. Hatshepsut was not buried in the complex herself. She prepared two tombs for herself in the valleys behind, an indication, perhaps, of her fears that her body would not be left undisturbed.

One of the most celebrated reliefs on Hatshepsut's complex commemorates an expedition to the land of Punt. There are references to this mysterious land as early as the Old Kingdom. Punt was probably along the African shores of the southern Red Sea, although no one site has ever been identified. Hatshepsut's reliefs suggest a journey through the Red Sea, and at Punt itself there are pictures of tree houses and tropical fauna (as well as the Queen of Punt, depicted with a swollen and curved body). The fruits of these expeditions included aromatic plants, used for incense, ebony, electrum, and shorthorned cattle, and it seemed that the traders lingered there for about three months at a time, perhaps waiting for favourable winds with which to return home.

Hatshepsut disappears from the record about 1458 BC. There is some suggestion that Senemnut turned against her and engineered the return of Thutmose III to power. The hieroglyphs representing Hatshepsut's name were now systematically erased from every monument, even from the tips of obelisks. This was a devastating fate for any Egyptian, as the survival of their inscribed name was one way in which an afterlife could be ensured. The comprehensive removal of Hatshepsut's name may be a sign of the spite of Thutmose for his powerful stepmother, but probably the main objective was to restore an ordered and comprehensible past focused once again on male kingship.

From War to Peace

In the reign of Thutmose III as sole ruler (1458–1425 BC) the New Kingdom was threatened with the loss of control in Asia. The kingdom of Mitanni, earlier defeated by Thutmose I, was now challenging Egypt for the control of the Levant [the region of Palestine and Syria]. It attempted to undermine Egyptian rule by stirring up rivalries between the cities of Palestine. Thutmose led no less than seventeen campaigns in Asia, proudly recording their results on the walls of the temple of Amun at Karnak. One of his most famous battles was at Megiddo, where the king, against all professional advice, took his armies through a difficult mountain pass to emerge behind his enemies and defeat them. With control over Palestine re-established, Thutmose took on Mitanni itself, even launching a successful crossing of the Euphrates. He also imposed his rule forcefully on Nubia. The land was now being exploited directly by Egyptian institutions, with the result that much of the indigenous culture was eradicated.

In royal mythology Thutmose was portrayed as one of the great kings of Egypt. He was far more than a successful conqueror. He had an acute sense of his place in history as the successor of a long line of Theban kings. A list of his ancestors was set up in the temple at Karnak and was treated with special reverence. He was also a man of culture and curiosity. He brought back examples of the flowers and plants of Syria, depicting them in a botanical scene on the temple wall at Karnak. He was an enthusiastic reader of ancient texts, and is believed to have composed literary works of his own.

Despite Thutmose's cultural interests, the ethos of the New Kingdom was essentially a military one. For the first time in Egyptian history, soldiers found themselves among the king's key advisers. Thutmose's successor, Amenhotep II (1427–1400 BC), gloried in the role of war hero. His ebullient Horus name, 'Powerful bull with great strength', is echoed in legends which tell how he hunted lions on foot and killed Syrian princes with his own hands. However, his propaganda could not gloss over the fact that much of northern Syria was lost during his reign. Under his successor Thutmose IV (1400–1390 BC), peace was made with Mitanni. The Mitannians were worried about the rise of the Hittite empire to the north, and they were quite content to hold northern Syria against the growing threat while allowing Egyptian rule to continue in Palestine. Peace was consolidated when Amenhotep III (1390–1352 BC) married the daughter of the Mitannian king.

THE ADMINISTRATION OF THE NEW KINGDOM

The reign of Amenhotep III marked the zenith of the New Kingdom. The structure of its administration is fairly well known. The king presided over three departments of government. The first was his own family. This could be large: Ramses II (1279–1213 BC), for instance, was said to have fathered 160 children. While the royal family had immense status, not many of its members seem to have been given political power. The king was presumably careful not to encourage those with royal blood to build up positions of influence. There were exceptions, however. The heir might be given command of the army, and there was a traditional role for the queen, or eldest daughter of the king, as Chief Priestess of Amun. . . . Through her the king had access to much of the wealth of the temples.

The second department of government oversaw the empire in Nubia and Asia. Apart from Nubia, where the ecology was very similar to what they were used to, the Egyptians were not successful colonizers. Their world was so dependent on the ordered environment of the Nile valley that they found it very difficult to adapt to life outside. When Egyptian armies reached the Euphrates they were completely bewildered by it, never having encountered water flowing southwards. In words reminiscent of the political newspeak of communist China, they described the river as 'water that goes downstream in going upstream'.

Ultimately the Egyptians depended on military force to sustain their rule, and for the first time in Egyptian history the kings raised a large army, of perhaps between 15,000 and 20,000 men. It was divided into battalions of infantry and charioteers, each battalion fighting under the name of a god. A large proportion of the troops consisted of levies raised within the empire itself. However, the army was expensive and difficult to maintain and soldiering was never popular. In practice most kings contented themselves with punitive raids into Asia or Nubia early in their reigns and then returned to a more settled life in their courts. The normal pattern of administration was indirect, with Egyptian governors, supported by envoys and garrisons, ruling through vassal princes. The governors were responsible for maintaining order and collecting taxes, tribute, and raw materials. Thutmose III, the most successful conqueror of Asia, initiated a policy of bringing back Palestinian princes to Egypt as hostages for the good behaviour of their home cities.

The empire was an important source of raw materials. This had always been the case with Nubia, but Asia also provided booty from the wars and openings for trade. The grain harvests of the plain of Megiddo were appropriated by Thutmose III, tin came from Syria, copper from Cyprus, and silver, valued in Egypt more highly than gold, from Cilicia in southern Anatolia [what is now Turkey]. If the temple inscriptions are to be believed, prisoners were brought back to Egypt in their thousands, and foreigners are to be found as artisans, winemakers, servants, and mercenaries. With them came Asiatic gods and goddesses, among them Astarte, the goddess of horse-riders, who were adopted within the Egyptian pantheon.

The third department of government was concerned with internal administration. This was subdivided into four offices, one each for the administration of the royal estates, the army, the overseeing of religious affairs, and internal civil administration. Each was headed by a small group of advisers, perhaps twenty to thirty at any one time, who were often intimates of the king. The country was divided into two administrative areas, one, Upper Egypt, based on Thebes and the other on Memphis. The success of civil administration was dependent on the personality of the ruler. It was he and only he who could infuse the necessary energy into maintaining the links with the provincial governments stretched out along hundreds of kilometres of valley. Smaller centres had mayors, who were responsible for collecting taxes, probably a tenth of total produce, and carrying out orders from above, although it is not clear how far mayors exercised power over the countryside outside their towns. . . .

AKHENATEN, THE RELIGIOUS REVOLUTIONARY

By the end of the reign of Amenhotep III (c. 1350 BC), the temples were so rich that they had become political and economic rivals of the king. The first signs of strain can already be seen in Amenhotep's reign. He seems to have distanced himself gradually from the influence of Thebes. He brought up his own son, also Amenhotep, in Memphis and is found patronizing other cults in northern Egypt—that of the sacred bulls at Saqqara and the sun god at Heliopolis, for instance. For the first time in Amenhotep's reign a new cult appears, the worship of the sun in its physical form, Aten. It was Amenhotep's successor, Amenhotep IV, better known as Akhenaten, 'Pious Servant of Aten' (1352–1336 BC), who was to attempt a religious and social revolution, installing Aten as a single god in place of the traditional gods of Egypt.

The worship of a sun god was well-established in Egyptian religion, and sun worship was also common among the cultures of the Middle East over which Egypt ruled. If Akhenaten had done no more than emphasize Aten among the other gods of Egypt he would probably have caused no stir. However, he chose to launch an attack on all other gods, in particular Amun, and to install himself as a direct mediator between his people and Aten. . . .

The impact was profound. Many temples were closed down and their goods were confiscated. The economic structure of the state was upset as lands were transferred direct to the king. The masses lost their festivals. As the reign went on the persecution of Amun became more intense. His name and even any reference to 'gods' in the plural was erased from the temples. . . .

The new religion did not catch on. For the mass of people there was no incentive to turn away from traditional religious practices which were so deeply integrated into everyday life. Egyptian religion was astonishingly flexible at a popular level. There was a plethora [large array] of gods which could take on different identities and attributes to meet different human and spiritual needs. They were grouped together or merged as composite gods in a rich mythology which covered creation and the afterlife. To replace them by a single physical entity, available only in one form was a cultural shock far greater than the Egyptians could absorb. Even the workmen building at Tell el-Amarna [Akhenaten's new capital city] stayed loyal to their traditional gods.

The failure of Aten does not make the reign of Akhenaten any less interesting. He was a strong king who focused the kingdom on himself as the only mediator with his god. By confiscating the goods of the temples he strengthened his political position and he appears to have been well in control of the administration. He was one of those rare Egyptians who introduced important cultural changes. He was represented with his wife Nefertiti and his family in much more informal and realistic poses than was conventional. It was as if the royal family now replaced the mythological families of the gods. . . .

One of the most interesting finds from Tell el-Amarna is the diplomatic archive of Amenhotep III and Akhenaten, 350 tablets of clay. . . . They give an intriguing picture of the political realities of control of the Egyptian empire. The Asian empire was ruled by three Egyptian governors who oversaw a host of native rulers. Many of the letters are from these rulers, professing their loyalty, complaining about their neighbouring rulers, or asking for help against the menace of raiding nomadic tribes. There are also communications from the major states of the area, among them Mitanni, Assyria, and Babylon, with their kings addressing the Egyptian ruler as 'brother' and often offering marriages between their families and his.

THE NINETEENTH DYNASTY AND RAMSES II

When Akhenaten died in about 1336 BC the country was left in some confusion. His successor lived only a few months and it was a boy, Tutankhaten, who succeeded. His name suggests that the worship of Aten was still officially practised, but within a year the king's name had been changed to Tutankhamun and the city at Tell el-Amarna had been abandoned. Tutankhamun never emerged as ruler in his own right. By the age of 19 he was dead, possibly from a cerebral haemorrhage. It was by sheer chance, probably because the site of the tomb was forgotten and blocked by the debris from later tunnelling, that his tomb in the Valley of the Kings survived intact until rediscovered in 1922 by the British archaeologist, Howard Carter. The completeness of the finds, the rich array of grave goods, and the poignant story of the king who had died so young led to a wave of 'Tutmania' which swept across the world in the 1920s.

On the death of Tutankhamun the Eighteenth Dynasty was virtually exhausted. The land was still in disruption, and it is hardly surprising that it was a general, Horemheb, who eventually succeeded. Horemheb saw himself as the restorer of traditional order. He even extended his reign backwards so as to delete that of Akhenaten and his successors and is officially recorded as a member of the Eighteenth Dynasty. Horemheb built heavily at Karnak, tearing down Akhenaten's temple to Aten and using its blocks for his own needs. With no male heir, he passed on the kingdom to a fellow general who, as king Ramses I, was to be the founder of the Nineteenth Dynasty, the last to see Egypt as a great power. . . .

The Egyptian empire was now under the threat of a new enemy, the Hittite empire, which at its height in the late fourteenth century extended across the central Anatolian plateau, over much of what had been the kingdom of Mitanni and south into the Levant. . . . Conflict along the northern boundaries of the Egyptian empire seemed certain, and already in the reign of Sety I new campaigns had to be launched into Asia to reimpose Egyptian control there. The most famous battle against the Hittites was that waged in about 1275 BC by Sety I's son, Ramses II (c. 1279–1213 BC), at Qadesh, the town in Syria which had been unofficially recognized as the border of the Egyptian empire. Ramses presented it on the temple walls of Egypt as a crushing victory, but with accounts surviving also from Hittite sources it is possible to see that the Egyptian army was lucky to escape intact from the mass of Hittite chariotry. In fact, the campaign was a stalemate, and Ramses was sensible enough to realize the dangers of campaigning against such a strong empire so far from home. About 1263 BC he made a Treaty of Alliance with the Hittites and brought his warlike career to an end.

Ramses is remembered because of the vast building programme he carried out during his long reign. Nearly half the temples which still stand in Egypt date from his reign. One of his most famous legacies is the great temple of Abu Simbel, rescued and rebuilt by UNESCO [an agency of the United Nations] in the 1960s when Lake Nasser threatened to engulf it after the building of the Aswan dam. Four colossal statues of Ramses, each 21 metres high, sit alongside each other in the rock face. Between them the temple entrance opens into a great hall and far inside there are four further statues of the gods. Twice a year the rays of the rising sun would strike inwards to illuminate the gods. The temple, at the southern extremity of Egyptian rule, was dearly designed to show off the reality of the king's power over his Nubian subjects.

To glorify his home area in the Delta, Ramses constructed an impressive new capital at Pi-Ramses. Here he had his palace and there were major temples to Amun, Seth, and Ra. As the king neared the thirtieth year of his reign he built a massive set of Jubilee Halls for the ceremony of *sed*, the celebration of thirty years of power. Naturally Ramses could not neglect planning for his death, and he followed the tradition of building a great royal tomb, perhaps the most opulent of them all, in the Valley of the Kings. As a more visible memorial he constructed a vast mortuary temple, the Ramesseum, on the west bank of the Nile at Thebes. Its granaries alone were so huge that 3,400 families could have been fed for a year from their contents. . . .

COLLAPSE OF THE NEW KINGDOM

In the next Dynasty, the Twentieth, only one able king, Ramses III (*c.* 1184–1153 BC), stands out. He carried out a series of brilliant victories against the intruders and managed to build some fine monuments, including a massive temple at Medinet Habu near Thebes, but his state was crumbling. The revenues of the temples of Amun were only a fifth of what they had been under Thutmose III. By the end of Ramses' reign there were growing signs of internal unrest. An assassination attempt was hatched within the royal harem, while, in a rare bureaucratic breakdown, grain rations failed to arrive for the craftsmen working on the royal tombs. In retaliation the workmen organized the first recorded strike in history.

The last nine kings of the Twentieth Dynasty all took the name Ramses, as if they hoped it would prove a lucky token against further decay, but they could do little to stop the decline. Part of the problem was that many were already elderly when they came to the throne. Their reigns proved too short and their energies too diminished for them to enforce their power. . . . The resources available to the kings were also contracting. The gold mines of Nubia were exhausted by the end of the New Kingdom. Rich areas such as the Fayum, a cultivated part of Egypt since the Middle Kingdom, gradually became indefensible against the Libyans. As central government faltered under ageing kings with diminishing resources, the empire disintegrated. The Asian empire was lost by the time of Ramses VI (1141–1136). The population of Nubia fell as gold mining ceased there and its provincial administration withdrew at the end of the Twentieth Dynasty. By 1060 Egypt had withdrawn into its original valley boundaries.

A vivid picture of the collapse of society within Egypt comes from records of tomb robberies. Such robberies had always taken place, but now their scale seems to have increased dramatically. It was the impoverished inhabitants of western Thebes who seem to have been most prominent in siphoning off grain supplies from the temples and robbing tombs of their furniture. Even royal tombs were not immune, a sure sign that respect for authority was crumbling. Among the goods recovered by officials were not only gold and silver but linen, vases of oil, wood, copper, and bronze. Corruption spread. Even the officials themselves became involved, and Nubian troops brought up to help deal with the problem themselves joined in despoiling tombs and monuments. In a desperate, but successful, attempt to preserve the bodies of the kings, their mummies, among them that of the great Ramses II, were collected from their original tombs and gathered in a new hiding place in the hills behind Deir el-Bahri, where they lay undiscovered until the nineteenth century. . . .

This was a devastating moment for a society which prided itself so much on its good order and respect for the past. Despite moments of national revival, the Egyptian state was never again to enjoy such power and sustained prosperity as it had in the New Kingdom.

KING TUT: REDISCOVERING AN EGYPTIAN RULER

BOB BRIER

The most famous of all the ancient Egyptian artifacts discovered in modern times was undoubtedly the tomb and remains of the pharaoh Tutankhamen (or Tutankhamun), known as "King Tut" for short. This relatively unimportant ruler, who reigned from 1336 to 1327 B.C., was buried in the Valley of the Kings (or Tombs), a New Kingdom burial ground on the Nile's west bank about three miles west of modern Luxor. What made him special was the fact that his tomb was discovered almost entirely intact, an unusual find considering that every other Egyptian royal tomb found up to that time had been pillaged by grave robbers. Bob Brier, of the American Research Center in Egypt, here recounts the details of that world famous discovery, made by English archaeologist Howard Carter and English antiquities collector and amateur archaeologist Lord George Carnarvon.

When Tutankhamen's mummy was discovered, there was no doubt about its identity. During his excavations in the Valley of the Kings, under a rock [wealthy American businessman and amateur archaeologist] Theodore Davis found a faience cup bearing Tutankhamen's name. Near that find spot he found a pit containing wine jars, bandages, a small mask, and other minor objects also bearing Tutankhamen's name. Davis concluded that he had found what little remained of a reburial of Tutankhamen. He published his discovery under the title *The*

Excerpted from *Egyptian Mummies*, by Bob Brier. Copyright © 1994 by Bob Brier. Reprinted by permission of HarperCollins Publishers, Inc.

Tombs of Harmhabi and Touatankhamanou, and it is here that he made his famous statement, "I fear that the Valley of the Tombs is now exhausted."

Tutankhamen's tomb was the one every Egyptologist knew was missing, and for which everyone was looking. Now that Davis believed he had found Tutankhamen's reburial site, he saw no reason to continue searching. He relinquished his concession, opening the door to Howard Carter. As an experienced excavator, Carter knew that Davis had merely found an embalmers' cache from Tutankhamen's burial, not a tomb. Carter, with Lord Carnarvon's support, eagerly took up the search.

The story of the discovery of Tutankhamen's tomb has been told many times and is well known. It should be noted, however, that the discovery of the tomb was in no way a stroke of luck. Carter and Carnarvon knew exactly what they were looking for and how to find it. Working from a detailed map of the valley prepared by Carter, they intended to clear every unexplored meter down to bedrock. After years of methodical work Carter and Carnarvon discovered the tomb that gave the world its single totally undisturbed pharaoh's mummy.

EXCAVATING THE TOMB

The first step leading down into the tomb was discovered on November 4, 1922, but it would be more than three years before Carter was able to see the boy king face to face. The tomb had four chambers, and the antechamber, which preceded the burial chamber, was packed with the goods a pharaoh needed in the next world. Chariots, statues, game boards, linens, jewelry—all had to be photographed, catalogued, and conserved in the tomb before removal. Sometimes it took as long as a week to coat a fragile wooden object with wax so it could be moved. It was not until February 16, 1923, that the task of clearing the antechamber was completed. Only then could the burial chamber be entered. Carter found evidence of at least two ancient minor robberies, but hoped that the thieves had not reached the body of the king and that behind the resealed wall of the burial chamber rested Tutankhamen's untouched body.

The official breaking through of the burial chamber wall took place on February 17, 1923—and when Carter and Carnarvon finally peered in, it seemed to them that they were face-to-face with a wall of gold. The small burial chamber was almost completely filled with a gilded wood shrine that, both hoped, encircled the body of Tutankhamen. When the excavators entered the chamber and examined the door to the shrine, they must have had their first serious doubts about finding the king's body intact. The expected seals were missing; perhaps thieves had violated the grave of the dead king. The bolt slid easily, and for the first time in 3,000 years the doors to the seventeen-by-eleven-foot shrine opened. That shrine enclosed another, covered with a linen pall; also of gilded wood, it bore religious texts the king needed for his resurrection. Unlike the first shrine, however, the two doors to this shrine were sealed.

The seals were broken, and the doors opened to reveal yet another gilded shrine, also with sealed doors. When these doors were opened the fourth and last shrine was revealed. It was clear that this was the last, the one containing the body of the king. Carter was greatly affected by being the first person in the presence of a pharaoh who died more than three millennia ago. He writes:

> The decisive moment was at hand! An indescribable moment for an archaeologist! What was beneath and what did that fourth shrine contain? With intense excitement I drew back the bolts of the last and unsealed doors; they slowly swung open . . . and there filling the entire area within, effectively barring any further progress, stood an immense yellow quartzite sarcophagus . . . intact, with the lid still firmly fixed in place, just as the pious hands had left it. It was certainly a thrilling moment. . . .

Carter had found the king for whom he had been searching so long.

Work on the sarcophagus had to wait until the shrines could be dismantled and removed from the chamber. Because of the confined space, this was an extremely difficult feat of engineering. The job had been easier for the ancient workmen, who had assembled the shrines from fresh, strong wood. Carter had to deal with the dry, brittle wood that now remained.

Still visible, painted in black and white inks on the shrines, were ancient instructions as to how to assemble them. On the front of the side panels was the hieroglyph ◿, meaning "front." On the rear was ⌇, meaning "rear." These hieroglyphs matched those on the roofs of the shrines—our equivalent of "Insert tab A in slot A." The workmen had been told to orient them with the doors opening to the west so the king could emerge into the next world. However, the ancient workmen got it backward; the doors opened to the east. Because the sun died in the west and was reborn each day in the east, the west was associated with death. Cemeteries were on the west bank of the Nile, for instance, and a common euphemism for the dead was "westerner." Tutankhamen would have walked into this world rather than the next.

THE COFFIN WITHIN A COFFIN

Once the shrines were dismantled and removed, the massive lid to the sarcophagus could be carefully examined and raised. The sarcophagus was carved from a single block of yellow quartzite, while the lid, which was not the one originally intended for the sarcophagus, was of pink granite painted to look like yellow quartzite. A crack across the middle had been repaired with plaster and painted to conceal the damage. The crack made it difficult to raise the lid, but eventually a block and tackle were brought in and ropes placed under the lid so it could be hoisted. Carter was one step closer to his goal—Tutankhamen himself. . . .

> None of us but felt the solemnity of the occasion [Carter later wrote], none of us but was affected by the prospect of what we were about to see—the burial custom of a king of ancient Egypt thirty-three centuries ago. How would the king be found? Such were the anticipatory speculations running in our minds during the silence maintained.
>
> The tackle for raising the lid was in position. I gave the word. Amid intense silence the huge slab, broken in two, weighing over a ton and a quarter, rose from its bed.

The group working in the tomb peered into the sarcophagus, but as if through a mist; they could not make out any details. Then they realized that they were looking at a linen shroud covering the coffin in the sarcophagus. When the shroud was rolled back, they were confronted with more than they could have hoped for. A seven-foot coffin of unsurpassed workmanship, bearing the likeness of Tutankhamen, came into view. On the forehead of the boy-king were the cobra and vulture, symbols of Upper and Lower Egypt—the pharaoh's dominion. Around these symbols of power was a small funeral wreath. Carter was evidently moved by the scene; it is one of the few times in his three-volume work about the tomb that he becomes overly sentimental. . . .

> Many and disturbing were our emotions awakened [he wrote] . . . most of them voiceless. But in that silence, to listen—you could almost hear the ghostly footsteps of the departing mourners. . . .

Carter's wait was not over. It was now February 12, 1924, and the next day would prove a pivotal point for the remainder of the excavation.

THE TASK OF SEPARATING THE COFFINS

There had been bad feelings between the two excavators, Carter and Carnarvon, and the Egyptian Antiquities Service, almost from the day the tomb was discovered. One source of conflict had been the handling of publicity. To avoid the nuisance of hundreds of reporters pouring into the Valley of the Kings, Lord Carnarvon decided to sell the exclusive rights to the story to the London *Times*. This allowed the team to deal with one reporter only, but it also alienated all the other members of the press. Reporters from the Egyptian newspapers, whose country owned the tomb and on whose soil the excavators worked, were not permitted to interview Carter or Carnarvon; only the foreign reporter from the London *Times* was allowed this privilege. This situation was viewed by the Egyptians as British colonialism at its worst.

When Carter invited his colleagues' wives to be present at the opening of the outer coffin, the Egyptian Antiquities Service refused permission. If Egyptian reporters were not to be allowed access, then neither would the wives of Carter's colleagues. The message to Carter was: This is not your tomb, but ours. By this time Lord Carnarvon had died of complications from an infected mosquito bite, and Carter was left to handle the situation alone. Carnarvon had possessed a soothing charm that enabled him to smooth things out; Carter was a meticulous excavator but he lacked charm, and that caused him political difficulty. He posted a notice at the Winter Palace Hotel stating that he and his colleagues could not work under such restrictions, and that he was closing the tomb. The Egyptians responded by sending guards to lock Carter out of it. It was now clear whose tomb it was. There was little Carter could do, so he left on a lecture tour of America. The Egyptian government knew that Carter was the best man for the excavation and eventually an agreement was worked out, but it was not until October, 1925, that the lid of the outer coffin was removed.

Removing the three coffins nested inside one another was a delicate task that consumed most of the 1925–1926 season. The outer lid included silver handles for lowering it onto the coffin; these proved strong enough for raising it. The second, equally beautiful, anthropoid coffin was revealed; it too bore floral wreaths. This coffin, however, gave Carter his first inkling that the mummy might not be in the best condition. Some of the inlays in this coffin had fallen out, a sign of moisture's destructiveness.

Because of the delicate condition of the second coffin, it was decided to remove the entire ensemble rather than just the lid. This was done, but no one could explain the incredible weight they seemed to be lifting. With the entire group of coffins suspended above the sarcophagus, planks of wood were placed on the stone sarcophagus and the coffins lowered onto them.

The problem now was that the second coffin had no handles but fitted inside the outer one with less than a half-inch to spare on any side. Carter screwed strong eyelets into the outer coffin, removed the planks, and lowered it back into the sarcophagus rather than raising its contents. The second coffin, still holding the innermost, remained suspended until a wooden platform could be placed under it. With room to maneuver now, the lid of the second coffin could be raised. The reason for the unexpected weight was discovered—the third, innermost, coffin was solid gold.

REMOVING THE MUMMY

The details on the gold coffin were obscured by a black coating, the remains of magical unguents that had been poured over it. These liquids had run into the bottom of the second coffin, gluing the two together. But the handles on the lid of the gold coffin allowed it to be lifted. At last the mummy of the king was uncovered. Carter wrote:

> At such moments the emotions evade verbal expression, complex and stirring as they are. Three thousand years and more had elapsed since men's eyes had gazed into that golden coffin. . . . Here at last lay all that was left of the youthful Pharaoh, hitherto little more than the shadow of a name.

Like the gold coffin, the mummy itself had been ritually dowsed with buckets of unguents, which explained the evidence of moisture noted in the second coffin. The famous gold mask protected the head of the pharaoh, but the rest of the body was in poor condition. An autopsy would prove to be difficult.

To soften the unguents, Carter took the coffins and mummy out into the sun. . . . Dr. Douglas Derry, who was then an anatomy professor at the Egyptian University, was given the responsibility for working with the body. He first tried to chisel the mummy free, then used heated knives, causing considerable damage to the body. Finally, Derry cut the mummy in half at the third lumbar vertebra so it could be removed in sections.

Unwrapping began on November 11, 1925. . . . The task was extremely difficult because of the fragile condition of the bandages. The unguents poured over them had caused a chemical reaction, and they were darkened, actually burned, by a slow spontaneous combustion. Because the bandages could not be unrolled, heated wax was brushed over their outer layer so it could be cut away in a large piece. When the wax had cooled, Derry made a longitudinal incision and peeled back the first layer of linen. The unwrapping continued for hours, with each successive layer revealing amulets and jewelry incorporated in the wrappings. In all, 143 splendid objects were removed with the bandages. Finally the mummy was revealed. . . .

REMAINS OF THE BOY KING

Because the mummy's arms and legs were disarticulated from their joints, Derry could clearly see the tops and bottoms of the long bones. The ends of these bones, the epiphyses, are not completely part of the long bone in early life, but instead ossify gradually. At birth they are attached by cartilage that converts to bone after growth stops. Since the average point at which the epiphyses join to the long bone is known, the degree of this union is a reliable criterion of age. In the case of Tutankhamen, the kneecap could be lifted off easily to examine the lower end of the femur. The epiphysis was separate from the shaft, and movable. Tutankhamen was indeed a boy king. Derry wrote:

> . . . As this latter portion of the tibia is generally found to fuse with the shaft at about age eighteen, Tut Ankh Amen, from the evidence of his lower limbs, would appear to have been over eighteen but below twenty years at the date of his death.

Arm bones can also indicate age, and they too agreed with the estimate from the leg bones.

Because of its poor condition, the mummy of Tutankhamen yielded few secrets or surprises. The most interesting discovery was a fact about the embalming process. The incision through which the internal organs were removed, in this case on the left, as is usual, was higher than normal, beginning near the navel and descending at an angle toward the hip bone. The incision was open and the flaps pushed inward, which probably occurred when the body cavity was packed with resin-soaked linen. Surprisingly, there was no gold plaque covering the incision, although one was found within the wrappings on the left side of the body.

Carter had hoped that Derry would be able to determine the cause of Tutankhamen's death, but because of the limited facilities in the Valley of the Kings, where the autopsy took place, and the poor condition of the mummy, this was not possible. The mummy of Tutankhamen has never left the valley. Because the King was found undisturbed in his original tomb, it was agreed he should remain there. Even so, preparing the coffin for the permanent storage of the mummy presented problems. The gold coffin was still stuck to the wooden one in which it rested, but

Carter invented a risky yet ingenious method for separating the two. . . . The second and third coffins were transported to the Egyptian Museum in Cairo. Tutankhamen's mummy, however, was allowed to remain in the tomb, in the outermost coffin, inside the yellow quartzite sarcophagus.

BURIAL RITUALS

Despite the poor condition of the mummy, from all the funerary equipment found in the tomb a great deal was learned about the rituals that accompanied the burial of a pharaoh. One new discovery was how liberally unguents were used. Gallons of oils were poured on the body and inner coffin of Tutankhamen, and this was not the only place they were employed. Past the burial chamber was a small room, named "the Treasury" by Carter, that, among other funerary items, contained the canopic chest holding the pharaoh's internal organs. Here, too, unguents had been poured over everything. Most interesting was the container for Tutankhamen's internal organs.

The canopic chest was carved from a single piece of calcite, divided into four shallow compartments to hold the king's mummified organs. . . . The four corners of Tutankhamen's canopic chest are carved with figures of the goddesses Isis, Nephthys, Selket, and Neith. Each was associated with one of the four sons of Horus, guardians of the internal organs. A carved calcite lid with the head of the king sealed each compartment. . . . The internal organs of Tutankhamen were not merely resting in the compartments, but had first been placed in a unique set of four tiny gold coffins, miniatures of the second of Tutankhamen's full-sized coffins. Each small coffin was wrapped with linen, then anointed with unguents and placed into a compartment. A magical spell emphasizing the connection between the protective goddesses and the four sons of Horus ran down the front of these little coffins. For example, the spell on the coffin containing the king's intestines reads: "Words spoken by Selket: I have placed my two arms around that which is inside. I protect Qebhsenuf who is in there. Qebhsenuf of the Osiris, the King, Neb-Kheperu-Re, true of voice." (It was believed that everyone, even pharaohs, would be judged before being allowed entry into the next world. The deceased would have to plead his case before a tribunal of gods and convince them that he was honest, good, truthful, etc. If he was successful, the gods would declare him "true of voice," a euphemism the ancient Egyptians had for those who died.)

Each miniature gold coffin depicted of one of the four goddesses with her protective arms (shown as wings) outstretched, accompanied by an elaborate magical spell. Nothing like these canopic coffins had ever been seen before, but there is evidence that they were not unique. One of Tutankhamen's had originally been made for his brother Semenkare, and traces of Semenkare's name can still be seen under Tutankhamen's. Thus Semenkare may have had a set, and the same may well be true of other kings of the late Eighteenth Dynasty.

The tomb of Tutankhamen provided archeologists with the burial of a king to study. However, those who were interested in the history of mummification were disappointed; nothing new was learned from the poorly preserved body of the boy king.

Early Mediterranean and European Peoples

CHAPTER 4

Minoans and Mycenaeans: The Early Greeks

Thomas R. Martin

The earliest advanced cultures in Europe appeared in Greece during the Bronze Age (ca. 3000–1100 B.C.). Noted Holy Cross scholar Thomas R. Martin composed the following well-written summary of what are sometimes referred to as the "proto-Greek" civilizations of the Bronze Age Aegean sphere. The Mycenaeans, who spoke an early form of Greek, at first inhabited mainland Greece (before expanding into the Aegean island sphere ca. 1400 B.C.). The non-Greek-speaking and culturally advanced Minoans were based on Crete and some nearby Aegean islands. Martin speculates about contacts and influences between the two peoples, describes their written scripts (Linear A and B), and concludes with a discussion of the still mysterious collapse of Greece's Bronze Age cultures beginning in about 1200 B.C.

People had inhabited the large, fertile island of Crete for several thousand years before the emergence about 2200–2000 B.C. of the system that has earned the title of the earliest Aegean civilization. This civilization, which was characterized by large architectural complexes today usually labeled "palaces," relied on an interdependent economy based primarily on redistribution. The first, "pre-palace" settlers in Crete presumably immigrated across the sea from nearby Anatolia about 6000 B.C. These Neolithic farming families originally lived in small settlements nestled close to fertile agricultural land, like their con-

Excerpted from *Ancient Greece: From Prehistoric to Hellenistic Times*, by Thomas R. Martin. Copyright © 1996 by Yale University. Reprinted by permission of Yale University Press.

temporaries elsewhere in Europe. In the third millennium B.C., however, the new technological developments in metallurgy and agriculture began to affect society on Crete dramatically. By about 2200 B.C. or somewhat later, sprawling, many-chambered buildings (the so-called palaces) began to appear on Crete, usually near but not on the coast. Today this Cretan society is called "Minoan" after King Minos, the legendary ruler of the island. The palaces housed the rulers and their servants and served as central storage facilities, while the general population clustered around the palaces in houses built one right next to the other, although there were also country houses and modest towns in outlying areas.

Earthquakes leveled the first Cretan palaces about 1700 B.C., but the Minoans rebuilt on an even grander scale in the succeeding centuries. Accounting records preserved on clay tablets reveal how these large structures served as the hub of the island's economy. Probably influenced by Egyptian hieroglyphs, the Minoans at first developed a pictographic script to symbolize objects, for the purpose of keeping such records. This system evolved into a more linear form of writing to express phonetic sounds. . . . This system of writing was a true syllabary, in which characters stood for the sound of the syllables of words. This script, used during the first half of the second millennium, is today called Linear A. Its language remains largely undeciphered, but recent scholarship suggests that it may have been Indo-European. In other ways, such as their religious architecture, the Minoans differed from the population on the Greek mainland. Since Minoan civilization had direct contact with and great influence on the mainland inhabitants, however, it is appropriate to treat it as part of the early history of Greece.

THE PALACE ECONOMIES

Linear A is sufficiently understood to show that it was used for records in the form of lists: records of goods received and goods paid out, inventories of stored goods, livestock, land holdings, and personnel. With their passion for accounting, the Minoans kept records of everything from chariots to perfumes. The receipts record payments owed, with careful notation of any deficits in the amount actually paid in. The records of disbursements from the palace storerooms cover ritual offerings to the gods, rations to personnel, and raw materials for crafts production, such as metal issued to bronze smiths. None of the tablets records any exchange rate between different categories of goods, such as, for example, a ratio to state how much grain counted as the equivalent of a sheep. Nor do the tablets reveal any use of bullion [precious metals] as money in exchanges. (The invention of coinage lay a thousand years in the future.)

The palace society of Minoan Crete therefore appears to have operated primarily on a redistributive economic system: the central authority told producers how much they had to contribute to the central collection facility and also decided what each member of the society would receive for subsistence and reward. In other words, the palaces did not support a market economy, in which agricultural products and manufactured goods are exchanged through buying and selling. Similar redistributive economic systems based on official monopolies had existed in Mesopotamia for some time, and, like them, the Cretan redistributive arrangement required both ingenuity and a complicated administration. To handle receipt and disbursement of olive oil and wine, for example, the palaces had vast storage areas filled with hundreds of gigantic jars next to storerooms crammed with bowls, cups, and dippers. Scribes meticulously recorded what came in and what went out by writing on clay tablets kept in the palace. This process of economic redistribution applied to crafts specialists as well as to food producers, and the palace's administrative officials set specifications for crafts producers' contributions, which amounted to work quotas. Although not everyone is likely to have participated in the redistribution system, it apparently dominated the Cretan economy. . . . Overseas trade probably operated as a monopoly through the palace system, too, with little role for independent merchants and traders. Egypt was a favorite destination for Minoan seafarers, who brought back objects for trade and are depicted in Egyptian tomb reliefs as bringing gifts or tribute to Egypt's rulers. . . . Minoan Crete was also in contact with the Near East and the island of Cyprus in the eastern Mediterranean, with traders and crafts specialists from those areas probably voyaging westward to Crete as often as the Minoans went eastward.

From all indications, Minoan civilization operated smoothly and peacefully for centuries. For example, contemporary settlements elsewhere around the Aegean Sea and in Anatolia had elaborate defensive walls. The absence of walls around the palaces, towns, and isolated country houses of Minoan Crete is therefore all the more striking and implies that Minoan settlements saw no need to fortify themselves against each other. The remains of the newer palaces, such as the famous one at Knossos on the north side of the island—with its hundreds of rooms in five stories, storage jars holding 240,000 gallons, indoor plumbing, and colorful scenes painted on the walls—have led many to see Minoan society as especially prosperous, peaceful, and happy. The prominence of women in palace frescoes and the numerous figurines of bosomy goddesses found on Cretan sites have even prompted speculation that Minoan society continued to be a female-dominated culture. . . . But the wealth of weaponry found in the graves of Cretan men shows that martial prowess and display bestowed special status in Minoan society. The weapons strongly suggest that men dominated in the palace society of Minoan Crete, and it is common to speak of "princes" or "kings" as the leaders of the palaces.

THE MAINLAND MYCENAEANS

The far-flung international trade of Minoan Crete developed extensive overseas contacts for the residents of the palaces, and this network of trade was greatly facilitated by yet another innovation of the third millennium, the longship. The sea travel of Minoans took them not only to Egypt and the other civilizations of the Near East in search of trade goods and pay, but also to the islands of the Aegean and southern Greece. On the Greek mainland they encountered another civilization today called *Mycenaean* after its most famous archaeological site. Inspired by the Greek poet Homer's tale of the Trojan War, archaeologists have uncovered the Bronze Age site of Mycenae in the Peloponnese (the large peninsula which is southern Greece), with its elaborate citadel on multiple terraces and fortification walls built of large stones meticulously fitted together. The discoveries at Mycenae gained such renown that *Mycenaean* has become the general term for the Bronze Age civilization of mainland Greece in the second millennium B.C., although neither Mycenae nor any other of the settlements of Mycenaean Greece ever ruled Bronze Age Greece as a united state.

The discovery in the nineteenth century of treasure-filled graves at Mycenae thrilled the European world. Constructed as stone-lined shafts, these graves entombed corpses buried with golden jewelry, including heavy necklaces festooned with pendants, gold and silver vessels, bronze weapons decorated with scenes of wild animals inlaid in precious metals, and delicately painted pottery. . . . The artifacts of the shaft graves point to a warrior culture organized in independent settlements ruled by powerful commanders, who enriched themselves by conducting raiding expeditions near and far, as well as by dominating local farmers. . . .

The construction of another kind of burial chamber, called *tholos* tombs—spectacular underground domed chambers built in beehive shapes from closely fitted stones—marks the next period in Mycenaean society, beginning in the fifteenth century B.C. The architectural details of the tholos tombs and the style of the burial goods found in them testify to the far-flung contacts that Mycenaean rulers maintained throughout the eastern Mediterranean. Reference to Mycenaean soldiers in Egyptian records indicates that mainland warriors could take up service far from home.

MINOAN INFLUENCES ON THE MAINLAND

Contact with the civilization of Minoan Crete was tremendously influential for Mycenaean civilization; Minoan artifacts and artistic motifs turn up on the mainland in profusion. The evidence for contact between Minoans and Mycenaeans raises a thorny problem in the explanation of cultural change. Since the art and goods of the Mycenaeans in the middle of the second millennium B.C. display many features clearly reminiscent of Cretan design, the archaeologist who excavated Knossos, Arthur Evans, argued that the Minoans had inspired Mycenaean civilization by sending colonists to the mainland, as they undeniably had to various Aegean islands, such as Thera. This demotion of Mycenaean civilization to secondary status offended the excavators of Mycenae, and a continuing debate emerged over the relationship between the two cultures. They were certainly not identical. They spoke different languages. The Mycenaeans made burnt offerings to the gods; the Minoans did not. The Minoans constructed sanctuaries across the landscape in caves, on mountain tops, and in country villas; the mainlanders built no shrines separate from their central dwellings. When in the fourteenth century B.C. the mainlanders started to build palace complexes reminiscent of those on Crete, unlike the Minoans the Mycenaeans designed their palaces around *megarons,* rooms with huge ceremonial hearths and thrones for the rulers. Some palaces had more than one megaron, which could soar two stories high with columns to support a roof above the second-floor balconies of the palace.

The mystery surrounding the relationship between the Minoans and the Mycenaeans deepened with the startling discovery in the palace at Knossos of tablets written in an adaptation of Linear A; the same script occurred on tablets from Mycenaean sites on the mainland and was termed Linear B. Michael Ventris, a young English architect interested in codes, stirred the scholarly world in the 1950s by demonstrating that the language being expressed by Linear B was Greek, not the Minoan language of Linear A. Because the Linear B tablets from Crete dated from before the final destruction of the Knossos palace in about 1370 B.C., they meant that the palace administration had for some time been keeping its records in a foreign language—Greek—rather than in Cretan. Presumably this change in the language used for official record keeping means that Greek-speaking Mycenaeans from the mainland had come to dominate the palaces of Crete, but whether by violent invasion or some kind of peaceful accommodation remains unknown. Certainly the Linear B tablets imply that the mainland had not long, if ever, remained a secondary power to Minoan Crete.

MYCENAEAN WARRIORS AND WARFARE

A glimpse at Mycenaean society in its maturity demonstrates the nature of its power. Archaeologists treasure cemeteries, not because of morbid fascination with death but because ancient peoples so often buried goods both special and ordinary with their dead. Bronze Age tombs in Greece tell us that no wealthy Mycenaean male went to the grave without his fighting equipment. The complete suit of Mycenaean bronze armor found in a fourteenth-century B.C. tomb from Dendra in the northeastern Peloponnese shows how extensive first-class individual equipment could be. This dead warrior had worn a complete bronze cuirass (chest guard) of two pieces for front and back, an adjustable skirt of bronze plates, bronze greaves (shin guards), shoulder plates, and a collar. On his head had rested a boar's-tusk helmet with metal cheekpieces. Next to his body lay his leather shield, bronze and clay vessels, and a bronze comb with gold teeth. Originally his bronze swords had lain beside him, but tomb robbers had stolen them before the archaeologists found his resting place. This warrior had spared no cost in availing himself of the best technology in armor and weaponry, and his family thought it appropriate to shoulder the expense of consigning this costly equipment to the ground forever rather than pass it on to the next generation.

Mycenaean warriors dressed like this man could ride into battle in the latest in military hardware—the lightweight, two-wheeled chariot pulled by horses. These revolutionary vehicles, sometimes assumed to have been introduced by Indo-Europeans migrating from Central Asia, first appeared not long after 2000 B.C. in various Mediterranean and Near Eastern societies. The first Aegean representation of such a chariot occurs on a Mycenaean grave marker from about 1500 B.C. Wealthy people evidently craved this dashing new invention not only for war but also as proof of their social status, much like modern people rushing to replace their horse-drawn wagons with cars after the invention of the automobile. It has recently been suggested that the Dendra armor was for a warrior fighting from a chariot, not for an infantryman, on the grounds that a foot soldier would not be able to move freely enough in the metal casing of such a suit. On this provocative and speculative argument, chariots carrying archers provided the principal arm of Mycenaean armies, supplemented by skirmishers fighting on foot, not unlike the tank battles of World War II in which infantrymen crept along into battle in the shadow of a force of tanks as mobile artillery. These supplementary infantrymen escorted the chariot forces, guarded the camps at the rear of the action, chased fugitive enemies after the main clash of battle, and served as attack troops on terrain inaccessible to chariots. Many of these Mycenaean-era foot soldiers may have been hired mercenaries from abroad.

War was clearly a principal concern of those Mycenaean men who could afford its expensive paraphernalia. The Mycenaeans spent nothing, by contrast, on the construction of large religious buildings like the giant temples of the Near East. The nature of Bronze Age mainland religion remains largely obscure, although the usual view is that the Mycenaeans worshipped primarily the male-dominated pantheon traditionally associated with the martial culture of the Indo-Europeans. The names of numerous deities known from later Greek religion occur in the Linear B tablets, such as Hera, Zeus, and Poseidon, as well as the names of divinities unknown in later times. The name or title *potnia*, referring to a female divinity as "mistress" or "ruler," is very common in the tablets, emphasizing the importance of goddesses in Bronze Age religion.

The development of extensive sea travel in the Bronze Age enabled not only traders but also warriors to journey far from home. Traders, crafts specialists, and entrepreneurs seeking metals sailed from Egypt and the Near East to Greece and beyond. Mycenaeans established colonies at various locations along the coast of the Mediterranean. Seaborne Mycenaean warriors also dominated and probably put an end to the palace society of Minoan Crete in the fifteenth and fourteenth centuries B.C., presumably in wars over commercial rivalry in the Mediterranean. By the middle of the fourteenth century B.C., the Mycenaeans had displaced the Minoans as the most powerful civilization of the Aegean.

THE CATASTROPHE OF C. 1200 B.C.

The Bronze Age development of extensive sea travel for trading and raiding had put the cultures of the Aegean and the Near East in closer contact than ever before. The wealth that could be won by traders and entrepreneurs, especially those seeking metals, encouraged contacts between the older civilizations at the eastern end of the Mediterranean and the younger ones to the west. The civilizations of Mesopotamia and Anatolia particularly overshadowed those of Crete and Greece in the size of their cities and the development of extensive written legal codes. Egypt remained an especially favored destination of Mycenaean voyagers throughout the late Bronze Age because they valued the exchange of goods and ideas with the prosperous and complex civilization of that land. By around 1200 B.C., however, the Mediterranean network of firmly established powers and trading partners was coming undone. The New Kingdom in Egypt was falling apart; foreign invaders destroyed the powerful Hittite kingdom in Anatolia; Mesopotamia underwent a period of political turmoil; and the rich palace societies of the Aegean all but disintegrated. The causes of the disruption are poorly documented, but the most likely reasons are internal strife between local centers of power and overexploitation of natural resources in overspecialized and centralized economies. These troubles, whose duration we cannot accurately gauge, apparently caused numerous groups of people to leave their homes, seeking new places to live or at least victims to plunder. These movements of peoples throughout the eastern Mediterranean and the Near East further damaged or even destroyed the political stability, economic prosperity, and international contacts of the civilizations of most of these lands, including that of the Mycenaeans. This period of disruption certainly lasted for decades; in some regions it may have gone on much longer. As a rough generalization, it seems accurate to say that the period from roughly 1200 to 1000 B.C. saw numerous catastrophes for Mediterranean civilizations. The consequences for the Mycenaeans were disastrous. . . .

It may be that one important origin of these catastrophes, which ended the power of Mycenaean civilization, was a relatively sudden reconceptualization of military tactics. That is, previously the preponderance of military might had lain with the chariots carrying archers that the kingdoms of the Bronze Age Mediterranean customarily mustered. These chariot forces had been supplemented by infantrymen, mostly foreign mercenaries. At some point around 1200, the argument goes, these hired foot soldiers realized that they could use their long swords and javelins to defeat the chariot forces in direct battle by swarming in a mass against their vehicle-mounted overlords. Emboldened by this realization of their power and motivated by a lust for booty, the motley bands of mercenaries attacked their erstwhile employers and plundered their wealth. They also conducted raids on other rich targets, which were no longer able to defend themselves with their old tactics dependent on chariots. With no firm organization among themselves, the rebels fatally weakened the civilizations they betrayed and raided but were incapable of or uninterested in putting any new political systems into place to fill the void created by their destruction of the existing ones.

Whether this explanation for the end of the Bronze Age will

win widespread assent remains to be seen, if only because one might ask why it took the mercenary infantrymen so long to grasp their advantage over chariots, if such it was, and to put it into play. But one important assumption of this scenario does ring true: what evidence we have for the history of the sea peoples points not to one group spreading destruction across the eastern Mediterranean in a single tidal wave of violence but rather to many disparate bands and conflicts. A chain reaction of attacks and flights in a recurring and expanding cycle put even more bands of raiders on the move. . . .

THE COLLAPSE OF THE PALACE ECONOMIES

In the end, all this fighting and motion redrew the political map of the Mediterranean, and perhaps its population map as well, although it is unclear how many groups actually resettled permanently at great distances from their original sites in this period. The reasons for all this violent commotion must still be regarded as mysterious in our present state of knowledge, but its dire consequences for Near Eastern and Greek civilization are clear. . . . The eventual failure of the palace economies had a devastating effect on the large part of the Mycenaean population that was now dependent on this system for its subsistence. Peasant farmers, who knew how to grow their own food, could support themselves even when the redistribution of goods and foodstuffs broke down, but the palaces fell into ruins. Warriors left unattached to their old rulers by the fall of the palaces set off to find new places to live or at least plunder, forming roving bands of the kind remembered by the Egyptians as sea peoples [foreign invaders who attacked Egypt in the 1180s B.C.]. The later Greeks remembered an invasion of Dorians (speakers of the form of Greek characteristic of the northwest mainland) as the reason for the disaster that befell Bronze Age Greece, but the Dorians who did move into southern Greece most likely came in groups too small to cause such damage by themselves. Indeed, small-scale movements of people, not grand invasions, characterized this era, as bands of warriors with no prospects at home emigrated from lands all around the eastern Mediterranean to become pirates for themselves or mercenaries for foreign potentates.

The damage done by the dissolution of the redistributive economies of Mycenaean Greece after 1200 B.C. took centuries to repair fully. Only Athens seems to have escaped wholesale disaster. In fact, the Athenians of the fifth century B.C. prided themselves on their unique status among the peoples of Classical Greece: "sprung from the soil" of their homeland, as they called themselves, they had not been forced to emigrate in the turmoil that engulfed the rest of Greece in the twelfth and eleventh centuries B.C. The nature of the Athenians' boast gives some indication of the sorry fate of many other Greeks in the period c. 1200–1000 B.C. Uprooted from their homes, they wandered abroad in search of new territory to settle. The Ionian Greeks, who in later times inhabited the central coast of western Anatolia, dated their emigration from the mainland to the end of this period. Luxuries of Mycenaean civilization like fine jewelry, knives inlaid with gold, and built-in bathtubs disappeared. To an outside observer, Greek society at the end of the Mycenaean Age might have seemed destined for irreversible economic and social decline, even oblivion. As it happened, however, great changes were in the making that would create the civilization we today think of as Classical Greece.

The Hardy Celts Spread Across Europe

Peter B. Ellis

Among the most important and prolific of the early peoples of Europe were the tribal Celts, who spread across large portions of the continent between 1200 and 100 B.C. As historian Peter B. Ellis, a noted authority on the Celts and their history, points out in this enlightening essay, the first impression many people form about this hardy, industrious people comes from the rather biased reports of later Greek and Roman writers, who viewed the Celts as illiterate barbarians. In reality, the Celts, though less advanced materially speaking, were no less civilized than the Greeks and Romans. Ellis begins by attempting to define the term *Celt*; then discusses the development of the Celtic language and the origins of Celts; and finally explores some common aspects of Celtic life, religion (including priest-rulers called Druids), and military customs.

T he Celts were the first European people north of the Alps to emerge into recorded history. But the first references to them appear in the sixth and fifth centuries BC when they began to encounter the peoples of the Mediterranean cultures, for the Celts did not leave any extensive written testimony in their own languages until the Christian era. When they emerge in historical record, they are first called Keltoi [KELL-tee], by the Greeks. Polybius also uses the term Galatae, which had, by his day, become widely used by Greeks. The Romans referred to them as Galli as well as Celtae. [The ancient writers] Diodorus Siculus, Julius Caesar, Strabo and Pausanias all recognize the synonymous use of these terms. Diodorus Siculus (*c.*60–30 BC) considered that the term Celt was the proper name for the people he was describing. Pausanias (AD *c.*160) certainly gives prior antiquity to the name Celt over the names Gauls or Galatians. And Julius Caesar (100–44 BC) comments that the Gauls of his day referred to themselves as Celtae.

THE CELTIC LANGUAGE

There is little doubt that the word Keltoi, or Celts as we will call them, was a word of Celtic origin. In searching for a meaning of the name some have pointed to the word meaning hidden—the word which gives us the Irish form *ceilt*, meaning concealment or secret, and the word which has given us the English word kilt. Thus some believe that Keltoi meant the hidden or secret people and that this name referred to the Celtic prohibition against setting down in written form their vast store of knowledge. Celtic history, philosophy, law, genealogy and science were transmitted in oral traditions until the Christian period. This was not because the Celts were illiterate but because of a religious prohibition. Caesar comments:

> The druids think it unlawful to commit this knowledge of theirs to writing (in secular and in public and private business they use Greek characters). This is a practice which they have, I think, adopted for two reasons. They do not wish that their system should become commonly known or that their pupils, trusting in written documents, should less carefully cultivate their memory; and, indeed, it does generally happen that those who rely on written documents, are less industrious in learning by heart and have a weaker memory.

So it was not until the Greeks and Romans commenced to write their accounts of the Celts, sometimes culturally misconceived and invariably biased, that the Celts emerged into recorded history. Archaeology has to fill the void before recorded history and so we are presented with great difficulties in identifying the Celts and their origins. For example, what is meant by the Celts? The strictest, as well as the easiest, definition is those people who speak or spoke a Celtic language. This is certainly the definition which has been used since recorded history identified the movements of a Celtic-speaking people. But once we go beyond historical record we have to rely on other methods of identification. Historians and archaeologists are agreed that the start of the Iron Age in northern Europe, identified as the Hall-statt Culture, using the town of Hallstatt, in upper Austria, as the centre point of its expansion, 700–500 BC, was a Celtic cultural expansion. They are agreed that another series of Iron Age objects, classified by their centre of distribution, La Tène, 500–100 BC, was also a Celtic cultural expansion. We must therefore ask whether there were Celts in Europe before 700 BC.

The direct answer is—of course! All the ancestors of the peoples of Europe were placed somewhere on the continent at this time. In the nineteenth century it became accepted that most past and present European languages, with the exceptions of Basque, Estonian, Finnish, Hungarian, Lapp and Turkish, were related to one another and were branches of a hypothesized common Indo-European language. When exactly 'common Indo-European' was spoken, and how it broke up into such diverse families as Latin, Slavic, Germanic, Celtic and so forth, is open to intense debate and speculation. And it is merely hypothesis. What we can say is that long before 700 BC there was in northern Europe a people whose language was developing into Celtic.

In more recent years archaeologists have generally accepted that the Urnfield Folk were Celtic or, as some quaintly phrase it, proto-Celtic, meaning that their language had not quite developed into a form which we would immediately recognize as Celtic today. The Urnfield Culture of northern Europe is roughly dated between 1200 and 700 BC. This people, if we may keep to generalities, were farming folk living in small communities who were also skilled in working bronze and, towards the end of the period, in working iron as well. In many places they lived in hill-forts and they buried their dead in the distinctive manner which gives them their name—urnfields. The cremated ashes and bones of their dead were buried in urns of clay accompanied by small personal items which belonged to the deceased in life.

This culture was identified by a concentration in the Danube basin, around eastern France and western Germany, spreading into eastern Germany and south across the Alps into the Po Valley, south-west to southern France and further south into the Spanish peninsula. It also arrived in the British Isles. This is now accepted as the spread of a Celtic culture. . . .

We can hypothesize that, at some stage of their historical development, the Celts spoke a Common Celtic language. Celtic scholars have supposed this Common Celtic to have been spoken just before the start of the first millennium BC, and then, soon after, two distinct dialects of Celtic emerged which are identified by their modern names—Goidelic and Brythonic, or the famous Q- and P-Celtic.

The Goidelic group is represented today by Irish, Manx and Scottish Gaelic, the Brythonic by Welsh, Cornish and Breton. Goidelic is said to have been the oldest form of Celtic with the Brythonic (which was of course closely related to continental Celtic, called Gaulish) developing from it at a later stage. . . .

WHERE DID THE CELTS ORIGINATE?

We now come to an important question. Where did the Celts begin to develop their distinctive culture? There are two contradictory traditions. One tradition, founded in history, places the point of origin on the north-west coast of Europe by the North Sea. The second tradition places the point of origin around the headwaters of the Danube.

[The Roman historian] Ammianus Marcellinus (AD c.330–95), quoting Timagenes of Alexandria as his source, claims that when the Celts began their expansion they came from the outermost isles beyond the Rhine, placing them on the coast opposite the North Sea. 'They were', he says, 'driven from their homes by the frequency of wars and violent rising of the sea.' Certainly the concept fits in with people living in the Low Countries. Ephoros of Cyme, one of the most influential Greek historians of the fourth century BC, believed that the Celts came from that area and he is quoted by Strabo (64 BC–AD c.24) but Strabo was somewhat sceptical. Ephoros describes the Celts as remaining obstinately in their lands and losing more lives in floods than in wars until, finally, they were forced to migrate.

When [the Greek writers] Hecataeus (c. 500–476 BC) of Miletus and Herodotus (c.490–425 BC) of Halicarnassus first mention the Keltoi they were already spread in an arc from the Iberian peninsula, through France and Belgium, Switzerland, Germany, Austria, northern Italy, and were moving eastwards along the Danube valley towards the Balkans. Herodotus indicates the Celtic homeland as being the upper Danube. If we accept the initial site of Celtic development as being the area around the headwaters of the Danube, the Rhine and the Rhône, we will not be far wrong. Here, Celtic names proliferate. The names of rivers, mountains and towns are Celtic. The Rhine, for example, Renos, means sea; the Danube, from Danuvius, means swift-flowing (cognate with the Irish *dana)* and the Rhur, from Raura, seems to be named after the Celtic tribe, the Raurici. The tributaries and subtributaries of the rivers still retain their Celtic origins. Laber (the Labara near Ratisbon) means talking river; the Glan means pure or clean river and so on. There is a strong concentration of Celtic place-names in this area, which weakens as one radiates from its central point. . . . This was the region, therefore, which was the 'cradle' of Celtic civilization and from which the Celts were eventually driven by the arrival of the Germanic people during the first century BC. When Julius Caesar was in Gaul, for example, the Celtic tribes were still moving westward as the Germanic tribes swept in behind them from the north-east to give their name and language to the lands taken from the former inhabitants. The last members of this general exodus were the Helvetii and Boii from Switzerland and Bohemia and the Tigurini from Bavaria. Only place-names and archaeological remains were left behind to mark the birth-place of Celtic civilization.

FAR FROM BEING BARBARIANS

It is a truism that a conqueror always writes the history and so we have to piece together the early history of the Celts from the hostile viewpoint of the Greeks and Romans. In trying to understand Celtic motivations, their attitudes, philosophies and laws, we are handicapped by the early prohibition of the Celts against committing their knowledge to written record. However, when the insular Celts of Britain and Ireland began to put their knowledge into written form in the Christian era it was not too late to form a perspective, bearing in mind the cultural changes from early times. And we can be wary about taking what the Greeks and Romans say about the Celts as a literal truth.

The Greeks and Romans represent the Celts as a barbaric people; as basically a fierce warrior society, proud, ignorant, illiterate, taking life cheaply, given to childish amusements and often drunk. In other words, Rome and Greece represented civilization while the Celts were depicted as exotic barbarians or noble savages. The image still remains with us. Yet today we realize that 'barbarity' or 'savagery' is just a matter of one's perception. Doubtless to the ancient Celts, the Romans and Greeks were equally as preposterous as the Celts were to the perceptions of the Romans and Greeks.

From the Urnfield Culture, the Celts emerge as an agricultural people—farmers cultivating their lands and living in a tribal society. By the start of the Hallstatt period in the eighth century BC, the development of ironworking enabled the Celtic peoples to make formidable axes, billhooks and other tools with which they could open roadways through previously impenetrable forests, effect extensive clearances and till the land with comparative ease. . . . The development of skill in metalworking, particularly in iron, also gave the Celts new armaments of swords and spears which rendered them militarily superior to most of their neighbours and therefore made them more mobile because there were few enemies to be feared.

It was the Celts who were the great road-builders of northern Europe. The ancient roads of Britain, for example, often ascribed to the Romans, had already been laid by the Celts long before the coming of the Romans. This is a fact only now slowly being accepted by scholars in the light of new archaeological finds. Yet Celtic roads were mentioned by Strabo, Caesar and Diodorus Siculus. It is obvious, looking at Caesar's account of his Gallic campaigns, that he was moving his legions rapidly through Gaul because there was an excellent system of roadways in existence. Similarly, when Caesar crossed to Britain, he found a highly mobile army of Celts opposing him in heavy war-chariots, some of them four-wheeled. For the Celts to be able to move in such vehicles with the speed and determination recounted by Caesar it becomes obvious, to the careful historian, that there had to be a well-laid system of roads in existence. . . .

ASPECTS OF CELTIC CULTURE

Archaeology has also shown much evidence of the prosperity of the rich farming communities of the Celts as well as their advances in art, Celtic pottery, jewellery, especially the enamelwork from north Britain and metal jewellery. This artwork found much favour in the ancient Mediterranean world. During the first century BC, before Caesar's invasion of Britain, British woollen goods, especially cloaks (*sagi*), were eagerly sought after in Rome. The ownership of a British woollen cloak was as prestigious in Rome in that period as the possession of a Harris-tweed suit was in the mid–twentieth century.

The Celts generally built their houses and settlements in wood but in some places they used stone, showing great sophistication in the construction of buildings. In Britain the remains of many such stone structures survive from the fourth to second centuries BC. One such structure survives to a height of forty feet, with lintelled entrances and inward-tapering wall, sometimes fifteen feet thick, with chambers, galleries and stairs. Staigue Fort, in Co. Kerry, Ireland, a circular stone fortress built some time during the first millennium BC, still stands with walls thirteen feet high, enclosing a space eighty-eight feet across, with two chambers constructed within the thickness of the walls. Most of these constructions were of drystone. The evidence demonstrates that the Celts were excellent builders.

The basis of their society was tribal. By the time the Celtic law systems were codified, with the Irish Brehon Law system being written down in the early Christian era, the Celtic tribal system was a highly sophisticated one. Comparing the Irish system with that enshrined in the Welsh Laws of Hywel Dda one can observe a common Celtic attitude to law. The good of the community was the basis of the law—in other words, a primitive yet sophisticated communism was practised. Chieftains were elected, as were all officers of the tribe. Women emerge in Celtic society with equality of rights. They could inherit, own property and be elected to office, even to the position of leader in times of war, such as Cartimandua of the Brigantes and her more famous compatriot Boudicca of the Iceni. . . .

The Celtic tribes varied in size. Some were small, others constituted entire nations. The Helvetii, for example, were said to be 390,000 strong when they began their exodus. Of special note was that the Celtic tribes cared for their sick, poor and aged and that, according to Irish records, hospitals, run by the tribes, existed in Ireland around 300 BC, many hundreds of years before St Fabiola founded the first Christian hospital in Rome. . . .

CELTIC RELIGION AND MYTHOLOGY

The Celtic religion is of importance in the understanding of Celtic attitudes. By the time the Greeks and Romans began to comment on the religion of the Celts, towards the end of the third century BC, it was, in its philosophy, a fairly standard one. It is true that the gods and goddesses were numerous, often appearing in triune form (three-in-one), although a 'father of the gods' is mentioned by many ancient observers. A lot of the gods and goddesses appear as ancestors of the people rather than as their creators—heroes and heroines. Celtic mythology, for example, surviving in Irish and Welsh texts, is an heroic one; for the Celts made their heroes into gods and their gods into heroes. In the lives of these gods and heroes, the lives of the people and the essence of their religious traditions were mirrored. Celtic heroes and heroines were no mere physical beauties with empty heads. They had to have intellectual powers equal to their physical abilities. They were totally human and were subject to all the natural virtues and vices. They practised all seven of the deadly sins. Yet their world was one of rural happiness, a world in which they indulged in all the pleasures of mortal life in an idealized form: love of nature, art, games, feasting, hunting and heroic single-handed combat.

The Celtic religion was one of the first to evolve a doctrine of immortality. It taught that death was but a changing of place and that life went on with all its forms and goods in another world, a world of the dead—the fabulous Otherworld. But when people died in that world, the souls were reborn in this world. Thus a constant exchange of souls took place between the two worlds: death in this world took a soul to the Otherworld; death in that world brought a soul to this world. Thus did Philostratus of Tyana (AD *c.*170–249) observe that the Celts celebrated birth with mourning and death with joy. Caesar, the cynical general, remarked that this teaching of immortality doubtless accounted for the reckless bravery of the Celts in battle.

The Celtic religion was administered, as was all Celtic learning, law and philosophy, by a group called the druids, first mentioned in the third century BC. To the Greeks and Romans, the druids were described as a priesthood, but they fulfilled political functions as well—indeed many tribal chieftains were also druids. . . . Druids were often called upon to take legal, political and even military decisions.

[The great Roman orator] Marcus Tullius Cicero (106–43 BC) reports the druids to have been great natural scientists, with a knowledge of physics and astronomy which they applied in the construction of calendars. The earliest-known surviving Celtic calendar, dated from the first century BC, is the Coligny Calendar, now in the Palais des Arts, Lyons, France. It is far more elaborate than the rudimentary Julian calendar and has a highly sophisticated five-year synchronization of lunation with the solar year. It consists of a huge bronze plate which is engraved with a calendar of sixty-two consecutive lunar months. The language is Gaulish but the lettering and numerals are Latin. Place-names, personal names and inscriptions testify to a certain degree of literacy in the Celtic language. Caesar explains: 'They count periods of time not by the number of days but by the number of nights; and in reckoning birthdays and the new moon and new year, their unit of reckoning is the night followed by the day.'. . .

CELTIC WARFARE

Turning to warfare . . . the Celts preferred to settle warfare by means of single-handed combat between the chieftains or champions of the opposing armies rather than a pitch battle between opposing forces. Diodorus commented: 'And when someone accepts their challenge to battle, they proudly recite the deeds of valour of their ancestors and proclaim their own valorous quality, at the same time abusing and making little of their opponent and generally attempting to rob him beforehand of his fighting spirit.'

In their early conflict with the Celts, some Roman commanders would accept the Celtic form of resolving the battle. But the custom was frowned upon by the Roman senate. Titus Manlius Imperiosus Torquatus (who had received his title Torquatus for taking the hero's torque from the body of a Celt he had slain in single combat) decreed in 340 BC that henceforth no Roman should enter into single combat with a Celt to settle military disputes. One might think that the Celtic method of two men, leaders of the armies, settling the outcome of a military conflict by this means was a little more civilized than the Roman method of total warfare and devastation by large armies.

Yet Celtic society did produce a warrior class, as well as bands of professional soldiers who sold their expertise to whomever would hire their services. Celtic warriors were recruited by Syracuse, Sparta, Carthage, Macedonia, Bythinia, Syria, Egypt and eventually Rome herself. They achieved a reputation for bravery among the peoples of the ancient world. . . .

Some of the bands of warriors, such as the Gaesatae (or spearmen) who took part in several Celtic wars . . . fought naked because of the religious ritual implications. Caesar records that some of the British warriors stained their body with a blue dye to give them a more fearsome appearance in battle. Diodorus Siculus gives a vivid description of the Celts as an army:

> Their armour includes man-sized shields decorated in individual fashion. Some of these have projecting bronze animals of fine workmanship which serve for defence as well as decoration. On their heads they wear bronze helmets which possess large projecting figures lending the appearance of enormous stature to the wearer. In some cases horns form one piece with the helmet, while in other cases it is relief figures of the foreparts of birds or quadrupeds.

> Their trumpets are again of a peculiar barbaric kind; they blow into them and produce a harsh sound which suits the tumults of war. Some have iron breastplates of chain mail, while others fight naked, and for them the breastplate given by nature suffices. Instead of the short sword they carry long swords held by iron or bronze chains and hanging along their right side. Some wear gold-plated or silver-plated belts round their tunics. The spears which they brandish in battle, and which they call *lanciae*, have iron heads a cubit or more in length and a little less than two palms in breadth; for their swords are as long as the javelins of other people, and their javelins have points longer than swords.

The Romans found the Celtic custom of taking the heads of their slain enemies as trophies somewhat distasteful, but it had a profound religious significance. To the Celts, the soul was contained in the head and not the heart. . . . The Celts, in their turn, regarded as no less barbaric the Roman custom of either slaughtering prisoners wholesale or selling them into slavery rather than ransoming them as hostages back to their own people in accordance with Celtic custom.

THE SEARCH FOR 'LIVING SPACE'

What made the Celtic tribes leave their original homelands and spread across Europe? At the start of the first millennium BC the peoples of Europe were in a great state of flux and would remain so until the middle of the first millennium AD. There occurred great movements of peoples across Europe, settling for a while, establishing homelands and then abruptly moving on. Perhaps a drought, several crop failures in consecutive years, would force farming communities to search for new lands and conditions; or perhaps the people would be forced to move on as more aggressive newcomers invaded their lands—this was the cause of the migrations of the Helvetii and Boii in the first century BC.

Even in the Mediterranean world the urge for movement and expansion was dominant. With the collapse of the Hittite empire at the end of the second millennium BC, there was a considerable movement of peoples through the eastern Mediterranean. Then the Phoenicians, from biblical Canaan, began to spread throughout the Mediterranean, settling colonies as far west as Gades (Cadiz) and also in North Africa at Utica and Carthage. The Greeks began a massive expansion in the eighth century BC, establishing colonies which dominated southern Italy and settlements in North Africa, in Spain and—one of their most famous colonies—Massilia (Marseilles). . . . So the expansion of the Celts was merely one of several major movements in the ancient world.

Unfortunately, as we have seen, we do not know anything about the reasons for the Celtic expansion before its collision with the Mediterranean. Latin writers, particularly [the first-century BC Roman historian] Livy, record a tradition that the expansions began because the original Celtic homelands had become overpopulated. The Celtic farming communities were looking for new fertile lands to cultivate and settle. This seems an acceptable theory. The Celts, once established in the new territory, did not set up trading colonies like the Phoenicians and Greeks, nor did they impose a military overlordship on the people they conquered, as did the Romans. They simply moved into the new lands, setting up pastoral and agricultural communities, defending them with tribal armies raised from the people. So it is likely that the search for 'living space' was the prime cause of the spread of the 'Celtic empire'.

ONE GOD: THE EMERGENCE OF THE HEBREWS AND MONOTHEISM

MAX I. DIMONT

The Jews (originally the Hebrews) are one of the oldest eastern Mediterranean peoples, probably originating somewhere in what is now Palestine (or perhaps migrating there from Mesopotamia) in the early second millennium B.C. According to the Old Testament, a patriarch named Abraham established a covenant (agreement) with the one true god (Jehovah) that Jews, Christians, and Muslims still recognize and follow. In this way, an idea born in a remote land some four thousand years ago came to transfigure the world. The following synopsis of the birth of the Jews and monotheism is by biblical scholar Max I. Dimont, author of the widely read *Jews, God and History*, which one critic called "the best popular history of the Jews written in the English language."

T he Jews elbowed their way into history late and inconspicuously. They went through no Stone or Bronze Age. They had no Iron Age. For the first eight hundred years of their existence they wandered in and out of the great civilizations surrounding them. They had no buildings, no cities, no armies, and possessed, in fact, no weapons. All they carried with them were their ideas, which eventually conquered the world without making them its masters.

Jewish history dates from the day, four thousand years ago, when a man named Abraham had an encounter with God, known to him as Jehovah. The dialogue between Jew and God begins then. This continuing dialogue is the history of the Jews, with the rest of the world as interested eavesdroppers.

But before we start the history of the Jews . . . let us briefly review what happened in history prior to their entrance upon the scene.

BEFORE THE ADVENT OF THE JEWS

The first signs of civilization, with all the classical symptoms—cities, agriculture, the calendar, refinement of weapons, armies, and taxes—began cropping up about 4500 B.C. History gave birth to two civilizations at the same time, both Semitic, one to the northeast of Palestine, the other to the southwest of it. It took 2,500 years before these civilizations—Mesopotamian and Egyptian—found out about each other. After that, the fight was on, with Palestine paying the price for being a buffer state.

Civilization in Mesopotamia, now part of modern Iraq, began with city-states. The oldest and most prominent were Susa, Kish, and Ur. It was around these cities that the first empires were formed. Just where they were located can be more easily visualized if we draw an east-west line through the middle of Mesopotamia. The northern part became Assyria, and the southern part, Babylonia. Now, imagine Babylonia also divided in half. The upper part was the former kingdom of Akkad, and the lower part the kingdom of Sumeria, the first two empire civilizations.

In the third millennium B.C. there arose in Akkad a great Semitic king by the name of Sargon I, who conquered the Sumerians and formed the Sumerian-Akkadian kingdom. The people in this kingdom had a high standard of living and a highly developed culture. They also had a powerful tool which transformed this Asiatic civilization from an agricultural economy to one of commerce and industry. This tool was cuneiform writing (from the Latin *cuneus*, meaning "wedge," descriptive of the shape of the characters), a great improvement over the Egyptian hieroglyphics.

It remained for a king and lawgiver named Hammurabi to unite, around 2100 B.C., all the city-states in this area into one vast Babylonian Empire. Hammurabi was the Moses of the Babylonians, giving them their code of law as a present from heaven, much as Moses was to give his code of law to the Israelites at Mount Sinai one thousand years later.

During these twenty-five hundred years, while the peoples in these civilizations built cities, enriched themselves with plunder, enjoyed their mistresses, wrote laws, drank wine, and dreamed of world conquest, the Jews were nonexistent.

ABRAHAM MEETS GOD

Then, about the year 2000, when a new and restless Semitic tribe, the Assyrians, lean and hungry, began to challenge the soft and rich life of the Babylonians, a man named Terah took his son Abraham, Abraham's wife Sarah, and his grandson Lot, the nephew of Abraham, and emigrated from the cosmopolitan city of Ur in Babylonia.

Who were they—Terah, Abraham, Sarah, Lot? History does not know and the Bible does not identify them beyond tracing Terah's genealogy to Shem, one of the three sons of Noah. Was Terah a Babylonian? What language did he speak? What was his occupation? Certainly not a sheepherder, living as he did in one of the most sophisticated cities of that age.

All these are questions the Bible leaves unanswered. But by the act of crossing the River Euphrates, Terah and his family group become the first people in the Bible identified as *Ivriim*, of which the English version is "Hebrews," the people "who crossed over," the people "from the other side of the river."

The wanderings of Terah and his small group took them six hundred miles northwest from Ur to the land of Haran, in the southern part of what is now Turkey. Here Terah, who had left Ur at no one's prompting, dies. Here Abraham has a strange experience. It is here that he meets the Lord God "Jehovah" for the first time. It was a meeting comparable to the later famous encounter of Paul with the vision of Christ on the road to Damascus. Abraham's experience was as portentous to the Jews as Paul's was to the Christians.

At this encounter between Abraham and God, it is God who proposes a covenant to the patriarch, who is now seventy-five years old. If Abraham will follow the commandments of God, then He, in His turn, will make the descendants of Abraham His Chosen People and place them under His protection. We must note here that God does not say that they shall be better—merely that they shall exist as a separate and distinct entity and be His people. How this is to be brought about is not revealed. God at this time stipulates only one commandment, and makes only one promise. The commandment is that all males of His Chosen People must be circumcised on the eighth day after birth, or, if converted into the faith, then circumcised upon conversion. The promise is the land of Canaan.

Did this really happen? Views vary all the way from the fundamentalist position of a literal acceptance of every word to the rejection of every word by the skeptics. We say it could have happened, but in a slightly different way. If we view this encounter through the lens of modern psychoanalysis, it might become understandable in modern terms. Psychiatrists are familiar with a psychological phenomenon known as "projection." Let us say that an individual is obsessed by a thought, which, because it is painful or forbidden, he does not want to acknowledge as his own. On the other hand, he can't give it up. He wants the thought, but doesn't want to be its owner. He longs for it unconsciously, but wants to reject it on a conscious level. His mind therefore resorts to an unconscious "trick." He "projects" the thought onto someone else, and then convinces himself that it is the other person who suggested the thought to him or accused him of it. These methods of hearing or perceiving such projected messages are known as auditory or visual hallucinations—that is, hearing voices, or seeing things, that are not there.

People who have such hallucinations are not necessarily neurotic or psychotic. They can be very intense or inspired people. From a psychoanalytic viewpoint, therefore, it could be that Abraham himself conceived the idea of a covenant with an Almighty Father figure, represented as Jehovah, and projected onto this father figure his own wish to safeguard his children and his children's children for future generations.

From a historical viewpoint, it makes no difference whether it was Abraham who projected this experience onto an imaginary Jehovah or a real Jehovah who proposed it to Abraham. The fact remains that after four thousand years the idea of a covenant between the Jews and Jehovah is still alive and mentioned daily in prayers in synagogues throughout the world. Though many aspects of Jews and Judaism have been changed or modified during their subsequent four-thousand-year history, this idea of a covenant with God has remained constant. This in turn gave rise to a *will to survive as Jews*, which has been the driving force in Judaism. Without it there can be no Judaism and no Jews. When this concept disappears, when the Jew, through a lack of this inner compulsion, no longer wishes to retain his identity as a Jew, then nothing will stand between him and assimilation, between him and his final disappearance. The methods whereby this wish has been perpetuated have changed through the ages; but the aim has not. Jewish history is a succession of ideas designed to perpetuate this aim.

THE "CRAZY" IDEA OF ONE GOD

"How goodly are your tents, O Jacob, and your dwellings, O Israel," exults a pagan priest in the Book of Numbers. This, of course, is poetic license, for nomadic life breeds neither art nor culture. For four hundred years Abraham and his descendants wandered about as nomads in the land of Canaan, without a country of their own or a stable form of government. They practiced their rite of circumcision and, though they were often esteemed by their neighbors, they were equally often regarded as a most strange people, perhaps even a little crazy, worshiping a God one could not see.

The Decalogue (the Ten Commandments of Moses) with its prohibition against other gods did not come into being until four hundred years after this nomadic period. The Book of Genesis abounds with examples of idols being part of the household goods of the patriarchs. Three things, however, kept the Jews together during the first four centuries of their existence: the ideas which Abraham had conceived (or, if one prefers, the ideas which had been vouchsafed to him—namely, that the Jews had the one and only exclusive God); the rite of circumcision; and the prohibition of human sacrifice (as so movingly told in the story of the binding of Isaac). Once the Jews accepted the idea of monotheism (the doctrine that there is only one god), they began to behave in a special way without consciously knowing they were doing so. This change in behavior was at first imperceptible, but became ever more noticeable, setting them farther and farther apart from others.

Because one has to treat an invisible god differently than a visible one, the Jews developed a ritual distinctly different from that of the surrounding pagans. Because Jehovah is immortal He never dies, and because He never dies He never has to be resurrected. Thus the Jews dispensed with the resurrection rites of the pagans. Because there is but one God, there can be no mythological wars between gods, and thus the Jews dispensed with the entire pagan hierarchy of gods and the wars between them. Because Jehovah is motivated by spirituality, He never indulges in sex life. Thus the Jews did away with all fertility rites.

The example set by Jehovah—that of being completely withdrawn from sexuality—led to a curbing of licentious impulses through an inner discipline by the Jews, rather than through fear of laws. Compare the path sexuality took in Jewish life with the path it took in Grecian civilization. . . . The Jews, even when they later came in contact with the Greeks, refused to indulge in the Grecian sexual excesses. The Jews also avoided the path of total sexual abstinence later taken by the early Christian Church. They steered a course between sexual excess and continence, following to the letter the Lord's commandment to have many children. In their zeal to follow this injunction literally, it is understandable if some erred a little on the side of liberality. Many a pagan mistress, disguised as a "handmaiden," dwelt in the tents of the lusty patriarchs who "begat" progeny in abundance at an age when modern man settles down to collect his Social Security.

THE HEBREWS ENTER EGYPT

The nomadic life agreed with the patriarchs, for all, according to the Bible, lived over a hundred years. By the time Abraham begat Isaac, and Isaac begat Jacob, and Jacob begat his twelve sons, including Joseph, four hundred years of Jewish history had slipped by. Then a famine swept the lands northeast of Egypt, and the hungry people of many lands, including the Hebrews, drifted toward the fertile Nile delta, toward Egypt, in search of food. History records that they were warmly welcomed by Egypt.

It was under the leadership of Joseph that the famine-stricken Hebrews emigrated from Canaan to Egypt. The Book of Genesis tells us the fascinating story of how Joseph was sold by his brothers into slavery in Egypt. Here he became a favorite of Pharaoh, rose to viceroy, and with Pharaoh's permission invited his brothers and fellow Hebrews to settle there. Here they tended their flocks peaceably until a new Pharaoh arose in the land who was not so kindly disposed to them and enslaved them. Except for the Bible, no source we know of makes any specific mention of this Jewish sojourn and subsequent captivity in Egypt, but the busy spade of the archaeologist has turned up convincing corollary evidence that these events did take place.

From the ingathering of the Jews into Egypt by Joseph in the sixteenth century B.C. until the outgathering of the Jews from Egypt under Moses, in the twelfth century, there is a four-hundred-year silence. The Bible compresses these fateful four centuries into a few sentences. This silence raises many perplexing questions. What portion of this period did the Jews in Egypt live in freedom and what portion in slavery? What religion did they practice? What language did they speak? Was there intermarriage? How did they maintain their Judaism as slaves? Who were their leaders until the advent of Moses? No one knows.

Not all the Jews left Canaan to go into Egypt with Joseph. Many remained behind, surviving the famine and keeping their covenant with Jehovah. This remnant of Jews, still known as Hebrews, remained free men, while their brothers were enslaved in Egypt. Is this enslavement of the Jews in Egypt the fulfillment of a prophecy made by Jehovah to Abraham four centuries earlier? For it is written in Genesis (15:13–14), "Know of a surety that thy seed shall be a stranger in a land that is not theirs, and shall serve them; and they shall afflict them four hundred years; and also that nation, whom they shall serve, will I judge; and afterward shall they come out with great substance." Or is this prophecy an interpolation by later authors, who write with the hindsight of history of the great fusion to take place in Canaan when Moses leads the Israelites, as they are now called, out of Egypt into the land of Canaan, to reunite them with the remnants of Hebrews who had stayed behind?

THE FIRST KINGDOM OF ISRAEL

ROBERTA L. HARRIS

After long years of wandering and many difficulties, in the last years of the second millennium B.C. the Hebrews managed to create a powerful state, now called the first kingdom of Israel to differentiate it from the modern state of that name. In this concise, well-informed article, biblical scholar Roberta L. Harris provides an overview of the relatively short-lived but important kingdom whose people and affairs play frequent and crucial roles in the Judeo-Christian Old Testament. She covers the early kings—Saul and David—who forged the kingdom during wars against the Philistines and other local peoples; and Solomon, who built the first great holy Temple in Jerusalem. After describing that city in some detail, she tells how the kingdom eventually split into two competing Hebrew states, which ultimately weakened both.

S ome of the best known Bible stories centre on King David, yet neither history nor archaeology can substantiate any of them. Scholars generally agree that he lived in the 10th century BC, and remains of structures of this date have been found in Jerusalem, though they may date to Solomon's reign. It is clear, however, that David was a man of enormous charisma. Few people have so gripped and held the imagination for over 3,000 years. Our view of David, the *Mashiach* (or Messiah, literally 'the Anointed One') is coloured by his successes, not least as an expert statesman and propagandist. His official biographies (mostly in 2 Samuel and 1 Chronicles) have an almost uniformly adulatory tone, showing the king as a hero of immense personal integrity and as a man who truly walked with God. Once he had consolidated his hold over his kingdom, he set about a vigorous expansion of his territory. The kingdom reached its greatest extent during his reign. Jerusalem, the city he made his own, is still the centre of three world religions.

David began life as a humble shepherd boy, the eighth and least of the sons of Jesse of the tribe of Judah, who lived in Bethlehem. The story of his youth is told in 1 Samuel 16–31. He was a fighter all his life, first on behalf of Saul and then, driven from Saul's entourage, as a mercenary in the pay of the Philistine king of Gath.

David gathered around him about 400 malcontents . . . and welded them into a highly professional army. After the death of Saul and Jonathan in battle against the Philistines at Mt Gilboa, David began to consolidate his hold on his own tribe of Judah, governing at first from Hebron, while still nominally a Philistine vassal. Following the assassination of Saul's only surviving son, Ish-Bosheth, the northern tribes also declared for David and he looked about him for a suitable place from which to rule over the now-united tribes of Israel. His choice fell on Jerusalem.

THE CITY OF DAVID

Before this time Jerusalem was a small Canaanite town called Jebus, owned by the Jebusites, one of the peoples of the hill country. Jerusalem was an excellent choice for David. It lay at the crossroads of important roads running through the hill country both north to south and west to east. It was also virtually on the border between the territory of Judah to the south and the tribes local to Saul (nearly all the rest) in the north and was thus neutral territory, claimed by neither side. David laid siege to it and took it with his own trained men, not with a levy of Israelite fighting men, so that the city became his personal holding and is still often called the City of David. He then made Jerusalem the centre of the worship of Jehovah, the God of all Israel, bringing to it the Ark of the Covenant. The Ark was a large but portable chest; it was also the holiest possession of the tribes of Israel, for it contained the Tablets of the Law—the Ten Commandments that Moses had brought down from Mt Sinai (2 Samuel 6). Thus the tiny town acquired a status that it could hardly have aspired to otherwise and one which it still retains to this day.

In terms of ancient town planning the siting of ancient Jerusalem was excellent, being virtually impregnable on all sides except the north. Until the Babylonian attacks [in the 6th century BC], no army was able to take it by assault. Low on its eastern flank in the Kidron valley is a perennial supply of water called the Gihon spring. . . .

The exact location of David's city within the larger area of ancient Jerusalem has been the subject of much research for over a century. . . .

Recently, excavation has concentrated on the ridge sloping southwards from the Dome of the Rock, bounded on the west by the Central valley and on the east by the Kidron. The late Professor Yigal Shiloh (1938–88), following on the work of Kathleen Kenyon between 1961 and 1967, conducted excavations in the area from 1978 to 1982. Through his excavations, Shiloh has proved conclusively that this was the site of the City of David.

The most important results came from Shiloh's Area G where two huge artificial terraces were found. These may have added as much as 2,150 sq. ft (200 sq. m) of ground to the vulnerable northeastern area of the ridge. They are made up of a series of stone-walled boxes, filled with rubble to form a solid foundation. Using these terraces as a base, David, or perhaps Solomon, constructed a glacis [defensive barrier] consisting of a stepped stone structure, semicircular in shape and still surviving to 44 ft (13 m) high. Shiloh believed that the Citadel of David, possibly called Zion (2 Samuel 5, 7), was built on top of the hill, utilizing the extended area of the stepped stone structure and looming above the old Jebusite city proper to the south. The citadel was perhaps the house built for David by Hiram, the Phoenician king of Tyre (2 Samuel 5, 11).

Solomon's palace complex was probably north of this citadel, with the Temple to the north again of that. These sections formed a sort of royal acropolis, being relatively inaccessible to the ordinary people of the town. . . .

The mighty city of David and Solomon was actually no bigger than a small village of today. David's Jerusalem probably covered about 15 acres (6 ha), and even Solomon's extension only reached 37 acres (15 ha). But by the time of King Hezekiah (727–698 BC) the city had grown to about 150 acres (65 ha) and new walls were built. This made Jerusalem more than six times larger than any other town in the kingdom. It also had extensive unwalled suburbs, especially to the north. The next largest city at the time, Lachish, covered only about 20 acres (8 ha). Most towns in the ancient Near East were fairly modest in size, except for the great capital cities of empires such as Babylon.

THE RISE OF SOLOMON

Solomon was a younger son of David. His mother was Bathsheba, whose first husband had been killed on David's orders, to leave her free to remarry the king (2 Samuel 11). Solomon (965–928 BC) was anointed at the Gihon spring while his father was still alive, and so became co-regent with him in the Egyptian style.

The empire Solomon inherited from his father covered virtually all of Canaan, west and east of the River Jordan, and stretched south through the Negev desert to the port of Ezion Geber at the head of the Gulf of Eilat (Aqaba). Solomon thus gained access to the lucrative seaborne trade of the Red Sea. His father's wars had ensured that the Philistines were no longer a problem, and the Phoenicians, especially Hiram of Tyre, were his allies. He ruled the Aramaean kingdoms of inland southern Syria and his economic influence reached as far as the River Euphrates. In the absence of other great regional powers, Solomon was indeed a force to be reckoned with. He secured his position even further by marrying an Egyptian princess, probably the daughter of Siamun (978–959 BC), one of the last pharaohs of the 21st Dynasty.

David, the man of war, had secured the kingdom; Solomon, the man of peace, by engaging in international trade, was able to modernize and develop it. He set up the formal framework of a court and reorganized the state into 12 districts, with a governor and an administrative centre for each. In this way, the traditional tribal system was all but abolished, making Israel more like other nations in the region.

Throughout his reign it seems Solomon was occupied with trading ventures and building projects. A large part of the king's wealth was dedicated to the conspicuous expenditure of an oriental monarch. His palaces and their furnishings, such as his ivory and gold throne flanked by 12 lions (1 Kings 10, 18–20), the Temple with its cedar-wood panels and gold decorations, and his 1,000 wives and concubines (1 Kings 11, 3), would all have been viewed at home and abroad as evidence of his royal rank and his kingdom's high status.

NUMEROUS CONSTRUCTION PROJECTS

Solomon devoted much effort and expense to fortifying the most strategic sites of the realm and to securing the vital trade routes. In these projects he used the skills of Tyrian craftsmen and the labour of a rotating levy of 30,000 Israelites (1 Kings 5, 13). Apart from Jerusalem, three places are singled out for special mention in the Bible: Hazor, Megiddo and Gezer (1 Kings 9, 15). The third of these, the town of Gezer, had been captured by the pharaoh, Siamun, who then gave it to Solomon as part of his daughter's dowry.

Excavations at these three towns revealed that in Solomon's day they had defensive walls and main gateways built to a standard plan and size, approximately 65 by 55 ft (20 by 17 m). All the gateways have three guard chambers on either side of the entry passage which could be barred by gates when the need arose. They also had projecting guard towers and the defensive walls associated with them are the double-skinned type called casemates. The space between the inner and outer wall could either be divided by short cross walls to make storage rooms or filled with rubble to strengthen the walls if the city was besieged. . . .

Solomon's construction programme in Jerusalem must have been spectacular. The Queen of Sheba visited the city and was astounded by the splendid buildings, which lived up to the report she had heard. Limited by the valleys to the west and east of the city, Solomon created an impressive acropolis area for his Temple and palace complex by expanding to the north, towards, and probably partially including, today's Temple Mount. His buildings may have stood in the area identified by some as the Ophel of Jerusalem (2 Chronicles 27, 3).

There is a detailed description of Solomon's building works in the Bible (1 Kings 7, 1–11), giving an impression at least of his grandiose scheme. There were several buildings, all with different functions, for instance 'the house of the Forest of Lebanon', 'the hall of the throne' and 'the hall of pillars'. . . . Phoenician masons and craftsmen, as well as raw materials, were probably employed on the work, and the decorative details of both the Temple and the palace were in the International Phoenician style. . . .

JERUSALEM'S GREAT TEMPLE

The Temple was undoubtedly one of the most important buildings in Solomon's royal complex. It was built to hold the supreme national and religious relic of Israel, the Ark, brought down by Moses from Mt Sinai and which had been recaptured from the Philistines by David. The Ark was the rallying point for all the tribes, and, in its new home, it was firmly under the control of the king.

It is not possible to make a complete reconstruction of the Temple even though it is described in great detail in 1 Kings, 6–7 and 2 Chronicles 3–4. Also in the Bible is the ideal plan of the Temple as remembered by Ezekiel (40–43), who had first-hand knowledge of the original, destroyed by the Babylonians in 587 BC. Excavations are not permitted today on the Temple Mount, the general area where Solomon's Temple stood, because of the sanctity of the place for Moslems and Jews, and also because it is protected under international law. . . . Remains of Herod's Temple may well still exist, and it is even possible that some signs of the foundations of Solomon's Temple may also be buried very deep.

As described in the Bible, Solomon's Temple was built of 'undressed stone' on a podium of ashlar masonry. It was rectangular in shape, and according to the Bible measured 60 by 20 cubits (approximately 100 by 33 ft or 30 by 10 m) and stood 30 cubits high (about 50 ft or 15 m), so it would have been easily visible above the city. The Temple had a tripartite structure consisting of a porch *(ulam)*, main hall or sanctuary *(hekhal)* and the Holy of Holies *(devir)*; the whole was considered as the House of God *(bayit)*, that is His dwelling place among His people. The Holy of Holies, which housed the Ark, may have been a separate room leading on from the main hall, perhaps via a short flight of stairs, or it may have been contained within it, if, as has been suggested, the *devir* was a prefabricated cedarwood room or 'cabinet'.

Two freestanding pillars named Yachin and Boaz stood at the entrance to the Temple; the names probably meaning '(God) established (the House) with might'. . . . With the exception of the porch, the Temple was surrounded by a three-storeyed annexe, which probably contained objects dedicated to the Lord. It also served as the national treasury. . . .

Wood was used throughout the Temple—cedar and pine covered the walls and pine the floors, with wild olive used for the doors. Apart from the doors this woodwork was ornamentally carved. Everything was overlaid with gold. The decorative motifs are well known from the so-called International Phoenician Style. For instance, the cherubim with wings outstretched over the Ark may have been similar to the winged and apron-wearing sphinxes seen on ivory carvings of the 9th and 8th centuries. . . .

THE KINGDOM DIVIDED

Following the death of Solomon in about 928 BC, his nation split into two parts. The north, which had been Saul's power base, became Israel. The tribe of Judah, virtually alone except for the tiny tribe of Benjamin, formed the southern kingdom of Judah and stayed loyal to the family of David. Even in David's time the northern tribes had never been fully assimilated and they resented the heavy burdens of tax and forced labour imposed on them. Jeroboam ben Nebat attempted rebellion during Solomon's reign, and, having failed, fled to Egypt. External forces were also threatening the security and prosperity of the empire. Edom revolted, while a new Aramaean dynasty was founded in Damascus. The trade monopoly in the region established by Solomon was beginning to break up and there were many who were keen to exploit this situation.

It was Rehoboam, Solomon's son and successor, who was responsible for the final schism. He summoned the northern tribes to the ancient cult centre of Shechem to affirm him as king by acclaim in the traditional way. However, led by the former rebel

Jeroboam ben Nebat, who had returned from exile, the tribes refused to recognize Rehoboam unless he agreed to remit some of their taxes. Foolishly the king instead threatened to increase their burdens, with the result that the tribes seceded from his kingdom. Rehoboam hurriedly returned to Jerusalem and was never able to bring the north back under his control.

Thus began the period of the Divided Kingdom. During the next two centuries there was frequent conflict between Israel and Judah, with each gaining the upper hand at different times. The southern state of Judah in its remote hill country was to remain under David's successors for nearly 350 years, until the time of the Babylonian conquest. The far larger and more exposed northern kingdom of Israel had a turbulent history. Without a secure ruling dynasty it was constantly prey to internal coups and external attacks until its eventual destruction by the Assyrians in the late 8th century BC.

THE PHOENICIANS: PIONEERING TRADERS OF THE MEDITERRANEAN

MAITLAND A. EDEY

It is a continuing frustration to modern archaeologists and other scholars that one of the most important early Mediterranean peoples—the Phoenicians—remains among the least well-documented and understood. In this excerpt from his impressively researched and informative book about this enterprising ancient trading people, scholar Maitland A. Edey clearly explains why so little tangible evidence of Phoenician ships and cities has survived. He also explains how and why the Phoenicians emerged as influential independent maritime traders at the time that they did, namely the two centuries following ca. 1200 B.C., when political upheavals rocked the eastern Mediterranean sphere. (The five principal Phoenician cities lying along the eastern Mediterranean coast were Aradus, Byblos, Berytus [modern Beirut], Tyre, and Sidon. In the western Mediterranean, the Phoenicians established Carthage, on the coast of what is now Tunisia, which later became one of the greatest cities of the ancient world and the archrival of Rome.)

O ne day, about 3,200 years ago, a small trading vessel was poking its way along the southern coast of what is now Turkey. There is no way of telling whether it was headed east or west when it got into trouble, in what season of the year it was traveling or what port it hailed from. But trouble did strike. It sank just off Cape Gelidonya in about 100 feet of water.

In 1960 two young Americans who have since become experts in the study of ancient wrecks, George Bass and Peter Throckmorton, decided to investigate the Cape Gelidonya wreck, whose existence had been reported to them by local sponge fishermen. They found that it had landed on a hard, rocky bottom where there had been little or no deposition of sand or mud to cover and preserve it. Therefore nearly all of the hull of the little ship had long since been eaten away by marine worms. All that was left of it was its cargo and, underneath that, some bits of its bottom planking, along with a layer of coarse twigs and branches. This stuff is known as dunnage and has been widely used down through marine history as packing to prevent cargo from bumping and banging during rough passages at sea. By carbon dating, these remaining bits of dunnage helped confirm the age of the vessel—an age that had already been given it after the divers had a chance to study its cargo.

For marine archeologists the Gelidonya wreck is a critically important one. With the possible exception of one other, located in shallow water near Marsala off the coast of Sicily, the Gelidonya wreck is the only known fragment of a ship that is believed to have been built by the Phoenicians.

THE WORLD WAS THEIR BAZAAR

Common knowledge about the Phoenicians is as skimpy as the remains of their vessels. Most people, if they have heard of the Phoenicians at all, know only two things about them: they were great seafarers and traders, and they invented the alphabet. . . .

They were indeed the greatest sea traders of the ancient world. They had their start in the eastern Mediterranean in what is now part of Lebanon. They began to appear on the historical scene around 1200 B.C. and became an important influence in the commerce, the culture and the history of their world for nearly a thousand years. Over that long span they spread westward throughout the Mediterranean, and so, for convenience's sake, it has been customary to speak of the cities that occupied the Lebanese coast as Phoenicia East, and the scattered settlements in the western Mediterranean as Phoenicia West. But, having so identified Phoenicia East and Phoenicia West, one must quickly say that there never was a country or an empire called "Phoenicia," only a collection of independent cities more interested in trade than in the development of an empire.

Furthermore, as traders they were their own worst competitors and were extremely jealous of one another, with the result that, though they spoke a common language and worshiped the same gods, they never did coalesce into a country. They spoke of themselves as Tyrians, Sidonians, Byblians, Carthaginians, Motyans and so on. The very word "Phoenician" was unknown to them; the label probably was pasted on them by the Greeks and preserved by the accident that the Greek language and its literature, and not the Phoenician, have been passed down to us. . . .

The Phoenicians have occupied a curious place in history for a long time. Through many references to them by others—in the Bible, in ancient literature and in the works of classical historians—they earned their reputation as the outstanding seafarers, traders, traveling artisans, explorers and shipwrights of their day. They went everywhere. They swapped goods with Egyptians, Greeks, Assyrians, Babylonians, Africans and Spanish tribesmen. The entire Mediterranean world was their bazaar. They even went beyond it, out into the Atlantic, far down the African coast and possibly north to Brittany and the British Isles. And yet, until comparatively recently, almost nothing directly was known about them because they appeared to say so little about themselves. . . .

It is from others—from people who in talking about themselves talk about the Phoenicians—that much of our knowledge has come. Wall carvings from Egypt and Mesopotamia give us better pictures of Phoenician ships and cities than any Phoenician source does. Only two significant collections of clay tablets that scholars are willing to ascribe to Phoenicians or their immediate ancestors have ever been discovered. One devotes itself to politics, the other to religion. Neither says anything about Phoenician daily life. No Phoenician tale has ever been found, no song. The soul of a people is revealed by the songs they sing, the jokes they crack. On the record the Phoenicians never cracked a single joke. I cannot believe they didn't. But there is no Phoenician Aristophanes to memorialize their humor, just as there is no Aeschylus to preserve their sense of tragedy, no Homer to talk about good food, good ships, good fighting, fine weapons and beautiful women. The Phoenicians were familiar figures in the ports of the Mediterranean when Homer wrote the *Iliad*. Surely they were as passionate about ships, the sea, war and women as the Greeks. But what they thought about them and what they said we simply do not know.

LOCATING PHOENICIAN SITES

No country, no civic records, no historians, no poets, no songs, no jokes. Who, then, were the Phoenicians? And if they were so well known to their contemporaries in the ancient world, how is it that they faded into such obscurity later on?

Fair questions. The Phoenicians faded because of the special circumstances they found themselves in, both geographical and historical—a particular climate, neighbors of a certain bent—and because of the particular kind of life they were able to work out for themselves in those circumstances. It is possible to write about them because, while their ships are still more or less a mystery, there has been recovered a growing collection of the trade objects that the Phoenicians carried about, assembled over the years by archeologists working throughout the Mediterranean. Some of these were of Phoenician manufacture, some the goods of others for whom they were acting as middlemen—all of them widely scattered throughout the ancient world, thus proving the classical presumption that the Phoenicians were extremely busy traders and travelers.

Then there are the Phoenician sites, many of them the merest traces of abandoned trading posts stretching ever westward like a string of beads along the African coast. An archeologist, finding one and knowing how far a trading vessel could be expected to travel in a day (about 30 miles), can quite accurately forecast the next likely spot where the trader might have been tempted to put in for the night. A number of sites have been located in this way. Finally there were the settlements and trading posts that eventually became cities. The location of some of these places and their identity as Phoenician have been well known throughout history. Others were lost and had to be rediscovered. One, Sarepta, only eight miles from Sidon, was turned up as a rich archeological site as recently as 1970. Today, though battered down by Greek and Roman, and by many an Arab and Crusader as well, the roots of those Phoenician towns still survive in the form of old walls, stairways, cisterns, temple foundations, tomb shafts and even paved dockyards for ships. The ghosts of the traders can still be heard whispering in those places, mingled with a hum of commerce and the creak of cordage, the clink of metals and the admiring sighs of people who came from far away to barter for rich purple cloth and shiny new toys. . . .

PHOENICIAN ORIGINS

As to the question of [who they were] . . . the Phoenicians were Canaanites, one group of a large number of Semitic-speaking peoples who had been spreading through the Near East for some thousands of years. Where they all came from is difficult to say, but many scholars believe that they represent successive waves of tribal expansion by semidesert herders, who over the centuries moved out from the enormous semiarid expanses of northern

Arabia eastward into the more fertile Tigris-Euphrates valley, and westward toward the Mediterranean into an area that now comprises Syria, Lebanon, Jordan and Israel. Thus, most of the people who walked the pages of early Near Eastern history were Semites: the Babylonians, the Assyrians, the Israelites, the Canaanites, the Moabites, the Amorites, the Ammonites, the Amalekites and others whose identities are not even known today. . . .

As far as can be learned, it was in about 5000 or 4000 B.C. that one group of Semitic people began trickling into what is now Lebanon and Israel, nearly 300 miles of seacoast along the eastern edge of the Mediterranean, with mountains and upland valleys behind it. This area, particularly its inland sections, should be well known to readers of the Bible as the Land of Canaan. Along the shore are excellent harbors. There is also good coastal farmland, but not much of it because a range of mountains marches parallel to the sea only a few miles inland. The original Canaanite invaders who got as far as the seacoast settled down there, either displacing or mingling with some aboriginal inhabitants who lived by a combination of farming and fishing. The Canaanites established towns, learned to build boats and go to sea, began trading up and down the coast with their neighbors. It was these people who became known to others as the Phoenicians. . . .

That part of their history that was played out prior to about 1100 or 1200 B.C. scholars properly identify as Canaanite. After this time scholars are willing to identify the Canaanite coastal peoples as Phoenicians. The event that made the name change appropriate was actually a whole series of events that did not take place in Canaan at all but in Egypt, in the Aegean world of the Bronze Age Greeks and on the upland plateau of Anatolia. In all these places great political upheavals were taking place. Rulers rose and fell and empires were collapsing.

The Canaanites, heretofore confined more or less to their own doorsteps by more powerful neighbors, suddenly found this constraint removed. They began flowing outward, cautiously at first, then with increasing boldness and rapidity into the vacuum left by their prostrate neighbors. Within a remarkably short period they had changed from local coastal traders to far-ranging seagoing merchant venturers with a network of trading posts throughout the Mediterranean. The existence of that trading network is the key to the identification of the Phoenicians as a recognizable people, though it should be emphasized again that they did not see themselves that way. That is why the Gelidonya wreck is so interesting. It is a small piece of positive evidence about the seagoing and mercantile habits of somebody from down the coast just at the moment when he was beginning to earn the label "Phoenician." By 1000 B.C. there would be no question whatsoever as to who a Phoenician was. . . . Within a few hundred years they were all over the place. Carthage was founded, toeholds were secured in Malta, Sicily, Sardinia, Corsica, the Balearic Isles and Spain. Expeditions were even made into the Atlantic.

BYBLOS IN TWO DIFFERENT AGES

The point of changeover from coastal Canaanite to Phoenician is critically important to an understanding of Phoenician history. . . .

There is hardly a better way of looking at this phenomenon than by making the acquaintance of two kings of Byblos: Rib-Addi (who ruled in about 1375 B.C.) and Zakar-Baal (who ruled in about 1075 B.C.)—the former unmistakably a coastal Canaanite king, the latter just as unmistakably a Phoenician.

Rib-Addi's world, like his own thinking, was dominated by Egypt and had been for a long time. Through various ups and downs extending back a thousand years or more, Egypt had been the mightiest power of the ancient world. Though it was never much of a naval power, it went through several periods of great military expansion on land, gaining control of the whole Canaanite coast and exacting tribute from the Canaanite ports. For centuries Egypt used them as sources of supply and as bases for its campaigns eastward against the Mesopotamian empires of Assyria and Babylon. In return it offered the Canaanite ports security against invasion by others.

In this long relationship the longest and closest ties were between Egypt and Byblos. Byblos was Egypt's principal supplier of prime timber—chiefly cedars of Lebanon—which grew in dense groves on the flanks of the mountains back of Byblos. They were consumed in such quantities by the Egyptians—for furniture, room paneling and especially river barges used for ceremonial purposes—that the ships sent up from the Nile to collect this wood were known as Byblos ships. The Egyptians paid well for Byblos' cedarwood, courted its kings with gifts of carved boxes and stone portrait busts inscribed with the personal seal of the pharaoh. In return, the Byblian kings were outstandingly loyal to the Egyptians. . . .

But jump ahead some 300 years and a different Byblos is encountered. Once-potent Egypt has slid still further. Subservient Canaanite princes like Rib-Addi have been replaced by independent Phoenician kings, the change vividly revealed in . . . an Egyptian papyrus dating from about 1100 B.C. and describing the adventures of an envoy who was sent up from Thebes to dicker with King Zakar-Baal of Byblos for cedarwood the pharaoh needed in order to build a ceremonial barge for the god Amon.

In former days, when the little Canaanite princes had to hustle to keep in the good graces of the Egyptians, we may be sure that the arrival of an Egyptian purchasing agent caused a great stir. How the local timber dealers, and perhaps the local king too, must have bowed and scraped to him.

How different now was the experience of the Egyptian agent whose name was Wen-Amon. The old visits, full of pomp and fine compliments, had washed out with the tide. There was not even an Egyptian ship of state to bring Wen-Amon; he had to make his own passage in a Syrian vessel, and thieves stole most of his money during the voyage. When he stepped ashore at Byblos there was nobody at all to welcome him. On the contrary, not only did the king, Zakar-Baal, refuse to see him, he ordered Wen-Amon to leave. For 29 days in a row the king sent curt messages down to the harbor telling Wen-Amon to get out immediately. The only reason Wen-Amon did not go was that he could not find a ship to sail in. . . .

FROM DEPENDENCE TO INDEPENDENCE

It is worth pausing a moment to compare Rib-Addi to Zakar-Baal. What a contrast there is between those two Byblian kings, separated by only 300 years in time. But for the emerging Phoenicians those 300 years measured the difference between dependence and independence. Rib-Addi is a petitioner, a leaner. For all his enterprise and his scurrying about, he knows that the real power lies elsewhere and that unless he has support he will go under. His letters are sprinkled with "My Lord, this" and "My Lord, that": "Let my Lord know that I would die for him. When I am in the city I will protect it for my Lord, and my heart is fixed on the King, my Lord."

Zakar-Baal stands squarely on his own feet. He will deal with the Egyptians if it suits him; if it doesn't, he won't—and the Egyptian envoy can rot in a dungeon forever, for all he cares. Zakar-Baal and the other Phoenician princes now emerging as heads of the various coastal cities are the survivors—the wiliest, most long-headed, the most accommodating and the most overbearing people in their societies. These traits have brought them to the top. They have survived 10 generations of turmoil. Power radiates from them. They have earned it and they know how to use it. And they will use it for nearly a thousand years.

ITALY'S MYSTERIOUS, SPLENDID ETRUSCANS

PAUL MACKENDRICK

At the same time that the Assyrians were carving out the greatest of their empires in Mesopotamia, the Celts were migrating through northern Europe, and Phoenician traders were plying the Mediterranean and founding cities on its shores, a magnificent and mysterious people rose to prominence in Italy. These were the Etruscans, whose homeland, Etruria (modern Tuscany), was located just to the north of Rome and the plain of Latium. As shown in the following pages by veteran classical scholar Paul MacKendrick, most of the generally sparse evidence for these proud, vibrant people comes from their tombs, several thousand of which were excavated in the twentieth century. What is clear, he explains, citing these and other archaeological finds, is that the Etruscans were strongly influenced by the Greeks, who established numerous cities in southern Italy during the 700s and 600s B.C.; and in turn, the Etruscans profoundly influenced the Romans, whose small state was emerging on the north rim of the Latium plain.

B etween Tiber and Arno there flourished, while Rome was still a collection of mud huts above the Tiber ford, a rich, energetic, and mysterious people, the Etruscans, whose civilization was to influence Rome profoundly. Their riches have been known to the modern world ever since the systematic looting of the fabulous wealth of their underground tombs began, as early as 1489. . . . Travellers to Tarquinia, on the Tuscan seaboard, can wonder at the strange, vivid paintings and seemingly inde-

Excerpted from *The Mute Stones Speak: The Story of Archaeology in Italy*, 2nd ed., by Paul MacKendrick. Copyright © 1960, 1983 by Paul MacKendrick. Reprinted by permission of W.W. Norton and Company, Inc.

cipherable inscriptions on the walls of mysterious and intricate underground chambers. . . .

ETRUSCAN ORIGINS?

Our knowledge of Etruscan civilization is almost entirely a triumph of . . . modern scientific archaeology, since written Etruscan, with no known affinities, is still largely undeciphered, though scientific methods have made large strides possible. In the last three generations archaeologists have attacked and in great measure solved the problem of the origin of the Etruscans, the nature of their cities, their political organization, their religious beliefs and practices, the degree of originality in their creative arts, their life and customs. The result is a composite picture of the greatest people to dominate the Italian peninsula before the Romans.

As to origins, the Etruscans might have been indigenous, or come down over the Alps, or, as most of the ancients believed, have come by sea from Asia Minor. The difference of their burial customs and, probably, their language from those of their neighbors makes it unlikely that their ruling class was native like, for example, the Villanovans [a prehistoric Italian people]; the archaeological evidence for their links with the North is very late. . . . There remains the theory of Near Eastern origin, first stated in the fifth century B.C. by the Greek historian Herodotus, and . . . given some slight support by Italian excavators' discovery of an inscription dated about 600 B.C. on the island of Lemnos, off the coast of Asia Minor opposite Troy. Though the Lemnian dialect is non-Indo-European, and therefore, like Etruscan, cannot be read, its archaic letters can be transliterated. . . . The inscription shows at the very least that on an island geographically intermediate between Asia Minor and Italy a language very similar to Etruscan was employed by some persons. The ancient tradition localizing the original home of the Etruscans somewhere in or near northwest Asia Minor receives here some archaeological support.

But the important thing is not where they came from, but how their culture was formed. The archaeological evidence justifies the hypothesis that they were a small but vigorous military aristocracy from the eastern Mediterranean, established in central Italy, where they built, by borrowing and merging, upon a structure created by the Villanovans. . . .

IMPRESSIVE CITY PLANNING

Archaeology tells us, too, that Etruscan civilization is a culture of cities. Ancient literary sources speak of a league of twelve Etruscan places, most of which have yielded important archaeological material: from Veii, the great terracotta Apollo; at Cerveteri, Vetulonia, Orvieto, and Perugia, the remarkable rock-cut tombs; at Tarquinia, Vulci, and Chiusi, strikingly vivid tomb-paintings; at Bolsena, Roselle, and Volterra, mighty fortification walls; at Populonia, the slag-heaps from the iron works which made Etruria prosperous. But the most interesting . . . evidence for Etruscan city-planning and fortifications comes from three sites, two in the northern Etruscan sphere of influence: Marzabotto on the River Reno, fifteen miles south of Bologna; Spina, near one of the seven mouths of the Po; and one in northern Etruria itself, Bolsena, ancient Volsinii. . . .

The striking discovery at Marzabotto was that the site (dated by pottery in its necropolis to the late sixth or early fifth centuries B.C.) had a regular, oriented, rectangular grid of streets, enclosing house-blocks *(insulae)* averaging 165 × 35 yards. The main north-south street, or *cardo,* and the main east-west street, or *decumanus,* were each over forty-eight feet wide, the minor streets one third as broad. The streets were paved, as they were not in Rome until 350 years later. Drains ran beneath all the streets. . . . The house-doors had locks and keys. A number of the buildings were recognizable as shops, with back rooms for living quarters. . . .

The city is dominated, on the high ground to the northwest, by an *arx* [citadel], bearing the footings, some of considerable size with impressive moldings, of five structures, temples or altars. One of them, facing south, and divided at the back into three *cellae* [temple chambers], is the prototype of the Roman Capitolium, decorated by an Etruscan artist, and dedicated to the triad Jupiter, Juno, Minerva (in Etruscan, Tin, Uni, Menerva). . . . In sum, Marzabotto is so perfect an example of an Etruscan town-site that it merits the name of the Etruscan Pompeii.

Marzabotto remained for many years the only known Etruscan site with a grid plan. Lying as it does outside Etruria proper, it was clearly the product of Etruscan expansion northward. Since 1922 reclamation by drainage canals has revealed the necropolis of another northern outpost, Spina, near one of the mouths of the Po. Working under the greatest difficulties from mud and seepage, archaeologists had unearthed the contents of no less than 1213 tombs, often finding golden earrings and diadems gleaming in the mud against the skulls in the burials. . . . Both Etruscans and Greeks lived in the site together, as is proved by *graffiti* in both languages scratched on the pottery. The spot, commanding the Adriatic, would be the ideal port of entry for foreign luxury goods imported to satisfy the taste for display of wealthy Etruscans. . . .

This rich and crowded cemetery was all that was known of

Etruscan Spina until further drainage operations in 1953, in the Pega Valley, south of the original site, brought to light not only 1195 new tombs, but also further surprises. In October, 1956, an air-photograph in color revealed beneath the modern irrigation canals the grid plan . . . of the port area of the ancient Etruscan city. . . . Later air-photographs showed evidence of habitation over an area of 741 acres, large enough for a population of half a million. Since the artifacts of this vast city are a little later in style than those of Marzabotto, we assume that Spina flourished a little later. Almost no weapons were found in the graves: Spina apparently felt secure on her landlocked lagoon, but she reckoned without attacks from the landward side. Few vases datable later than the late fifth century are found in the graves: the inference is that Spina fell, about 390 B.C., before the same Gallic invasion that despoiled Marzabotto. The two sites together reinforce each other in giving evidence for the use by Etruscan city-planners of the kind of square or rectangular grid of streets later made famous by Roman colonies and Roman camps; unfortunately the question is still open whether the Etruscans invented the grid used in Italy or whether it was a Greek import. . . .

EVIDENCE FROM TOMBS

It is about Etruscan religion, and especially funerary rites, that we are best informed. The Etruscans had the reputation of being the most addicted to religious ceremonial of any people of antiquity, and we learn much about Etruscans living from Etruscans dead. We know what sort of documentation to expect on religious matters from an Etruscan tomb, by extrapolating back from rites which the Romans believed they had inherited from Etruria, especially in the area of foretelling the future by examining the livers of animals (hepatoscopy) or observing the flights of birds (augury). One of the most curious surviving documents of Etruscan superstition is the bronze model of a sheep's liver found in 1877 near Piacenza, on the upper Po, and now in the Civic Museum there. The liver is split in two lengthwise. From the plane surface thus provided three lobes project. The plane surface itself is subdivided into sixteen compartments; over each compartment a god presides. The same sixteen subdivisions were used in the imaginary partition of the sky for augury, and the same principle governed the layout and orientation of cities like Marzabotto and probably Spina. The same superstition found in Babylonia directs our attention once more to the probable Near Eastern origin of the Etruscan ruling class. . . . From the Piacenza liver and the orientation of Marzabotto we can deduce both the orderliness of the Etruscan mind and the ease with which it degenerated into rigidity and superstition. For this deadly heritage the Etruscans apparently found in the Romans willing recipients; often, but not always, for old Cato [a famous Roman senator] said, " I cannot see how one liver-diviner can meet another without laughing in his face."

The vast number of Etruscan tombs and the richness of their decoration and furnishings tell us much about another aspect of the Etruscans' religion: their view of the afterlife. About this the fabulous painted tombs of Tarquinia tell us most. . . . Electrical-resistivity surveying with a potentiometer, sensitive to the difference between solid earth and empty subterranean space, makes possible the rapid tracing of a profile showing where the hollows of Etruscan tombs exist underground. A hole is then drilled large enough to admit a periscope; if the periscope shows painted walls, or pottery, a camera can be attached to make a 360-degree photograph. . . .

The Tomb of Hunting and Fishing at Tarquinia, discovered in 1873, gives us our most attractive picture of how Etruscans in their palmiest days viewed the next world. The tomb is dated by the black-figured Attic vases it contained in the decade 520–510 B.C., when the Etruscan ruling class was still prosperous. A more charming invitation to the brainless life could hardly be imagined. The most vivid scene is on the walls of the tomb's inner room, which are conceived as opening out into a breezy seascape, with a lively population of bright birds in blue, red, and yellow, frisky dolphins, and boys, friskier still, at play. Up a steep rock striped in clay-red and grass-green clambers a sunburnt boy in a blue tunic, who appears to have just pushed another boy who is diving, with beautiful form, into the hazy, wine-dark sea. On a nearby rock stands another boy firing at the birds with a sling-shot. Below him is a boat with an eye painted on the prow. . . . Of the boat's four passengers, one is fishing over the side with a flimsy handline, while beside the boat a fat dolphin turns a mocking somersault. All is life, action, humor, vitality, color; such is the notion of blessed immortality entertained by a people for whom God's in his heaven, all's right with the world. . . .

THE VIBRANCY OF ETRUSCAN SCULPTURE

What can archaeology tell us about Etruscan cultural life? Of art for art's sake there seems to have been very little, of literature none, except for liturgical texts. The Etruscans excelled in fine large-scale bronze work . . . , but their minor masterpieces in bronze deserve mention also, especially the engraved mirrors, the cylindrical cosmetic boxes called *ciste*, and the statuettes whose attenuated bodies appeal strongly to modern taste. Their painting at its best shows in its economy of line how intelligently they borrowed from the Greeks, in its realism how sturdily they maintained their own individuality. In architecture, Etruscan temples, having been made of wood, do not survive above their foundation courses, but recent discoveries of terracotta temple-models at Vulci tell us something about their appearance, and masses of their terracotta revetment survive, brightly-painted geometric, vegetable, or mythological motifs, designs to cover beams, mask the ends of half-round roof tiles, or . . . to follow the slope of a gable roof. Made from molds, the motifs could be infinitely repeated at small expense, an aspect of Etruscan practicality which was to appeal strongly to the Romans.

But the Etruscans' artistic genius shows at the best in their architectural sculpture in painted terracotta, freestanding or in high relief. Their best-known masterpiece in this genre is the Apollo of Veii, designed for the ridgepole of an archaic temple. Discovered in 1916, it is now in the Villa Giulia museum in Rome. The stylized treatment of the ringlets, the almond eyes, the fixed smile are all characteristic of archaic Greek art, and the fine edges of the profile, lips, and eyebrows suggest an original in bronze. But this is no mere copy. It is the work of a great original artist, probably the same Vulca of Veii who was commissioned in the late sixth century B.C. to do the terracottas for the Capitoline temple in Rome. . . . The god is shown as he tenses himself to spring upon his opponent; the anatomical knowledge, the expression of mass in motion, and the craftsmanship required to cast a life-size terracotta (a feat which even now presents the greatest technical difficulties) are all alike remarkable. . . .

[Another] Etruscan masterpiece in terracotta, of later date, but still showing the same striking vitality as the [Apollo of Veii] . . . is the pair of winged horses in high relief . . . which come probably from the pediment of the temple called the Ara della Regina, on the site of the Etruscan city . . . of Tarquinia, and now in the Tarquinia museum. The proud arching of the horses' necks, their slim legs, their rippling muscles are rendered to make them the quintessence of the thoroughbred, so that we forget that the delicate wings would scarcely lift their sturdy bodies off the ground. In these . . . masterpieces art is none the less vibrant for being put at the service of religion. Here is created a new Italic expressionistic style, so admirable that many would hold that Italian art did not reach this level again until the Renaissance.

THE FOUNDING OF ROME, THE ETERNAL CITY

ARTHUR E.R. BOAK AND WILLIAM G. SINNIGEN

Rome's period of greatest power and influence (ca. 200 B.C. to ca. A.D. 400) came a good deal later than the heydays of early civilizations such as those of the Indus Valley, Mesopotamia, Egypt, Israel, and Minoan Crete. However, Rome's own earliest years did coincide with the consolidation of much of the Near East by the Assyrians, the fall of Assyria and rise of the Neo-Babylonian realm, the glory days of the Etruscans in northern Italy, and the last few centuries of existence for the Jewish kingdoms in Palestine. Considering its monumental importance to the later history and cultures of North Africa, the Near East, and Europe, Rome's early beginnings, though humble, cannot be ignored. This overview of those beginnings is by former University of Michigan professor Arthur E.R. Boak and former Hunter College professor William G. Sinnigen.

R ome, the Latin *Roma*, is situated on the Tiber [River] about fifteen miles from the sea, where the river makes its way through a cluster of low hills. There, on the left or eastern bank are the three isolated eminences called the Capitoline, Palatine, and Aventine. Stretching out toward them from the high ground farther east are the spurs known as the Quirinal, Viminal, Esquiline, and Caelian. All these formed part of Rome of the later Republic and the Empire, the City of the Seven Hills, which also extended across the Tiber to the west bank where it included

From *A History of Rome to A.D. 565*, by Arthur E.R. Boak and William G. Sinnigen (New York: Macmillan, 1921).

both the low ground along the river and the height of Mount Jan-
iculum. This extent was the result of a long period of growth; the
beginnings of Rome were much more humble.

GROWTH OF THE CITY

The origins of Rome go back to prehistoric times. As Rome grew
in importance, men's curiosity on this point was aroused, and
speculation began to supply the want of historical evidence. Legends arose which ultimately came to form the traditional version
of the founding of Rome. In this can be detected contributions
from both the Romans and their Greek neighbors in Italy and
Sicily. Before the close of the fourth century B.C., the Romans attributed the foundation of the city to a figure called *Romulus*,
whose name is derived from that of Rome itself. Romulus, son of
the god Mars and the daughter of a king of Alba Longa [the chief
city of the plain of Latium, south of Rome], was credited with the
establishment of a city on the Palatine hill. Meanwhile the Greek
desire to explain the origin of Rome by linking it with their own
past had given rise to myths in which the founder of the city appears as the descendant of a Greek hero. The most significant of
these Greek tales was the one whose roots go back to the sixth century and which eventually established a connection between
Rome and the Trojan prince Aeneas, son of the goddess Aphrodite.
In his wanderings after the destruction of Troy, Aeneas made his
way to Italy, where either his son or his grandson founded Rome.
Owing to the Greek cultural ascendancy over the Romans, the latter partially accepted the Greek myth and by the end of the third
century B.C. combined it with the native tradition. The resultant
composite version was that Aeneas came to Latium and founded
Lavinium, his son Ascanius founded Alba Longa, and Romulus,
his descendant after many generations, was the founder of Rome.
In this legend there is little of historical worth, except perhaps a
faint reflection of the early importance of Alba Longa in Latium
and the memory of a prehistoric settlement on the Palatine. Roman writers of the late third and the second centuries B.C. differed
widely on the date of the founding of Rome, but in the first century the date 753 B.C. came to be accepted generally and to serve
as the basis for reckoning events in terms of years "from the
founding of the city." If by the "foundation" of Rome is meant the
appearance of an Iron Age settlement on the Palatine, then this
date may well be approximately correct; at the very least it is not
contradicted by the surviving archaeological evidence. In default
of written records we must rely mainly upon such evidence in any
attempt to picture the early stages in the growth of the city.

The recent find of some Apennine Bronze Age pottery in a fill

on the low ground near the Tiber indicates that there was a settlement on the site of Rome about 1500 B.C., but its location is unknown, and there seems to be no continuity between this settlement and those of the early Iron Age. Excavations have shown
that in the latter period, from the ninth to the seventh century B.C.,
there were several distinct communities on the hills overlooking
the marshy area which later became the site of the celebrated Forum of the city Rome. One of these, and at first probably two, occupied the Palatine Hill. Here the foundations of the dwellings
show that they were rectangular huts with rounded corners and
walls of interwoven branches plastered with mud and supported
by upright posts, conforming in general to the type of hut revealed by the hut-shaped cinerary urns from Latium. The cemetery of the Palatine community lay on the northeast side of the
Forum area. Here the earliest graves contained cremation burials
[in which the dead were burned, their ashes buried], the ashes of
the dead being deposited in the customary hut-shaped urns. Inhumation burials [in which the bodies were buried] began later,
but cremation continued along with the new rite.

Similar cemeteries on the Quirinal, Viminal, and Esquiline
seem to indicate the presence of comtemporary settlements on
these hills also, although some authorities deny the existence of
any on the Viminal and the Esquiline, considering the latter to be
an extension of the Palatine settlement. The cemetery on the Esquiline contained inhumation burials almost exclusively, but in
that on the Quirinal at first cremation alone was practiced. The
use of these contrasting burial rites contemporaneously suggests
that the early occupants of the Roman hills were of different cultural traditions, and supports the view of the Romans themselves, who believed they were a people of heterogeneous origins. The inhumers may possibly have been Sabine intruders in
a region predominantly Latin.

These early communities were sprawling villages with no regular ground plan. It may be assumed that each was an independent political unit. . . .

About the middle of the seventh century B.C., the Old Palatine
cemetery ceased to be used and an extensive part of the Forum
area was built over with huts of the Palatine type. This points to
an expansion of the Palatine community and its absorption by
conquest or peaceful amalgamation of those on the other hills.
This union may be regarded as the first important step in the formation of the historic city of Rome.

The next step was the organization of the earliest city which
can with certainty be called Rome. It is the city of the Four Regions, known in historic times as Palatina, Esquilina, Collina, and

Sucusana (later Suburana). These included the Quirinal, Viminal, Esquiline, Caelian, and Palatine hills, as well as the intervening low ground. This probably was the area included from the earliest historic times within the *pomerium*, the ritually consecrated boundary of the city. Within the *pomerium* but not embraced in any of the four regions was the Capitoline hill which was fortified and served as the citadel of the community. Thus Rome of the Four Regions may be regarded as an expansion and consolidation of the town formed earlier by the union of the Palatine with its adjacent communities. The cessation of burials in the cemeteries lying within the *pomerium* about 600 B.C. or a little later indicates that the unification took place then, for burials within the city were contrary to Roman practice. . . . The new city was not surrounded by a continuous wall, although the individual hills were protected by the sixth century by earthen embankments with ditches in front. The Aventine Hill, as well as part of the plateau back of the Esquiline, was included within the city walls of the fourth century B.C. but remained outside the *pomerium* until the time of the Emperor Claudius in the first century A.D.

The archaeological evidence shows that the Roman tradition of a strong Sabine element in the population of the early city has a substantial basis. But though it is true that the population of Rome was the result of a fusion of different elements, Latin and Sabine mainly but with a slight admixture of Etruscan and probably even pre-Italic, nevertheless the Romans were essentially a Latin people. In language, in religion, in political institutions, they were characteristically Latin, and their history is inseparably connected with that of the Latins as a whole.

The location of Rome, on the Tiber at a point where navigation for seagoing vessels terminated and where an island made transit easy, made it commercially important. It was also the gateway between Latium and Etruria [homeland of the Etruscans, located directly north of Rome] and the natural outlet for the trade of the Tiber valley. Furthermore, its central position in Italy gave it a strategic advantage in its wars. But the greatness of Rome was not the result of its geographic advantages; it was the outgrowth of the energy and political capacity of its people, qualities which became a national heritage because of the character of the early struggles of the Roman state.

THE EARLY MONARCHY

"In the beginning," wrote the Roman historian Tacitus, "kings ruled the city Rome." The accuracy of this statement is attested by the mention of the *rex* or king in an inscription of the sixth century B.C. and by the survival of this term in later times in the title *rex sacrorum* or "king of the sacrifices," which was borne by one of the higher priests, as well as by the strength of the Roman tradition regarding an early period of monarchical rule. It is quite impossible, however, to present any reliable history of Roman monarchy because, when Roman historians began to write they found scarcely any records of the regal age, and oral tradition had become confused. Consequently the Roman account of the reigns of the kings is a reconstruction by annalists and antiquarians who sought to attribute the origins of Roman political and religious institutions to these rulers.

According to the accepted Roman version, seven kings ruled Rome between the founding of the city and the establishment of the Republic about 509 [B.C.]. The first of these, Romulus, and his alleged Sabine colleague Titus Tatius, may not have been historical personages. The six successors of Romulus—Numa Pompilius, Tullus Hostilius, Ancus Marcius, Lucius Tarquinius Priscus, Servius Tullius, and Lucius Tarquinius (Superbus)—probably were historical, although we can place little reliance upon the characteristics and exploits assigned to each. Apparently the first three were pre-Etruscan and may have ruled the Palatine community before and after the absorption of its neighbors; the last three date from the sixth century when Rome was under [strong Etruscan influence]. . . . By name, as well as by tradition, the Tarquinii were Etruscan, and Servius Tullius may well have been an Etruscan whose name has survived in a Latin form.

In spite of the unreliability of the Roman account of the age of the kings, it is possible to draw a general picture of conditions in Rome under its kingly rulers, based on the survival in later times of religious, political, and social institutions that had their origin in the early stages of the Roman state, and on the results of archaeological studies that have revealed much of the character of early Roman civilization.

The political institutions of the early Roman state bore a strong resemblance to those of other city kingdoms built up by immigrants from the north in Greece and Italy. They comprised the kingship, a council, an assembly of the people, and the smaller units into which the citizens were grouped for the better performance of their obligations and the exercise of their rights.

The Roman monarchy apparently was not purely hereditary but elective within the royal family, like that of primitive Greek states, where the king was the head of one of a group of noble families, chosen by the nobles and approved by the people as a whole. The king was war-lord, chief priest, and judge in matters affecting the public peace. His authority, called the *imperium*, included the right of scourging and execution. Its symbols were the

fasces, small bundles of rods enclosing an axe, carried by atten-
dants called lictors. The royal power was not absolute, for its exercise was tempered by custom, by the lack of any elaborate ma-
chinery of government, and by the practical necessity for the king
to avoid alienating the community.

The council was called the Senate (*senatus*), which, as its name
indicates, was originally a council of elders but, following the
pattern of similar councils in the city states of Greece, had become a council of nobles. The details of its organization are not
known, but its functions were primarily advisory. From a very
early date the Roman people were divided into thirty groups
called *curiae*, which at one time may well have corresponded to
territorial divisions. Membership in the *curiae* was probably
hereditary, and each *curia* had its special cult, which was maintained long after the *curiae* had lost their political importance. Apparently the *curiae* were grouped into three larger units called
tribes, ten *curiae* to each tribe. The names of these tribes, *Ramnes*,
Tities, and *Luceres*, survived in later times as the names of cavalry
corps in the army, which was recruited at first on a tribal basis.

When the members of all the *curiae* met, they constituted the
popular assembly known as the Curiate Assembly *(comitia curi-
ata)*. It was convoked at the pleasure of the king to hear matters
of interest to the whole community such as adoptions, wills, and
grants of citizenship. It did not have legislative power, but such
important steps as the declaration of war or the appointment of
a new *rex* required its formal sanction.

EXPANSION UNDER THE KINGS

According to later tradition, Rome grew to be the chief city in
Latium under the kings, having absorbed several smaller Latin
communities in the immediate neighborhood, extended her territory along the lower course of the Tiber to the seacoast, where later
the port of Ostia was founded, and even conquered Alba Longa,
the former religious center of the Latins. This tradition conflicts
with archaeological evidence, which indicates that other towns
were dominant in the Latin League during the sixth century and
that Rome did not attain such dominance until after 500. The legend of Rome's greatness under the monarchy seems to have been
the creation of the earliest Roman historians, who sought to provide their city with a past worthy of its later greatness.

Early Greek Culture: The Birth of the West

CHAPTER 5

PEOPLE AND LIFE IN MINOAN CRETE

RODNEY CASTLEDEN

When one mentions the birth of Western civilization and its unique culture, ancient Greece usually comes to mind. But before the rise of a high civilization on the Greek mainland, the Minoans, based on Crete, dominated the Aegean sphere and created the first advanced culture in Europe. In the following essay, Rodney Castleden, a noted scholar of early European cultures, discusses the Minoan people and their lives, including their appearance, grooming habits, weapons, leadership, social structure, slaves, and religious festivals and ceremonies. He cites the tablets inscribed with Linear B (a writing system proven to be an early form of Greek) and some of the other surviving evidence for Minoan society. He mentions some of the main Minoan sites, among them Knossos (or Knossus, in northern Crete), Pylos (on the southern rim of the Greek mainland), and Thera (a small island lying directly north of Crete).

<hr>

Although the Minoan civilization had its origins as long as five thousand years ago and had come to an end by 1000 BC, we nevertheless have a very clear idea of what the Minoan people looked like. There are in the region of a hundred statuettes in stone, metal and clay, showing us ordinary Minoans worshipping. There are also representations of Minoans on sealstones and decorative metalwork, as well as in the best-known medium of all, the frescoes. Among these, there is plenty of evidence of the sort of clothes they wore and of their general appearance or, to be more precise, of the way in which the Minoans liked to see themselves.

The Minoans depicted themselves as straight-nosed (often with a high bridge), and with large almond-shaped eyes. They had conspicuous eyebrows and long, wavy black hair falling in curling locks to their shoulders and sometimes to their waists. Their tanned bodies were athletic and tense with nervous energy; their arms, shoulders and thighs were strong and muscular, their waists and lower legs slim and lithe. It is above all a physically attractive type that we are shown, graceful whether in repose or engaged in energetic activity, and graceful in a rather self-conscious, theatrical way: it is the grace of a matador or a ballet dancer.

Whether the majority of Minoans actually possessed these characteristics is another matter. Perhaps we should see them as goals or ideals against which individual Minoans were measured. Perhaps, alternatively, it is only the young Minoans that are depicted. . . .

Wherever possible, the Minoans' fashions in clothes, jewellery and face-painting were designed to accentuate the bodily characteristics that were specially favoured. The very fact that the men often wore very skimpy clothes revealing as much of their physique as possible indicates their intense love of physical beauty. . . .

MEN'S CLOTHING

The Minoans' main cloth-making fibre was wool. Spinning and weaving were well-established cottage industries by the beginning of the bronze age: clay spindle whorls and loom weights are found at a great many Minoan sites. The wooden upright looms on which the cloth was produced have not survived, but there is a stone in the Agia Varvara house at [the Minoan palace site] Mallia with two slots which may well have held a loom's upright posts. Wool is known to have been available from the many references to flocks of sheep on the clay tablets at Knossos; possibly woollen cloth was one of the Minoans' main exports. . . .

Possibly silk was produced in Crete: it is known to have been produced in Cos, just to the north-east of Crete, after the Minoan civilization collapsed. Animal furs and skins were used to make garments for rituals, although leather was no doubt used for making sandals and boots for everyday wear.

In the Early and Middle Minoan Periods, men nearly always wore a loincloth, either rolled and tucked round the waist or held up by a belt. There were several different styles of loincloth and it may be that they were fashionable at different times or in different areas. Sometimes the loincloth was folded out on each side to cover the upper thighs. Sometimes it was simply wrapped round like a mini-skirt. From this it was a straightforward development to turn the skirt or kilt into a pair of shorts by sewing the centre at the front and back together between the legs. The Lion Hunt Dagger, made in Crete although found at Mycenae [in southern Greece] clearly shows Minoan hunters wearing patterned shorts; the third hunter from the left in particular is shown to have shorts made in two layers, a curious parallel with the flounced or layered skirts worn by the women. The archer depicted on a carved steatite jar from the Knossos area is shown wearing similar shorts.

The codpiece was another enduring feature of male attire. The early design was a straight and narrow genital-guard held up by a belt: it was often worn without a loincloth. . . . After 1700 BC the codpiece was developed into a more exaggerated feature. Wider and more prominent, it was often worn with a kilt made of a stiff material. The kilt left the codpiece exposed, covering the front of the thigh but rising to expose the side of the thigh: the 'tail' was somehow made to curl back. . . .

By 1500 BC the codpiece was not always exposed. Several representations of men from this time show them wearing kilts but no codpieces. From 1500 BC a new, bulkier kilt was introduced and, for a time, it seems that both old and new styles were worn. The new kilt had a hem that sloped down from back to front and reached the knees; the codpiece was replaced by a decorative beaded tassel. . . .

WOMEN'S FASHIONS

Women's fashions, though covering more of the body than male attire, nevertheless showed an equal interest in display. Their clothes are not the clothes of women kept in purdah, but of women who expect to take the centre of the social stage. Generally, designs accentuated full hips, slender wasp-waists and prominent breasts; in fact the most conspicuous and best-known feature of Minoan attire is that it usually left the breasts exposed.

At the time of the first temples, women wore long robe-like dresses held in at the waist by girdles wound twice round and tied in a knot, leaving the girdle-ends hanging down in front. The dress tops, which were sometimes separate bodices, had short and fairly tight sleeves, rather in the style of a modern T-shirt, but with a deep slit at the front right down to the navel. This gave two options. The bodice front could be arranged to cover the breasts, leaving only the cleavage showing, which I suspect was the normal practice; alternatively, it could be pulled sideways, deliberately to display the breasts, as was the custom during religious ceremonies. Often the bodice rose to a high peak at the back of the neck.

The Snake Goddess statuette, which shows how a priestess dressed for a religious ceremony to transform herself into a deity, shows some extra garments. She has a wide belt to accentuate her slender waist and from it, descending at the front and back, is an elaborately embroidered double apron, which may be a sacral garment worn only by priestesses. Underneath this she wears a heavy flounced skirt made of seven overlapping layers of material, each layer composed of different coloured and patterned cloth in 12–15 centimetre squares to make a very striking check pattern.

This style was evidently a very enduring one. It appears on an early ivory seal from Knossos and continued in use through both the temple periods. By 1550 the layered skirts began to develop a marked 'V' in front, which may indicate that a new way of tying on the overskirt was being tried out. . . .

An assumption is often made that the heavy flounced skirt was normal to female attire, but this is by no means certain: its use may have been restricted to religious ceremonies. How the priestesses managed to dance in them is hard to imagine, but this is shown in several rings and frescoes. . . .

GROOMING AND JEWELLERY

Both women and men usually had very long dark-brown or black hair falling to the shoulders and below, with curling locks hanging down each side of the face in front of the ears. But some men are shown with short hair, and it may have been felt that it was more appropriate, perhaps even essential for safety, for men in certain occupations to have their hair cut relatively short. This is to an extent borne out by the Chieftain Cup. The 'prince' has the beautiful long flowing locks that we might expect of a leisured aristocrat, but the officer reporting to him has short hair and seems to have a broad diadem or visor across the front of his head: this may have had the purely practical purpose of keeping the hair off his face. The hunters on the Lion Hunt Dagger also have short hair, and it may have been customary for soldiers—if indeed there were regular soldiers—to have their hair short. In the circumstances, it seems extraordinary that the bull-leapers had long hair, which must have made their vaulting and somersaulting even more difficult to bring off successfully; but bull-leaping was a religious rite, and there was some ritual reason why the bull-leaping teams—boys and girls alike—wore their hair long.

Men were usually clean-shaven, but at least some had moustaches and beards, such as the man shown on the plaque . . . dating to about 2000 BC. This may have been a matter of personal preference or of social group: perhaps instead there were certain localities where beards were preferred. Small bronze blades were used as razors. For a time they were leaf-shaped, although in the Late Minoan III Period an Egyptian type of razor shaped like a small chopper became fashionable. Tweezers too were used for removing hair and possibly shaping the eyebrows which, as the frescoes clearly show, were regarded as a very important facial feature—and there is no reason to suppose that Minoan men were any less concerned about the beauty of their appearance than Minoan women.

The pigments used to colour the face and eyes were evidently ground on specially made rectangular stone palettes and later in stone bowls. The priestess known as 'La Parisienne' is obviously wearing heavy make-up. The eye is enlarged and emphatic and the arc of the eyebrow is exaggerated; some sort of black eye-liner must have been used to create this impression. The lips too have been emphasized with rouge. To help with this beautifica-tion, the Minoans used mirrors of polished bronze, just as their Egyptian contemporaries did, held on handles of wood or ivory. The long hair must have required careful combing and it is as-sumed that to begin with the Minoans used wooden combs: ivory combs did not appear in Crete until around 1500 BC.

Both women and men—even the scantily-clad men—wore jewellery. The Minoans reveal their love of physical beauty in many ways, but to an exceptional degree in their addiction to jewellery. They decorated themselves with gold-topped hairpins, earrings that were often large and elaborate—sometimes double and triple earrings were worn—armlets, wristlets and anklets, fancy beaded collars and necklaces made of copper, silver, gold or semi-precious stones. . . .

The overall picture is one of remarkable richness and inven-tiveness. The Minoan style is unmistakable, original and in-tensely sensual. There is a delight in the sheer physical beauty of the human body—all the rest is there to emphasize it—and a de-light in the beauty of jewels, coloured textiles, feathers, cosmet-ics and gold. In all this it would be easy to overlook detail, but the Minoans were careful to make even the smallest detail of a garment interesting to look at. The frescoes show a great variety of fabric patterns, many of them intricate, interlocked repeating patterns in many colours. Some of the fabric patterns may have been woven, some hand-printed with wooden blocks; others may have been produced by a mixture of techniques, with em-broidery and beads sewn onto a printed or woven pattern.

WARFARE AND WEAPONS

To judge from the available evidence, which is far from com-plete, the towns of bronze age Crete were not fortified. As yet no traces have been found of city walls or defensive towers at Knossos or at any of the other Minoan centres. We may be lulled by this into believing that life on Minoan Crete was entirely peaceful. In fact many of the sites were destroyed by burning and we have no way of knowing whether those fires were accidental, starting as a result of carelessness, or deliberate acts of arson by an enemy, or precipitated by a convulsive earthquake upsetting lamps and domestic hearths. The archaeological evidence is often ambiguous. . . .

Even so, we should not rule out the possibility—likelihood, even—of warfare between one Cretan city-state and another. It is known . . . that the Cretan city-states of the third and fourth centuries BC were at war with each other constantly, struggling for supremacy. Bitter fighting over long periods may leave no archaeological trace. We also know that the Minoans were equipped for war. . . . Bronze helmets were made in eight pieces: four to make the conical crown with its mount for a horsehair or feathered plume, two cheek-pieces which hung down in front of the ears, and two other pieces which may have protected the back of the neck. . . . Similarly shaped helmets were also made out of boar's tusks, just as depicted in [a surviving] ivory plaque of a warrior's head . . . and as described by Homer on the Cretan hero Meriones. A socket on the helmet's crown was a mount for a crest or plume. Remains of a Minoan boar's tusk helmet were found in a tomb at . . . Knossos.

The Lion Hunt Dagger from . . . Mycenae, dating to around 1550 and produced in Crete, shows three shield shapes: the figure-of-eight shape which appears in Knossian frescoes, rectangular and rectangular with a curved raised section on the top. These shields were light and made of cattle hides stretched over wooden frames, with at least one handle-strap on the back. . . . The lion hunters are shown with their shields hung over one shoulder, the handle-strap over their heads, to free both hands for spear-throwing. . . .

The Minoans had daggers and swords, some of them richly decorated. At Mallia a beautiful matching set of sword and dagger was found. The sword handle was covered in gold sheet decorated top and bottom with an incised herringbone design, the pommel being fashioned out of a large piece of rock crystal. Since the sword and dagger were found close to a ceremonial leopard-axe, it may be that all these weapons from the Mallia temple had a ceremonial rather than a military use. . . .

The Minoans used chariots in battle. The shape of their chariots is clearly shown in the ideogram for 'chariot' on the Linear B tablets. The Minoan chariot . . . had a lightweight body, with sides and front possibly made of wickerwork or layers of hide on a wooden frame, and two simple four-spoked wheels mounted on a central axle. A wooden bar or frame extended forwards between the two ponies who drew the chariot along. It seems from the detailed descriptions of chariot spare-parts at Pylos as if the aristocracy had chariots equipped with special wheels; they are described as 'Followers' wheels'. . . .

LOCAL LEADERS

In spite of the abundance of artefacts, images and even inscriptions from the Cretan bronze age, it is still very difficult to reconstruct the society with any confidence. The Linear B tablets offer fleeting glimpses of deities, officials and bureaucrats from the fourteenth century. Since some of the officials' titles have been found at Pylos on mainland Greece as well as at Knossos, it may be fair to assume provisionally that Minoan society had a rather similar structure to that of Pylos.

A few tablet references imply the existence of a king or Wanax at both Pylos and Knossos, but little more than this can be said. The adjective 'royal' is used of certain craftsmen—a royal fuller and a royal potter at Pylos—and even of certain textiles and pottery at Knossos. There is no mention of a king or of the adjective 'royal' at Mycenae at all. Sometimes the word 'king' was used for a deity such as Poseidon, so we cannot be sure, even where the word occurs, that a secular king existed. . . .

However sparingly, the word 'royal' was nevertheless used at Knossos, so we should perhaps assume that there was a king of Knossos, even if he was a fairly shadowy, background figure dominated by the priesthood and by other officials. The great temple centres of Knossos, Phaistos, Mallia and Zakro were certainly major administrative, economic, and political centres and it is likely that each had its own ruler. The classical Greek tradition had it that Minos co-ruled Crete with his brothers Rhadamanthys and Sarpedon; King Minos became associated with Knossos, King Rhadamanthys with Phaistos and King Sarpedon with Mallia. It is likely that Middle Minoan Crete was a loose confederation of city-states, each with its own ruler and often with its own great temple-complex. . . .

At Knossos, one tablet lists the names of men attached to two officials who are given the title qa-si-re-wi-ja. This may be the word 'guasileus', later to become the Homeric word 'basileus', an alternative title for a king. In Minoan-Mycenean times, the guasileus seems to have been a less exalted figure than a king, but still an important figure, perhaps a local chief. . . .

In the Early Minoan Period, to judge from burial practices, society was structured mainly round clans or extended families. It may be that as the urban centres evolved and became foci of wealth, certain families emerged as wealthier and more successful commercially than others and that the Guasileus emerged from these rich families. It would certainly make sense for progressive economic and social differentiation to result in the emergence of individual social leaders. The clans remained important [for a long time] . . . and this may have been partly thanks to the clan-focus supplied by the person of the Guasileus.

The most outstanding leader, though, was in a stratum above the Guasileus. He was the Lawagetas, literally 'the leader of the people'. In later Greek, for instance in the *Iliad*, the word translated as 'people' often refers to 'the people arrayed for battle' or 'the war host', so some have understandably assumed that this Minoan-Mycenean title designates the commander of the army. But the tablets do not confirm this interpretation. There is nothing, apart from the much later connotation accruing to the word 'people', to connect the Lawagetas with the command of the army. He may have been the leader of the people in a political rather than a military sense, a kind of prime minister under the Wanax or possibly even a president, if the Wanax was a ceremonial figure-head with circumscribed powers. There is really too little evidence to go on, but what we have is compatible with a Wanax who was a monarch with very limited secular power, a constitutional monarch who formed a charismatic focus for public ceremony, and a Lawagetas who was the effective secular ruler. . . .

COURTIERS AND OTHER OFFICIALS

Surrounding the Pylian Wanax was an important group of courtiers known as Hequetai (e-qe-ta in the tablets) or 'Followers'. These noblemen presumably formed an entourage for the leader, providing him with support, security and company, and who probably also functioned as senior administrators and military commanders. . . . According to the tablets, the Followers at Pylos had slaves, special clothes and wheels, i.e. chariots, which implies either high status or a military role or both. The Knossian Followers . . . had a supervisory role in, for example, textile production, which certainly implies a less exalted status. On the other hand, the distinction made in the tablets between 'cloth for export' and 'cloth to do with the Followers' could be interpreted differently: it may be that certain cloth was reserved for use in making garments for the aristocracy because of its high quality. . . .

It is not known how many Followers there were at Knossos or at any of the other centres on Crete; they may have formed an elite corps, a mobile fighting force, or each may have commanded a regiment. The Followers were probably town-based and . . . as a group, they could have been a threat to the king's (or leader's) power. . . . The Followers may have acted on the king's (or leader's) behalf sometimes in counteracting any tendency for a Land-holder to behave independently of the central administration.

Another group of rural officials, the Koreters or Governors, existed at Pylos, and may also have existed in Crete. It is not clear how the role of the Koreter differed from that of the Guasileus, but it may be that the Koreter was an official appointed by the central administration and allocated to a district, whereas the Guasileus emerged as it were dynastically out of the district's clan system. The district Governors or Superintendents had deputies called, among other things, Prokoreters: the Minoans were great bureaucrats.

THE LOWER CLASSES

Of the great mass of ordinary people, little is known. The lower classes were, on the whole, not the concern of the tablet scribes; masons are mentioned in the Knossos tablets, but few other trades-people. . . . The society of classical Crete had three lower classes. There were free citizens, and then two classes of serfs, one with some rights, though not the right to possess arms, the other with no rights and these were the chattel slaves. This three-tiered lower class may have been inherited from the Minoans, although there is no reason to think so, except that Aristotle made a passing reference to the laws of Minos still being in force among Cretan serfs. Certainly some slaves at Knossos were bought and sold; the phrase 'he bought' crops up in four places in tablets listing men and women by name, which is strongly suggestive of slavery. 'Women' and their children are mentioned on the tablets too, without any reference to menfolk, implying slavery and absent males. The male slaves were probably removed to work elsewhere, possibly to reduce slave solidarity, possibly to reduce morale, possibly to supply a work-force for the Minoan galleys. We know that Minoan ships were rowed as well as sailed. . . . We also know . . . that as many as 600 rowers were required for a fleet. The 'women' were probably on their own because their men were deployed at sea, as galley slaves.

At Knossos, a fragmentary fresco shows a white (i.e. Caucasian) officer exercising a troop of black soldiers at the double. The negroes are probably Nubian slaves given to the Minoans by the Egyptians in exchange for manufactured goods such as pottery and metalwork. At Pylos, slaves were listed in order to make calculations for rations. It seems that significant numbers of the

Pylian slaves were servants of a deity and therefore not ordinary slaves at all. It may well be that at Phaistos, Mallia, Zakro and Knossos many slaves became temple servants—and probably considered themselves fortunate. . . .

RELIGIOUS CEREMONIES AND INITIATIONS

The great public festivals, such as those shown on the Grandstand and Sacred Dance Frescoes at Knossos, played an important part in displaying and reinforcing the social hierarchy. Public ceremonies tend to have this function even in the modern world. . . . It is reasonable, given the fresco evidence, to assume that the Minoans . . . had a range of festivals and religious ceremonies. . . .

In the Theran Naval Festival Fresco, we can see the central, queenly figure of a priestess on a balcony with the sacral horns beside her. Below the town walls a procession of naked, uninitiated youths takes an animal to be sacrificed. Elsewhere there are men in kilts who . . . may be initiated young people of higher social rank; there are common towns-people in tunics, nobles in long robes and rustics in sheepskins. We do not need to believe that rural farm workers actually wore shaggy hide garments as they went about their work, or that boys normally went naked until their manhood initiation; the fresco artist was simply spelling out the concepts of social stratification and of social unification during the festival. Possibly the Theran artist was deliberately focusing on the appropriate dress for certain rituals. For instance, the priest in the harvest festival on the Harvesters Vase is wearing a symbolically bizarre garment; the boys stripped for their initiation rituals, such as boxing, tests of strength, and head-shaving. The girls had their own ritual which took place indoors. . . . Possibly they had to draw blood, symbolizing the onset of menstruation. This is shown graphically by the wounded, bleeding girl sitting on a rock. . . . Her blood sacrifice is shown again in a different way on the wall over the adyton, where sinister, blood-spattered sacral horns stand forbiddingly on top of a blood-spattered altar. . . .

The mainly small-scale, private and intimate ceremonies of initiation undertaken in the temples enabled people to step as individuals and peer-groups from one social, spiritual and status class to another. The transition from childhood to adulthood was probably marked by a graded series of initiation rites. . . . The strong elements of an initiatory character detected in later Cretan society were probably a survival from the Minoan civilization. . . .

The private, small-scale ceremonies took place within the framework of the larger, public ceremonies. In the Cretan towns, many of the private and public rites must have taken place at the great temples. The inner chambers . . . of the temples were places where individual and small-group initiations and rites of passage were conducted. The Central and West Courts were places where the large public ceremonies took place. The Grandstand Fresco appears to show a crowd of spectators . . . gathered in the Central Court of the Knossos Labyrinth. The Sacred Dance Fresco appears from the design of the pavement to have been set in the West Court, either at Knossos or at a similarly designed temple. The temples were thus major foci, socially as well as spiritually.

Again and again, women are shown in dominant roles—in the Theran Naval Festival Fresco, and in the Knossos frescoes too. That priestesses were dominant in the temples cannot be doubted—the Grandstand and Sacred Dance Frescoes make their position very plain—and it is left for us to speculate on the possible role of women in society outside the temple. In state affairs, for instance, were women able to take their place as equals alongside men? Or perhaps even as their superiors? There is no hint in the tablets that women held important political positions, but we know that the picture they give is incomplete. . . . It is tempting to see the powerless Wanax, with his mainly ceremonial role, living in the shadow of a Labyrinth run by powerful priestesses as an earthly parallel to the Minoan myth of a relatively insignificant male god, Velchanos, who was subordinate to a more powerful goddess.

A MYTH REFLECTS REAL EARLY GREEK POLITICS?

PLUTARCH

Because the Bronze Age Greeks left no historical records, almost nothing of a concrete nature is known about political and other interactions between Crete and the mainland or between separate kingdoms. Many scholars suggest that faint echoes of such relations can be found in the famous Greek legend of Theseus and the Labyrinth. The Labyrinth was the huge and complex palace at Knossos, in northern Crete, which was supposedly inhabited by a fierce creature—the Minotaur, half-man and half-bull. In the story, the Cretan overlord, Minos, periodically demands hostages from mainland Athens, where Theseus's father, Aegeus, reigns. Only with the help of the Cretan princess Ariadne does Theseus manage to kill the Minotaur and rescue the hostages. The fullest surviving ancient telling of the story is that of the first century A.D. Greek writer Plutarch, excerpted below (from Ian Scott-Kilvert's translation). Plutarch had access to various ancient synopses and analyses of the legend, now lost, which he refers to regularly in his own version. His mention of battles on land and sea, an agreement signed between Crete and mainland Athens, and tribute (payment acknowledging submission) in the form of hostages paid by the latter, may reflect strained relations between Crete and the mainland, or perhaps Crete's political domination of Athens.

Excerpted from "The Life of Theseus," in *The Rise and Fall of Athens: Nine Greek Lives*, by Plutarch, translated by Ian Scott-Kilvert (Penguin Classics, 1973). Translation copyright © Ian Scott-Kilvert, 1973. Reprinted by permission of Penguin Books Ltd.

S oon after this the collectors arrived from Crete for the third time to take away the customary tribute. Most writers agree that the payment of this tribute originated from the occasion when Androgeus [a Cretan lord] was supposed to have been treacherously murdered in Attic [Athenian] territory. Because of this, not only did Minos carry on a war of devastation against the Athenians, but they were also visited with divine vengeance; the land would not bear fruit, there was a great plague and all the rivers dried up. Apollo then declared to them that if they placated Minos and became reconciled with him, the wrath of heaven would cease and they would be delivered from their sufferings. Thereupon they sent heralds and appealed to Minos and entered into an agreement to send him a tribute every nine years, consisting of seven young men and seven girls. According to the most dramatic version of the story, when these young men and women reached Crete, they were thrown into the Labyrinth and there killed by the Minotaur, or else wandered about and finally perished because they could find no way out. . . .

However, according to [the ancient writer] Philochorus, the Cretans deny this and declare that the Labyrinth was indeed a dungeon, but had nothing wrong with it except that the prisoners could not escape. Minos, they explain, founded funeral games in memory of Androgeus, and the prizes he gave to the victors consisted of these young Athenians, who in the meanwhile were imprisoned in the Labyrinth. . . . Aristotle himself in his treatise *On the Constitution of Bottiaea* evidently does not believe that these young people were put to death by Minos, but that they lived on into old age as slaves in Crete. . . .

So when the time came for the payment of the third tribute, and those fathers, whose sons were not yet married, were obliged to present them so that the victims could be drawn by lot, the cry went up once more against Aegeus. The unhappy people complained that the king, who was the cause of all their troubles, was the only man to be exempted from the penalty; he was content to see them robbed of their lawful children and left destitute, while he made over his kingdom to a bastard son of his own, who was not even an Athenian. Theseus was deeply troubled by this; he thought it only right that he should share the fate of his fellow citizens and not stand aloof from them, and so he came forward and offered to go to Crete himself, regardless of how the lot might fall. The Athenians were struck with admiration at his courage and delighted at his public spirit, and Aegeus, finding that his prayers and entreaties could do nothing to change his son's mind or turn him from his purpose, proceeded to cast lots for the rest. . . .

On the two earlier occasions, there has seemed to be no hope of deliverance, and so the Athenians had sent out their ship with a black sail, believing that it was carrying their youth to certain doom. But this time Theseus urged his father to take heart and boasted that he would overcome the Minotaur, and so Aegeus gave the pilot a second sail, a white one, and ordered him on the return voyage to hoist the white canvas if Theseus were safe, but otherwise to sail with the black as a sign of mourning. . . .

When he [Theseus] arrived in Crete, as most of the historians and poets tell us, Ariadne fell in love with him; it was she who gave him the famous thread and taught him how to find his way through the mazes of the Labyrinth, and there he killed the Minotaur and sailed away with Ariadne and the young Athenians. [The writer] Pherecydes tells us that Theseus also stove in the bottoms of the Cretan ships and thus prevented them from pursuing him. And [the writer] Demon adds that Minos's general Taurus was killed in a naval battle in the harbour as Theseus was sailing away. However, in Philochorus's version, Minos was holding the funeral games and Taurus was expected once again to beat all his rivals, but this success was far from being popular. Taurus's disposition had made his authority hated and there was a scandalous rumour that he was too intimate with Pasiphae, the queen. So when Theseus asked leave to challenge him, Minos granted his request. As it was the custom in Crete for women as well as men to watch the games, Ariadne was present and was not only captivated by Theseus's appearance, but filled with admiration at his strength as he overcame all his opponents. Minos, also, was especially pleased because he had defeated Taurus at wrestling and humiliated him, and so he restored the Athenian youths to Theseus and released Athens from the tribute.

[The writer] Cleidemus, on the other hand, gives an unfamiliar and more ambitious account of these events, which begins a long way back. There was, he says, a decree in force throughout Greece that no trireme should sail from any port carrying a crew of more than five men. The only exception was made for Jason, the commander of the *Argo,* who sailed the seas clearing them of pirates. But when Daedalus escaped from Crete in a merchant ship and made for Athens, Minos, in defiance of the decree, set off in pursuit with his warships and was driven off his course by a storm to Sicily, where he lost his life. His son, Deucalion, who was by no means averse to a war with the Athenians, sent them a message demanding the surrender of Daedalus and threatening, if they refused, to put to death the young Athenians whom Minos had taken as hostages. Theseus replied in mild terms, but declined to give up Daedalus, who was his own cousin and blood-relation, his mother being Merope, the daughter of Erechtheus. In the meantime Theseus set himself to build a fleet, part of it in Attica at the time of Thymoetadae, far away from any public high road, and part of it under the direction of Pittheus at Troezen, as he wanted to keep his plans secret.

When the ships were ready he set out, taking Daedalus and a number of Cretan exiles as his guides. The Cretans had no warning of his movements and supposed that the oncoming fleet was friendly, so that Theseus was able to seize the harbour, disembark his men, and reach Cnossos before his arrival was discovered. There he fought a battle at the gates of the Labyrinth and killed Deucalion and his bodyguard. As Ariadne now succeeded to the throne, he made a truce with her, recovered the young Athenians, and concluded a pact of friendship between the Athenians and the Cretans, who swore that they would never in future begin a war with Athens.

There are many different accounts of these events, and of the story of Ariadne, none of which agree in their details. According to some versions she hanged herself when Theseus deserted her, while others tell us that she was taken to Naxos by sailors, that she lived there with Oenarus, the priest of Dionysus, and that Theseus had abandoned her because he was in love with another woman. . . .

On his way back from Crete, Theseus touched at Delos. There, when he had sacrificed to Apollo and dedicated in his temple the statue of Aphrodite which he had received from Ariadne, he and the Athenian youths with him executed a dance, which they say is still performed by the people of Delos, and which consists of a series of serpentine figures danced in regular time and representing the winding passages of the Labyrinth. The Delians call this kind of dance the Crane, according to Dicaearchus, and Theseus danced it round the altar known as the Keraton, which is made of horns all taken from the left side of the head. They also say that Theseus founded games at Delos and that he began there the practice of giving a palm to the victors.

The story goes that as they approached the shore of Attica Theseus was so overcome by joy that he forgot, and so, too, did his pilot, to hoist the sail which was to signal their safe return to Aegeus and he in despair threw himself down from the cliff and was killed. Theseus meanwhile put in to the shore and himself offered up the sacrifices he had vowed to the gods at Phalerum when he sailed away, and sent a herald to announce his homecoming. The messenger found many of the people mourning the king's death, and others who were naturally enough overjoyed and ready to welcome him and crown him with garlands for their deliverance. He accepted the garlands and wreathed them around his herald's staff, but on his return to the seashore, he found that Theseus had not yet poured his libations to the gods, and so, as he did not wish to disturb the sacrifice, he waited outside the precinct. Then after the libations had been made, he announced the news of Aegeus's death, whereupon Theseus and his companions hurried with cries and lamentations into the city. So it is, the tradition says, that to this very day at the festival of the Oschophoria the Athenians do not crown the herald himself, but his staff, and at the libations; the bystanders cry out 'Eleleu! Eleleu!': the first of these is the cry of eager haste or of triumph, the second of trouble or confusion.

THE POET: HOMER ESTABLISHES WESTERN LITERATURE

MICHAEL GRANT

Greek literature, and indeed all of Western literature, begins with Homer's *Iliad* and *Odyssey*. The first of these masterful epic poems revolves around the wrath of Achilles, the most formidable warrior among the Greek chieftains who besieged the city of Troy (in northwestern Asia Minor). The *Odyssey* follows the adventures of another of these chieftains, the crafty Odysseus (king of the island kingdom of Ithaca) in the decade following Troy's fall. This highly informative examination of "the Poet" (as the ancients referred to Homer) and his timeless works (including brief synopses of their plots) is from *The Rise of the Greeks*, by the prolific and popular classical historian Michael Grant.

A number of cities in the eastern Aegean area claimed to be the birthplace of Homer, to whom the *Iliad* and *Odyssey* were ascribed, and internal evidence from the poems—especially their vivid, varied similes—indicates that this coastal area was the region of their origin. . . .

The most convincing claims to Homer's birthplace were those of Chios and Smyrna, and despite the contradictory and fragmentary nature of our sources . . . it seems probable that, although he may have been born at Smyrna, he lived and worked on Chios . . . later the dwelling-place of the guild of the Homeridae, devoted to reciting his poetry, who claimed to have originated from his descendants. In the seventh century the poet Semonides ascribes a passage of the *Iliad* to 'the man of Chios', and at about the same time the Pythian (Delphic) section of the *Hymn to Apollo* . . . speaks of him as a supreme poet who 'dwelt in rocky Chios' and was blind. . . .

DATING THE EPICS

The poems seem to have reached their final, or nearly final, form in *c.* 750/700 BC—more than 200 years, that is to say, after the arrival of the Ionians upon the island of Chios, and half a millennium later than the supposed events that their poet purported to describe. . . . Shorter lays by earlier anonymous or at least unknown poets, which were evidently combined and amended by Homer to form parts of the *Iliad* and *Odyssey,* may already, before his time, have been amalgamated into longer units, pointing the way towards the two complete epics that subsequently emerged during the vast period that extended between the alleged date of the Trojan War and the time of eventual compilation and composition. But on the whole it seems more likely that the amalgamation of these shorter works into the majestic, complex structure of the two great epics should be regarded as the specific achievement of Homer.

During the intervening centuries, the bards who gave performances had been illiterate, but the vanished songs that they sang had been orally transmitted from one generation to another. They no doubt included numerous recurrent formulas which served as mnemonic guides and landmarks to help the impromptu singers; and such formulas—epithets, phrases and word groups ('rosy-fingered dawn', 'wine-dark sea'), in addition to whole set themes and action sequences—continued to abound in the *Iliad* and *Odyssey.* Indeed, their 28,000 lines include 25,000 of these repetitive formulaic units.

Exhaustive efforts, with the aid of every archaeological technique, to date the objects, institutions, customs and rituals described in Homer's poems have produced mixed results, leading, above all, to the conclusion that he was not concerned to reproduce the features and values of any actual society which existed, or had existed, at any specific date. For, whereas his verses include certain allusions, of a more or less garbled character, to the Mycenaean way of life that had come to an end so long ago . . . there are other, more numerous (though far from systematic) references to the poet's own eighth-century surroundings. On the other hand, a number of further elements derive neither from recollections of the long-past Mycenaean age nor from phenomena existent in the poet's own time, but from a wide variety of chronological points during the half-millennium intervening between those two epochs. Other episodes evidently reflect no historic period at all, and are timeless.

Homer was apparently assisted towards his supreme achievement by a stroke of fortune: for his lifetime seems to have coincided with the reintroduction of writing into the Greek world. In this situation the poet, providentially personifying the impact of a literate upon an illiterate culture, may have utilized this new technique in person, and committed his verses to writing (or, more probably, dictated them to others who could write)—an opportunity which helped him, beyond measure, to create coherent, monumental poetic structures far beyond the reach of his oral predecessors.

Nevertheless, it was the antique oral tradition of which he himself was still the heir, and he no doubt composed his poetry for (and perhaps partly while) reciting or chanting aloud, accompanying his words with a simple form of lyre (*citharis, phorminx*). These performances may have taken place at noblemen's feasts or at a major festival, such as the Pan-Ionian meetings on Mount Mycale. On such an occasion, one of the two epics could have been recited in about fifteen two-hour sessions, that is to say during the course of three or four days.

The poems that these audiences were privileged to hear were miracles of clarity, directness and speed, and contain some of the most exciting and moving passages ever composed, as well as many delicate touches of sophisticated humour. . . .

THE STORY OF THE *ILIAD*

The *Iliad* narrates events that supposedly took place at some distance to the north of the poet's own home-country, in the neighbourhood of Ilium (Troy) on the Asian mainland, overlooking the Hellespont (Dardanelles). The poem describes a brief and late stage in the siege of Troy by the combined armies of numerous states of the Achaeans (as Homer calls these pre-Dorian peoples of the Greek homeland), commanded by Agamemnon, king of Mycenae. In association with his brother Menelaus of Sparta, he had prompted the leaders of other Achaean states to join this naval expedition against the Trojan monarch Priam because Paris, one of Priam's sons, had abducted Menelaus' wife, the beautiful Helen.

For nine years the Greek troops have been encamped beside their fleet outside the walls of Troy. But they have not, so far, been able to capture the city, although they have seized and plundered a number of neighbouring towns, mainly under the leadership of Achilles, prince of the Myrmidons of Thessaly, the most formidable and unruly of Agamemnon's allies. The loot from one of these townships provokes a quarrel between Achilles and his commander-in-chief. The dispute concerns Chryseis, a girl whom the Achaeans have made captive. She has been allocated to Agamemnon as his prize, but he is reluctantly compelled to return her to her father Chryses, in order to propitiate the anger of [the god] Apollo. . . . Agamemnon seeks compensation by taking possession, instead, of a girl named Briseis, who was one of the prizes of Achilles, whereupon Achilles furiously withdraws from the battle against the Trojans, taking his Myrmidon followers with him. This is the wrath which forms the first word of the poem, and it is a wrath, as Homer pronounced, which enveloped countless other Achaeans in disaster.

A truce between the two armies, designed to enable Menelaus and Paris to settle their dispute by single combat, comes to nothing, and the war is resumed. Lacking the aid of Achilles, however, the Achaeans find themselves hard-pressed, but Achilles still refuses to help, despite an offer of handsome amends from Agamemnon. A rampart the Achaean soldiers are forced to construct around their ships and living quarters is stormed by Priam's son Hector. At this juncture Achilles relents to the extent of allowing his beloved older friend and associate Patroclus . . . to lead the Myrmidons to the rescue of their endangered compatriots. Patroclus is successful, but he dashes too far ahead, and meets his death at the hands of Hector beneath the city walls.

Thereupon, convulsed by grief and fury, Achilles himself finally enters the fray once again, throws the fleeing Trojans back into their city, slays Hector and savagely ill-treats his corpse, thus carrying his anger beyond the bounds of humanity. However, the dead man's father, Priam, in his sorrow, is prompted by Zeus to visit Achilles in his camp at night, in order to appeal for the return of his son's body. Achilles concedes his request, and the poem ends with Hector's funeral, amid an uneasy truce.

OF HEROES AND GODS

Excavations confirm that the small but advantageously located fortress of later Bronze Age Troy ('Troy VIIA') was destroyed in c.1250/1200. Its destroyers *may* have been products of the Mycenaean culture from the Greek mainland—speaking a form of Greek—though this cannot be confirmed. But the Mycenaean civilization itself (together with the form of writing that it practised) collapsed not long afterwards, and it was not . . . until five hundred years later that the *Iliad* and *Odyssey* assumed approximately their present shape.

Nevertheless, this great distance of time did nothing to frustrate Homer's unparalleled descriptive talent. With lively yet disengaged comprehension, each personage is depicted as a distinct individual. The most arresting is Achilles, who possesses in extreme degree all the virtues and faults of a Homeric hero, and most completely embodies the heroic code of honour. A hero, as reconstructed by Homer . . . dedicated his entire existence, with all the aid that his birth and wealth and physical prowess could afford him, to an unceasing, violently competitive, vengeful struggle to win applause, together with the material goods which were its standard of measurement, by excelling among his peers, especially in battle, which was his principal occupation (though oratory also ranked high).

Yet the *Iliad*, at times, seems to debate rather than lay down such principles of heroic conduct. This lust and zest for fighting, which at its zenith seemed to elevate the heroes to a pinnacle not too far short of the gods, is overshadowed by pathos: for they still have no way of escaping the mortal, fatal destiny that awaits them.

This destiny is identified with (or occasionally overrides) those very gods themselves. . . . Amoral, unedifying, they squabble sordidly as they divide their support between the two warring sides in the Trojan War, and strike out viciously in sporadic, frightening, often unpredictable interventions. That is partly why a sense of the fragility of all human endeavour pervades the *Iliad*. The gods never die, but death pounces, in the end, upon men and heroes on earth, becoming the ultimate test of merit, the final and most searching ordeal and fulfilment. Achilles knows he has not long to live: and when, at the deeply moving end of the poem, he meets old Priam, whose son Hector he has slain, the exultant din of war has faded into misery and compassion.

Hector, although he made military mistakes and was inferior to Achilles, had been a noble hero (and a noble enemy of the Greeks), in whom warlike and elegiac elements are blended together. Agamemnon and Menelaus are flawed. There are authentic women in the *Iliad*. The last meeting of Andromache with her doomed husband Hector is poignant. As for Helen (transformed from a moon-goddess into the most seductive of human beings), she was responsible for everything, since it was only because of her that the war had ever taken place.

THE STORY TOLD IN THE *ODYSSEY*

The *Odyssey* tells of Odysseus' return to his home on the island of Ithaca from the Trojan War. His mythical wanderings lasted for ten years, but the action narrated concerns only the last six weeks of this time. At the outset of the poem, he has come to the island of the goddess Calypso, who compels him to stay there as her lover for nearly eight years, in spite of his longing to get back to Ithaca. There, in the meantime, his son Telemachus has grown up, and his home is filled with uninvited guests, the suitors of his wife Penelope. Eating and drinking at the expense of their absent host, they continually urge her to marry again and eventually insist that she must now choose one or another of themselves.

Odysseus owes his troubles to the enmity of [the sea god] Poseidon, for in the course of his travels he had blinded the god's son, the Cyclops Polyphemus. While Poseidon is away, however, the other gods and goddesses are convinced by the hero's staunch patron, Athena, that they should show him pity and render him assistance. She directs Telemachus to visit Pylos (the kingdom of Nestor) and Sparta (to which Menelaus and Helen had by now returned home) in order to seek information about his father's whereabouts. Meanwhile, Zeus commands Calypso to release her captive. He constructs a raft and sets out, but Poseidon creates a storm, and his ship is wrecked. Eventually, after terrible experiences, he is cast up on the coast of Scheria, inhabited by a well-conducted people, the Phaeacians. On reaching the shore he encounters the princess Nausicaa, and she leads him to the palace of her father, the king of the Phaeacians, Alcinous.

During a banquet in Odysseus' honour, the hero describes his travels and adventures since leaving captured Troy. He tells of his perilous encounters with Lotus-Eaters, Polyphemus, the wind-god Aeolus, the cannibal Laestrygones, the witch Circe, the phantoms of the dead . . . the Sirens, monstrous Scylla and the whirlpool Charybdis. And Odysseus describes, too, how his men had eaten the cattle of the sun-god Helios, paying for this sacrilege by a storm which destroyed them, so that only he himself had survived to make his way to the island of Calypso, and thence later to come ashore on Scheria.

Soon afterwards, despite continuing divine wrath, the Phaeacians arrange his transportation to Ithaca, where, unheroically disguised as a grimy beggar, he discovers how Penelope's suitors have been behaving in his absence. Guided by Athena, Telemachus gets back to the island from Sparta, and so Odysseus and his son, reunited, plan the destruction of their unwelcome guests. In Odysseus' palace, there is no recognition of the returned hero except from his dog (which thereupon closes its eyes in death) and his nurse Eurycleia. Penelope, once again pressed by the suitors to remarry one of their number, proposes an archery contest, allegedly to enable her to make her choice, but no one except Odysseus can string his own mighty bow. He himself, however, contrives to get hold of the weapon, and lets fly a volley of arrows to massacre the suitors. Then Penelope identifies her long-lost husband, and Odysseus rules his island kingdom once again.

A WORK OF QUIETER VIRTUES

Although tacked on to traditions of the Trojan War in order to justify its epic form, the *Odyssey* is founded on a standard folktale: the story of the man who is away for so long that he is believed to be dead, and yet eventually, after fantastic adventures, returns home and rejoins his faithful wife. Dozens of other wondrous ancient stories, often displaying near-eastern analogies, are transformed and incorporated into the fabric of this most exciting of poems.

The *Odyssey* resembles the *Iliad* in its commendation of physical courage, and a savage pleasure in bloodshed is by no means lacking. However, there has been a shift (if the *Odyssey* is the later of the two poems) from the doom-fraught heights of passionate heroism towards quieter virtues such as endurance and self-control and patience, while love of comrades and of honour now seems to take second place to love of home and wife—the other type of woman, who menaces male society, being rejected in the person of Circe. In a picture that oscillates between kingship and the aristocratic regimes which sometimes or often, it would seem, succeeded monarchical systems, our attention is engaged by the social and family lives of the noble landowners, living on their estates. And stress is placed on good breeding, courtliness and hospitable guest-friendship, with its elaborate web of gifts and countergifts. Nor are humbler folk, such as beggars and suppliants, ignored; more distinctive than the dim soldier-assemblymen of the *Iliad*, they are individually protected by a Zeus who is concerned, to this extent, with morality.

But before the poet comes to the more static second half of the *Odyssey*, in which such themes predominate, the hero is tossed upon many seas, and thrown up on strange lands. . . .

This archetypal wanderer, the formidable, unconquerably strong and enduring Odysseus, cleverer and more resourceful, too, than any other Homeric hero . . . is the permanent exemplar of the complete man who has struggled against all the hazards of life and has vanquished them, one after another—thus finding out many things, and discovering himself. For all Odysseus' sturdy independence, however, a novel note in Greek thinking (and religion) is struck by the exclusive, protective companionship, admiring and often humorous, that is lavished upon him by the goddess Athena.

The magical Circe, too, is vividly delineated, and so is amorous Calypso, the pair whose sexual domination over Odysseus for a time shockingly reversed, in the Greek view, the natural process. But fully developed personalities are for the first time accorded to females who are human beings and not witches, notably Nausicaa and, above all, the complex, ingenious and resolutely chaste Penelope. Women, it is true, are often still not much more than masculine chattels, dependent on their husbands' prowess. Yet they play a major part in the social system, since they are able to link powerful families in alliance, evoking rich presents.

Moreover, watching and enduring on the sidelines, they possess minds and characters of their own, interpreting the significances and consequences of masculine actions. Less of a sexual chauvinist than almost any other male writer of antiquity, Homer gives his women some freedom. . . .

A GREAT CIVILIZING INFLUENCE

Once composed, the *Iliad* and *Odyssey* in due course became the property of a guild or clan of reciters, practitioners of the most skilled Ionian craft of the age. These, as we saw earlier, were the Homeridae—prototypes and models of those professional reciters of poetry the rhapsodes, named after the *rhabdos* (baton) which they held in their hands instead of singing to the lyre. Possibly, in origin, singers of Homer's own circle, the Homeridae claimed to be his descendants, and belonged to the island of Chios. But they and the rhapsodes after them also travelled . . . so that knowledge of the *Iliad* and *Odyssey* spread rapidly.

And indeed, throughout the entire subsequent millennium of ancient history, these two poems . . . divided into twenty-four books each in the third century BC—supplied the Greeks with their greatest civilizing influence, and formed the foundation of their literary, artistic, moral, social, educational and political attitudes. For a long time, no histories of early times seemed at all necessary, since the *Iliad* and *Odyssey* fulfilled every requirement. They attracted universal esteem and reverence, too, as sources of general and practical wisdom, as arguments for heroic yet human nobility and dignity, as incentives to vigorous . . . manly action, and as mines of endless quotations and commentaries: the common property of all Greeks everywhere.

DEATH OF A HERO: ACHILLES SLAYS HECTOR

HOMER

Following is one of the most famous and memorable scenes from Homer's *Iliad*, taken from the widely acclaimed translation by Robert Fagles of Princeton University. Achilles (son of Peleus), greatest of the Greek warriors besieging Troy, seeks revenge against the Trojan champion Hector (son of Priam, king of Troy), who slew Achilles' closest friend, Patroclus. In their battle to the death, Achilles and Hector each hope that Zeus (leader of the gods) and the other gods will come to his aid. This mode of warfare, namely champions fighting one-on-one, is characteristic of warriors in this and other stories from Greece's Age of Heroes, which modern scholars know to be the late Bronze Age.

Now, at last, as the two came closing for the kill
it was tall Hector, helmet flashing, who led off:
"No more running from you in fear, Achilles!
Not as before. Three times I fled around
the great city of Priam—I lacked courage then
to stand your onslaught. Now my spirit stirs me
to meet you face-to-face. Now kill or be killed!
Come, we'll swear to the gods, the highest witnesses—
the gods will oversee our binding pacts. I swear
I will never mutilate you—merciless as you are—
if Zeus allows me to last it out and tear your life away.
But once I've stripped your glorious armor, Achilles,

I will give your body back to your loyal comrades.
Swear you'll do the same."

A swift dark glance
and the headstrong runner answered, "Hector, stop!
You unforgivable, you . . . don't talk to me of pacts.
There are no binding oaths between men and lions—
wolves and lambs can enjoy no meeting of the minds—
they are all bent on hating each other to the death.
So with you and me. No love between us. No truce
till one or the other falls and gluts with blood
Ares [god of war] who hacks at men behind his rawhide
   shield.
Come, call up whatever courage you can muster.
Life or death—now prove yourself a spearman,
a daring man of war! No more escape for you—
Athena [goddess of war and wisdom] will kill you with
   my spear in just a moment.
Now you'll pay at a stroke for all my comrades' grief,
all you killed in the fury of your spear!"

A CONTEST OF SPEARS

With that,
shaft poised, he hurled and his spear's long shadow flew
but seeing it coming glorious Hector ducked away,
crouching down, watching the bronze tip fly past
and stab the earth—but Athena snatched it up
and passed it back to Achilles
and Hector the gallant captain never saw her.
He sounded out a challenge to Peleus' princely son:
"You missed, look—the great godlike Achilles!
So you knew nothing at all from Zeus about my death—
and yet how sure you were! All bluff, cunning with words,
that's all you are—trying to make me fear you,
lose my nerve, forget my fighting strength.
Well, you'll never plant your lance in my back
as I flee *you* in fear—plunge it through my chest
as I come charging in, if a god gives you the chance!
But now it's for you to dodge *my* brazen spear—
I wish you'd bury it in your body to the hilt.
How much lighter the war would be for Trojans then
if you, their greatest scourge, were dead and gone!"

Shaft poised, he hurled and his spear's long shadow flew
and it struck Achilles' shield—a dead-center hit—
but off and away it glanced and Hector seethed,

his hurtling spear, his whole arm's power poured
in a wasted shot. He stood there, cast down . . .
he had no spear in reserve. So Hector shouted out
to Deiphobus [another Trojan prince] bearing his white
    shield—with a ringing shout
he called for a heavy lance—
                        but the man was nowhere near him,
vanished—
            yes and Hector knew the truth in his heart
and the fighter cried aloud, "My time has come!
At last the gods have called me down to death.
I thought he was at my side, the hero Deiphobus—
he's safe inside the walls, Athena's tricked me blind.
And now death, grim death is looming up beside me,
no longer far away. No way to escape it now. This,
this was their pleasure after all, sealed long ago—
Zeus and the son of Zeus, the distant deadly Archer—
though often before now they rushed to my defense.
So now I meet my doom. Well let me die—
but not without struggle, not without glory, no,
in some great clash of arms that even men to come
will hear of down the years!"

A Mortal Wound

                                    And on that resolve
he drew the whetted sword that hung at his side,
tempered, massive, and gathering all his force
he swooped like a soaring eagle
launching down from the dark clouds to earth
to snatch some helpless lamb or trembling hare.
So Hector swooped now, swinging his whetted sword
and Achilles charged too, bursting with rage, barbaric,
guarding his chest with the well-wrought blazoned shield,
head tossing his gleaming helmet, four horns strong
and the golden plumes shook that the god of fire
drove in bristling thick along its ridge.
Bright as that star amid the stars in the night sky,
star of the evening, brightest star that rides the heavens,
so fire flared from the sharp point of the spear Achilles
brandished high in his right hand, bent on Hector's death,
scanning his splendid body—where to pierce it best?
The rest of his flesh seemed all encased in armor,
burnished, brazen—*Achilles'* armor that Hector stripped
from strong Patroclus when he killed him—true,
but one spot lay exposed,

where collarbones lift the neckbone off the shoulders,
the open throat, where the end of life comes quickest—*there*
as Hector charged in fury brilliant Achilles drove his spear
and the point went stabbing clean through the tender neck
but the heavy bronze weapon failed to slash the windpipe—
Hector could still gasp out some words, some last reply . . .
he crashed in the dust—
                              godlike Achilles gloried over him:
"Hector—surely you thought when you stripped Patroclus'
    armor
that you, you would be safe! Never a fear of me—
far from the fighting as I was—you fool!
Left behind there, down by the beaked ships
his great avenger waited, a greater man by far—
that man was I, and I smashed your strength! And you—
the dogs and birds will maul you, shame your corpse
while Achaeans bury my dear friend in glory!"

Struggling for breath, Hector, his helmet flashing,
said, "I beg you, beg you by your life, your parents—
don't let the dogs devour me by the Argive ships!
Wait, take the princely ransom of bronze and gold,
the gifts my father and noble mother will give you—
but give my body to friends to carry home again,
so Trojan men and Trojan women can do me honor
with fitting rites of fire once I am dead."

Staring grimly, the proud runner Achilles answered,
"Beg no more, you fawning dog—begging me by my parents!
Would to god my rage, my fury would drive me now
to hack your flesh away and eat you raw—
such agonies you have caused me! Ransom?
No man alive could keep the dog-packs off you,
not if they haul in ten, twenty times that ransom
and pile it here before me and promise fortunes more—
no, not even if Dardan Priam should offer to weigh out
your bulk in gold! Not even then will your noble mother
lay you on your deathbed, mourn the son she bore . . .
The dogs and birds will rend you—blood and bone!"

HECTOR'S DEATH

At the point of death, Hector, his helmet flashing,
said, "I know you well—I see my fate before me.
Never a chance that I could win you over . . .
Iron inside your chest, that heart of yours.

But now beware, or my curse will draw god's wrath
upon your head, that day when [the Trojan prince] Paris
    and lord Apollo [god of light]—
for all your fighting heart—destroy you at the Scaean
Gates!"

    Death cut him short. The end closed in around him.
Flying free of his limbs
his soul went winging down to the House of Death,
wailing his fate, leaving his manhood far behind,
his young and supple strength. But brilliant Achilles
taunted Hector's body, dead as he was, "Die, die!
For my own death, I'll meet it freely—whenever Zeus
and the other deathless gods would like to bring it on!"

    With that he wrenched his bronze spear from the corpse,
laid it aside and ripped the bloody armor off the back.
And the other sons of Achaea, running up around him,
crowded closer, all of them gazing wonder-struck
at the build and marvelous, lithe beauty of Hector.
And not a man came forward who did not stab his body,
glancing toward a comrade, laughing: "Ah, look here—
how much softer he is to handle now, this Hector,
than when he gutted our ships with roaring fire!"

ARCHAIC GREECE: A PEOPLE ON THE VERGE OF GREATNESS

DON NARDO

The splendid Greek culture that burst upon the scene in the fifth century B.C. and produced democracy, the Parthenon, *Oedipus Rex*, and the philosophers Socrates and Plato appeared neither miraculously nor overnight; instead, like the early Sumerians, Egyptians, Chinese, Assyrians, Jews, Romans, and others, the Greeks underwent a centuries-long development process in which they slowly accumulated the customs, ideas, skills, and achievements necessary to build a strong, successful civilization. That formative process began in the years following the collapse of Greece's Bronze Age Mycenaean kingdoms (ca.1200–1100 B.C.) and lasted until the beginning of the Persian Wars (early fifth century B.C.). In the following essay, I present a concise overview of pre-classical Greece, covering life in the Dark Age, the rise of city-states and a new class of independent farmers, the emergence of writing, literature, and philosophy, widespread colonization of distant shores, and a great deal of political experimentation. All of these developments, along with others, set the stage for the emergence of the first great—and still the most influential—society produced by Western civilization.

Modern historians divide the roughly six hundred years following the collapse of Greece's Bronze Age society into two broad historical periods. In the first, the Dark Age (ca. 1100–ca. 800 B.C.), Greek civilization was in a sense sleep-

Reprinted from *The Ancient Greeks,* by Don Nardo (San Diego: Lucent Books, 2001) with permission.

ing within a cultural cocoon and quietly reinventing itself; in the second of the two periods, the Archaic Age (ca. 800–ca. 500 B.C.), it awakened and began to reach for new horizons, eventually surpassing the achievements of prior ages. New communities, called city-states, arose all over the Greek sphere—some of these states boldly planted colonies on distant Mediterranean shores— and Greek artists and architects began to develop the skills and styles that would later reach maturity in one of history's greatest cultural golden ages.

During these same years, Homer's epic poems appeared and became widely known. These works not only provided the Greeks with a link to a dimly remembered cultural past, but also reminded them that, regardless of political and other differences, they all spoke the same language and worshiped the same gods. Besides the Homeric poems, very little literature was produced in the Dark and Archaic Ages: most of what *was* produced was not written down; and most of what was written down has not survived. So the chief sources of evidence for this still somewhat obscure part of the Greek saga are archaeological—the remains of pottery, tools, weapons, houses, tombs, temples, sunken ships, and so forth.

WHY THE DARK AGE WAS DARK

Unfortunately, even archaeological evidence remains scarce for the Greek Dark Age, which is so labeled partly for this very reason; hence scholars still know very little for certain about life in this period. It also appears to have been "dark" in the sense that civilization temporarily declined during its early years. For the most part, Greek society experienced a general loss of literacy, major decreases in population (for at least the first century or so), widespread poverty, and an overall deterioration of both the standard of living and cultural standards.

These negative developments were, of course, the result of the collapse of the Bronze Age Mycenaean political and administrative apparatus between ca. 1200 and ca. 1100 B.C. In short, the palace-centered bureaucracies were vital to society because they had become the main means of maintaining record keeping, collective agriculture, and architectural and artistic skills; and when they disappeared, there was nothing to replace them. "It seems clear," writes University of Missouri scholar William R. Biers,

> that the mainland palaces represented the heart of the Mycenaean system, and when that system ceased to exist, society changed. When the palaces fell, their bureaucracy disappeared, and with them the need for and eventually the knowledge of writing. The same

thing happened to large-scale architecture and representational art.

Still, Greece was neither primitive nor stagnant during the Dark Age. As early as the mid- to late eleventh century B.C., new ideas and skills were filtering in from the outside. The most obvious example is the introduction of iron smelting (from the Near East, where it had long been known; probably via Cyprus, the large island lying south of Asia Minor), which spread across Greece between ca. 1050 and ca. 950. This was a major advance, since tools and weapons made of iron are tougher and keep their edges better than those made of bronze.

The early Dark Age was also a time of large population movements. The reasons for these migrations are far from clear, but many mainland Greeks appear to have been displaced by other migrants who were *entering* Greece, including a tribal people, the Dorians, from the Balkan region south of the Danube River. Most of those who were displaced crossed the Aegean and settled on the coasts of western Asia Minor. This area, in which dozens of Greek communities eventually grew and prospered, later came to be called Ionia. Other mainlanders may have migrated in search of better farmland and other opportunities for a fresh start.

Dark Age Society and Its Leaders

Social and political life during the Dark Age was centered on individual villages (in contrast to the citylike palace-centers of Mycenaean times). The local leader was known as the *basileus.* "The Greek word *basileus,*" Sarah B. Pomeroy and her colleagues write,

> is usually translated as "king" wherever it appears in literature, including [Homer's] *Iliad* and *Odyssey*. It would be misleading, however, to call the Dark Age leaders "kings," a title that conjures up in the modern mind visions of monarchs with autocratic powers. A more appropriate name for the Dark Age *basileus* is the ... term "chief," which suggests a man with far less power than a king. The *basileus*, nevertheless, was a man of great stature and importance in the community. ... The construction and renovations of the chieftains' homes required the time and labor of a substantial number of persons, unlike the ordinary houses, which could be built by the occupants themselves. The chiefs' houses may also have had some communal functions.

Archaeologists discovered the remains of a powerful Dark Age chieftain, his wife, and possibly their house in 1981 at Lefkandi, a site in the western part of Euboea (the large island lying along the eastern coast of the Greek mainland). The centerpiece of the find was a finely decorated bronze amphora (jar) containing a man's ashes. These cremated remains were wrapped in strips of cloth, some of which have survived in an excellent state of preservation. (Physical examination of the cloth, coupled with comparisons to painted depictions of cloth on vases, has greatly increased knowledge of early Greek textiles.) Beside the amphora rested an exquisite iron sword and spearhead, which surely only a well-to-do or powerful person could have afforded to own at that time. Also close beside this burial were two others—the skeleton of a woman who had been buried wearing a golden necklace and other fine jewelry, and the skeletons of four horses, probably the man's chariot team.

These magnificent burials, clearly those of socially prominent individuals, were made beneath the floor of a large houselike structure that was deliberately knocked down and covered by a mound of earth and stones directly after the funeral. The largest Dark Age building yet discovered, the structure, erected ca. 1000 B.C., measured about 146 by 30 feet and had a high roof supported by wooden pillars. Although it may have served as the chief's home and/or served some communal functions, its connection to the burials and the manner of its destruction suggest that it was also a *heroon*, a special site designed to honor or worship the memory of a hero or royal personage.

Scholarly opinion generally holds that the large size of the Lefkandi building and the unusual finery attending the burials it contained were exceptional for the early Dark Age. If so, the buried man, sometimes referred to as the "Hero of Lefkandi," may have been the leader of a small pocket of Mycenaean society that had survived the catastrophe of the previous century. Such a situation is not all that surprising; for scholars have long suspected that the Mycenaean settlement at Athens also survived the upheavals for a while, until the inhabitants slowly lost most of their heritage and began to build a new culture. Archaeologists may eventually bring to light other temporary pockets of Mycenaean survival, succeeding, as they did at Lefkandi, in making the Dark Age seem a little less dark.

It is almost certain that most of the Dark Age villages and their leaders were a good deal less splendid than those at Lefkandi. The political or governing institutions for villages and groups of villages described in Homer's epics, which scholars believe roughly reflect average examples from the late Dark Age, were fairly simple. A group of local chiefs, headed by an overall chief, met in a council (*boule*) to decide policy for the whole community or people (*demos*). To achieve a consensus in the community, the chiefs presented their ideas and decisions to an assembly of the fighting men, who gave their approval. The overall chief probably also led public sacrifices to the gods and conducted "diplomatic" relations with chiefs from neighboring regions. As portrayed in Homer's works, society was male dominated and generally characterized by a competitive spirit, the desire to be recognized as "best" (*aristos*) and thereby to acquire honor and respect (*time*). As would prevail in later ages in much of Greece, women had no political voice and for the most part obeyed the rules set by their fathers, husbands, and other male relatives.

THE TRANSFORMATION OF FARMING AND FIGHTING

Eventually, Greek society began to grow more complex, vigorous, prosperous, bold, and creative, marking the start of one of history's most profound economic, political, and cultural transformations. First, during the late Dark Age and early Archaic Age, the population began to rise again, which helped to spur important agricultural developments. These included more intensive cultivation of olives and vines and a corresponding reduction in the prevalence of pastoralism (the raising and herding of livestock), which had been the main means of food production in Mycenaean times and the early Dark Age.

Agricultural changes promoted the spread of small independent farmers, who created a veritable revolution in agriculture, and warfare as well. Noted classical scholar Victor D. Hanson calls it "an enormous transformation . . . nothing less than the creation of an entire class, which through sheer preponderance of numbers overwhelmed" the chiefs and other traditional aristocratic rulers. This class, one unlike any the world had yet seen, was made up of tough, independent men who neither needed nor wanted control by aristocratic or other ruling elites.

These self-reliant farmers became not only the economic backbone of the typical community, but also the source of its military strength. The practice of individual farmers, and later small communities of farmers, taking up arms to protect their lands, private property, and heritage against aggressors (most often other farmers) steadily led to the development of citizen militias. By the seventh century B.C., well-organized military units and tactics had developed, built around heavily armored infantry soldiers called hoplites, who wielded thrusting spears and short swords. The hoplites fought in a special formation known as a phalanx, most often composed of eight ranks, or rows, of soldiers. When standing in close order, their uplifted shields created a formidable unbroken protective barrier. As the formation marched toward an enemy, the men in the front rank jabbed their spears at their opponents, while the hoplites in the rear ranks pushed at their comrades' backs, giving the whole unit a tremendous and lethal forward momentum. The members of local phalanxes, full-time farmers and part-time but highly effective fighters, Hanson states, "helped to establish agrarian control of the political life of their respective" communities.

AN IMMENSELY FERTILE AGE

At the same time that these independent farmers and fighters were emerging, Greece was growing increasingly prosperous and steadily rising from its formerly backward state. Once again, scholars know this because of archaeological discoveries, especially excavations of grave sites. The sharp rise in prosperity near the end of the Dark Age "can be seen in the number of luxury goods that now turn up in graves," Biers explains.

> Imports [from foreign lands] are also found again [for the first time since the end of the Bronze Age], and precious metals reappear. Thin bands of gold foil shaped by being hammered in stone molds appear in Athens in the ninth century [B.C.]. . . . By the second half of the eighth century [B.C.] they were being decorated with animal friezes [decorative strips containing carvings or sculptures], which are generally considered to indicate [Near] Eastern influence.

Another Near Eastern import, an alphabet borrowed from the Phoenicians (a maritime trading people who inhabited the coasts of Palestine), made possible the reemergence of reading and writing in Greece. In turn, this led to the beginnings of written literature, including the commission of Homer's epics to paper (actually papyrus, a parchment made from an aquatic plant) some time in the Archaic Age.

The immensely fertile Archaic Age witnessed a veritable host of other economic and cultural developments. Accompanying the return of literacy was the expression of new, more rational (what might be termed scientific) views about the universe, as opposed to traditional supernatural conceptions. In the late seventh century B.C., Thales of Miletus (the leading city of Ionia), perhaps the world's first philosopher-scientist, theorized that everything in the natural world might be a form of one universal, underlying physical substance; and he is said to have invented geometry, based partially on Egyptian mathematical ideas. The Archaic Greeks also began to develop monumental architecture, most conspicuously in religious temples, which were at first made of wood but eventually of stone. In addition, the on-going expansion of both the population and foreign trade set in motion a burst of colonization. In the late 700s and early 600s B.C., settlers from various Greek cities established new towns along many of the coasts of the Mediterranean and Black Seas. Still an-other hallmark of the Archaic Age was the growth of Panhel-lenism, the concept that all Greeks were culturally united, if not politically so. This concept was exemplified by shrines, oracles, and athletic games attended by all Greeks, including the famous shrine and oracle at Delphi (in central Greece), which dispensed divine prophecies, and the Olympic Games, initiated, according to tradition, in 776 B.C.

WIDESPREAD POLITICAL EXPERIMENTATION

Meanwhile, the Archaic Age was also a time of political growth and experimentation and the crucial formative period of Greek democratic institutions. The region's many isolated communities, which had developed separate, individual identities during the Dark Age, emerged as full-blown city-states in the eighth century B.C. The Greeks called the city-state the polis (plural is poleis). Most typically, each polis consisted of a town built around a cen-tral hill, or acropolis, and surrounded by small villages and farm-land. But though the majority of city-states had such physical similarities and felt linked by their common language, religious beliefs, and heritage of myths from the Age of Heroes, they evolved differing local governments and traditions. This is why they came to think of themselves as tiny separate nations and were so often reluctant to unite.

A crucial part of what differentiated the polis of Archaic and later times from the simple Dark Age community was the de-velopment of increasingly sophisticated political institutions to meet the needs of a local people. In most states, power passed from the hands of chieftains to ruling councils composed of sev-eral community leaders (at first exclusively aristocrats). This form of government is known as oligarchy, from a Greek word meaning "rule of the few." Some states, for example Corinth (in the northern Peloponnesus), retained their oligarchic councils for several centuries.

In many other Greek states, however, where the common people steadily grew disenchanted with aristocratic rule, new forms of government evolved. Beginning in the mid-600s B.C., for instance, ambitious individuals in several leading cities gained power by exploiting growing anti-aristocratic sentiments. The Greeks came to call these men, who were essentially petty dictators, "tyrants." The negative definition of the term "tyrant"—an "oppressive leader"—developed later, for a number of tyrants, at least at first, upheld most local laws, supported the arts, and enjoyed wide popular support. But as a form of government, tyranny was unstable and short-lived in Greece. This is because a tyrant needed popular support, especially from his community's soldiers, to stay in power. The citizen bodies of many city-states, which included the soldiers, increasingly came to eliminate the tyrants and to assume governing authority themselves.

This trend toward democratic ideals and government was spearheaded by Athens, which began its rise to greatness in late Archaic times. There, in 594 B.C., with the aristocrats and common people poised on the brink of civil war, the opposing factions called on a prominent citizen named Solon to arbitrate a solution. He proceeded to cancel all debts, create a new, fairer system of laws, and to increase opportunities for nonaristocrats to climb the social ladder. "To the mass of the people I gave the power they needed," Solon is reported to have remarked afterward,

> neither degrading them, nor giving them too much rein. For those who already possessed great power and wealth I saw to it that their interests were not harmed. I stood guard with a broad shield before both parties and prevented either from triumphing unjustly.

Solon's social and legal reforms laid the necessary groundwork for the emergence of a full-fledged democracy, the world's first, in Athens some eight decades later. This event would prove to be part of the prelude to the Classic Age, in which Greek civilization would reach its political and cultural zenith.

CHRONOLOGY

B.C.

ca. 2,000,000

Primitive humans begin making and using stone tools.

ca. 40,000–30,000–ca. 10,000

The so-called Upper Paleolithic period, the last phase of the Old Stone Age, in which human hunter-gatherers make important advances, including more effective tools and the production of the first art.

ca. 8000

The agricultural revolution begins in the Near East, initiating the Neolithic period, or New Stone Age.

ca. 5600–5500

People from the upland areas surrounding the Mesopotamian plains begin to descend from the hills and settle in the Tigris and Euphrates river valleys.

ca. 3300–3000

The Sumerians build the first Mesopotamian cities in the plain just northwest of the Persian Gulf; they also begin using a complex writing system that evolves into what modern scholars call cuneiform.

ca. 3100

The pharaoh Menes (or Narmer) unites Upper and Lower Egypt into a single nation-state.

ca. 2600

The greatest of the Egyptian pyramids, the tomb of the pharaoh Khufu (or Cheops), is completed.

ca. 2500

In India's Indus River Valley, the Harappan culture, characterized by large cities constructed of burnt brick, rises to prominence.

ca. 2400–2200

In Mesopotamia, Akkadian rulers, most prominent among them Sargon the Great, conquer Sumeria and unite northern and southern Mesopotamia.

ca. 2100

Ur-Nammu, king of the city of Ur, establishes a new empire, the Third Dynasty of Ur.

ca. 2000

An unknown Babylonian scribe collects the epic tales of the early Mesopotamian hero Gilgamesh.

ca. 1813–1781

Reign of Shamshi-Adad, founder of Assyria's first great royal dynasty and the first of that nation's rulers about whom any details are known.

ca. 1759

Babylonian king Hammurabi, famous for his law code, conquers the kingdom of Mari (on the upper Euphrates) and soon afterward absorbs the Assyrian cities.

ca. 1600

Babylon is sacked by the Hittites, an ambitious people from central Anatolia (what is now Turkey); in India, the Harappan civilization rapidly declines; on the Aegean island of Crete, the Minoans rebuild their palaces, which had been damaged by earthquakes.

ca. 1523

Along China's Yellow River, a group of rulers known as the Shang conquer most of the small city-states in the region, creating a strong kingdom.

1550–1069

Years of Egypt's New Kingdom, in which a series of energetic pharaohs expand the country's power and influence, building an empire that stretches northward into Syria.

ca. 1400

The Mycenaeans, the Greek-speaking inhabitants of the Greek mainland, expand outward into the Aegean and take control of the Minoan sphere.

1336–1327

Reign of the Egyptian boy-king Tutankhamen (King Tut), whose tomb will lie almost undisturbed until rediscovered by English archaeologist Howard Carter in 1922.

ca. 1250–1200

Traditional period for the Trojan War, probably a Mycenaean raid or siege that would later be immortalized in the epic poetry of the Greek bard Homer.

ca. 1200–1100

Many Near Eastern and Mediterranean cities are sacked and burned as the region undergoes catastrophic upheaval, the causes of which remain unclear; Assyria and Egypt largely escape the destruction; a devastated Greece sinks into a dark age of poverty and illiteracy; in northern Europe, the tribal Celts begin a long series of folk migrations that will carry them across the continent and eventually into the British Isles.

ca. 1000

Rise of the ancient kingdom of Israel (in Palestine) under the biblical King David.

776

Traditional date for the first Olympic Games, part of Greece's new age of economic and cultural revival.

753

Traditional date for the founding of Rome by the legendary figure Romulus on seven low hills near the Tiber River in western Italy.

ca. 722–705

Reign of Sargon II, founder of the greatest Assyrian dynasty.

ca. 694

Sargon's successor, Sennacherib, destroys Babylon.

615

Media's King Cyaxares attacks Assyria from the east; the following year he captures and sacks Assur, the most sacred of Assyria's cities, and forms an alliance with Babylonia.

612

A combined Babylonian-Median army ravages the Assyrian heartland, destroying Nimrud and Nineveh.

558

Cyrus the Great rises to the throne of Persia, a small kingdom of southern Iran that was then a subject of Media.

539

Having conquered and absorbed Media, Cyrus captures the great Mesopotamian city of Babylon.

508

The Greek city of Athens establishes the world's first democracy.

490

The Athenians defeat the Persians at Marathon (northeast of Athens), one of the first major events of the classical age.

ca. 485

Birth of the Greek historian Herodotus, later called "the Father of History," who visits the Near East and sees and writes about the ancient civilizations that had long ago risen in that region.

FOR FURTHER RESEARCH

Early China, India, and the Far East

William T. de Bary, ed., *Sources of Indian Tradition*. Vol. 1. New York: Columbia University Press, 1958.

A.L. Basham, *The Wonder That Was India*. New York: Taplinger, 1967.

Patricia B. Ebrey, *The Cambridge Illustrated History of China*. New York: Cambridge University Press, 1996.

L. Carrington Goodrich, *A Short History of the Chinese People*. New York: Harper and Row, 1969.

Valerie Hanson, *The Open Empire: A History of China to 1600*. New York: Norton, 2000.

John Keay, *India: A History*. New York: Atlantic Monthly, 2000.

Kenneth S. Latourette, *A Short History of the Far East*. New York: Macmillan, 1964.

H. Maspero, *China in Antiquity*. Amherst: University of Massachusetts Press, 1978.

Franz Schurmann, ed., *The China Reader*. 4 vols. New York: Random House, 1967–1974.

Vincent A. Smith, *The Oxford History of India*. New York: Oxford University Press, 1981.

Early Egypt

Bob Brier, *Egyptian Mummies: Unraveling the Secrets of an Ancient Art*. New York: William Morrow, 1994.

Charles Freeman, *Egypt, Greece, and Rome: Civilizations of the Ancient Mediterranean*. New York: Oxford University Press, 1996.

Nicolas Grimal, *A History of Ancient Egypt*. Trans. Ian Shaw. Oxford, England: Blackwell, 1992.

Barbara Mertz, *Red Land, Black Land: Daily Life in Ancient Egypt*. New York: Dodd, Mead, 1978.

Don Nardo, *Egyptian Mythology*. Berkeley Heights, NJ: Enslow, 2000.

Roland A. Oliver, *Africa in the Iron Age, ca. 500 B.C. to A.D. 1400*. New York: Cambridge University Press, 1975.

Byron E. Shafer, ed., *Religion in Ancient Egypt*. Ithaca, NY: Cornell University Press, 1991.

Ian Shaw and Paul Nicholson, *The Dictionary of Ancient Egypt*. New York: Harry N. Abrams, 1995.

David P. Silverman, ed., *Ancient Egypt*. New York: Oxford University Press, 1997.

Desmond Stewart, *The Pyramids and the Sphinx*. New York: Newsweek Book Division, 1971.

Early Greece

Rodney Castleden, *Minoans: Life in Bronze Age Crete*. New York: Routledge, 1993.

Charles Freeman, *The Greek Achievement: The Foundation of the Western World*. New York: Viking/Penguin, 1999.

Michael Grant, *The Rise of the Greeks*. New York: Macmillan, 1987.

Peter Green, *The Greco-Persian Wars*. Berkeley and Los Angeles: University of California Press, 1996.

Herodotus, *The Histories*. Trans. Aubrey de Sélincourt. New York: Penguin Books, 1972.

Homer, *Iliad*. Trans. Robert Fagles. New York: Penguin Books, 1990.

———, *Odyssey*. Trans. E.V. Rieu. Baltimore: Penguin Books, 1961.

Pierre Leveque, *The Birth of Greece*. New York: Harry N. Abrams, 1990.

Thomas R. Martin, *Ancient Greece: From Prehistoric to Hellenistic Times*. New Haven, CT: Yale University Press, 1996.

Don Nardo, *Life in Ancient Athens*. San Diego: Lucent Books, 2000.

———, ed., *The Complete History of Ancient Greece*. San Diego: Greenhaven, 2001.

———, ed., *The Decline and Fall of Ancient Greece*. San Diego: Greenhaven, 2000.

John G. Pedley, *Greek Art and Archaeology*. New York: Harry N. Abrams, 1993.

Plutarch, *Parallel Lives*, excerpted in *The Rise and Fall of Athens: Nine Greek Lives by Plutarch*. Trans. Ian Scott-Kilvert. New York: Penguin, 1960.

Sarah B. Pomeroy et al., *Ancient Greece: A Political, Social, and Cultural History*. New York: Oxford University Press, 1999.

Early Italy and Central Europe

Arthur E.R. Boak and William G. Sinnigen, *A History of Rome to A.D. 565*. New York: Macmillan, 1965.

Nora K. Chadwick and Barry Cunliffe, *The Celts*. New York: Penguin, 1998.

T.J. Cornell, *The Beginnings of Rome: Italy and Rome from the Bronze Age to the Punic Wars (c. 1000–264 B.C.)*. London: Routledge, 1995.

Norman Davies, *Europe: A History*. New York: HarperCollins, 1998.

Peter B. Ellis, *The Celtic Empire: The First Millennium of Celtic History, c. 1000 B.C.–51 A.D.* Durham, NC: Carolina Academic, 1990.

Daithi O. Hogain, *Celtic Warriors: The Armies of One of the First Great Peoples of Europe*. New York: Dunne Books, 1999.

Anthony Kamm, *The Romans: An Introduction*. London: Routledge, 1995.

Martin Kitchen, *The Cambridge Illustrated History of Germany*. New York: Cambridge University Press, 2000.

Paul MacKendrick, *The Mute Stones Speak: The Story of Archaeology in Italy*. New York: St. Martin's, 1960.

Don Nardo, *The Ancient Romans*. San Diego: Lucent Books, 2001.

Early Mesopotamia

Jean Bottéro et al., eds., *The Near East: The Early Civilizations.* New York: Delacorte, 1967.

Jacquetta Hawkes, *The First Great Civilizations: Life in Mesopotamia, the Indus Valley, and Egypt.* New York: Knopf, 1973.

Tom B. Jones, ed., *The Sumerian Problem.* New York: John Wiley, 1969.

Samuel N. Kramer, *Cradle of Civilization.* New York: Time-Life, 1967.

Seton Lloyd, *The Art of the Ancient Near East.* London: Thames and Hudson, 1961.

———, *Foundations in the Dust.* New York: Thames and Hudson, 1981.

Don Nardo, *The Assyrian Empire.* San Diego: Lucent Books, 1998.

———, *Empires of Mesopotamia.* San Diego: Lucent Books, 2001.

J.N. Postgate, *Early Mesopotamia: Society and Economy at the Dawn of History.* New York: Routledge, 1992.

Georges Roux, *Ancient Iraq.* New York: Penguin, 1980.

John M. Russell, *Sennacherib's Palace Without Rival at Nineveh.* Chicago: University of Chicago Press, 1991.

William Ryan and Walter Pitman, *Noah's Flood: The New Scientific Discoveries About the Event That Changed History.* New York: Simon & Schuster, 1998.

Daniel C. Snell, *Life in the Ancient Near East, 3100–332 B.C.* New Haven, CT: Yale University Press, 1997.

Wolfram von Soden, *The Ancient Orient: An Introduction to the Study of the Ancient Near East.* Grand Rapids, MI: William B. Eerdmans, 1994.

Early Palestine

Emmanuel Anati, *Palestine Before the Hebrews.* New York: Knopf, 1963.

Maria E. Aubert, *The Phoenicians and the West.* Trans. Mary Turton. New York: Columbia University Press, 1993.

Max I. Dimont, *Jews, God, and History.* New York: New American Library, 1962.

Trude Dothan and Moshe Dothan, *People of the Sea: The Search for the Philistines.* New York: Macmillan, 1992.

Maitland. A. Edey, *The Sea Traders.* New York: Time-Life, 1974.

Roberta L. Harris, *The World of the Bible.* London: Thames and Hudson, 1995.

Kathleen M. Kenyon, *Archaeology of the Holy Land.* New York: Praeger, 1979.

James B. Pritchard, ed., *Ancient Near Eastern Texts Relating to the Old Testament.* Princeton, NJ: Princeton University Press, 1969.

Roland de Vaux, *Ancient Israel: Its Life and Institutions.* New York: McGraw-Hill, 1961.

General Ancient Civilizations

Paul G. Bahn, ed., *The Cambridge Illustrated History of Archaeology.* New York: Cambridge University Press, 1996.

Nels M. Bailkey, ed., *Readings in Ancient History, from Gilgamesh to Diocletian.* Lexington, MA: D.C. Heath, 1976.

L. Sprague de Camp, *The Ancient Engineers.* New York: Ballantine Books, 1963.

Lionel Casson, *The Ancient Mariners.* New York: Macmillan, 1959.

Peter Clayton and Martin Price, *The Seven Wonders of the Ancient World.* New York: Barnes & Noble, 1993.

Peter James and Nick Thorpe, *Ancient Mysteries.* New York: Ballantine Books, 1999.

William H. McNeill, *The Rise of the West: A History of the Human Community.* Chicago: University of Chicago Press, 1963.

H.W.F. Saggs, *Civilization Before Greece and Rome.* New Haven, CT: Yale University Press, 1989.

Chester G. Starr, *A History of the Ancient World.* New York: Oxford University Press, 1991.

Michael Wood, *Legacy: The Search for Ancient Cultures.* New York: Stirling, 1992.

Tim Wood, *Ancient Wonders.* New York: Penguin Books, 1991.

Stone Age Cultures

J.M. Coles and E.S. Higgs, *The Archaeology of Early Man*. London: Faber and Faber, 1969.

B.M. Fagan, *The Journey from Eden: The Peopling of Our World*. London: Thames and Hudson, 1990.

John Haywood, *The Illustrated History of Early Man*. New York: Smithmark, 1995.

J.B. Hutchinson et al., *The Early History of Agriculture*. London: British Academy, 1977.

Patricia D. Netzley, *The Stone Age*. San Diego: Lucent Books, 1998.

K.P. Oakley, *Man the Tool-Maker*. Chicago: University of Chicago Press, 1976.

David Oates and Joan Oates, *The Rise of Civilization*. New York: E.P. Dutton, 1976.

Richard Rudgley, *The Lost Civilizations of the Stone Age*. New York: Simon & Schuster, 1999.

Ann Sieveking, *The Cave Artists*. London: Thames and Hudson, 1979.

INDEX

Historian Don Nardo has written extensively about the ancient world. His studies of ancient Greece and Rome include *Life in Ancient Athens*, *The Age of Augustus*, *Greek and Roman Sport*, and *Life of a Roman Soldier*; he is also the editor of Greenhaven Press's massive *Complete History of Ancient Greece* and *The Encyclopedia of Greek and Roman Mythology*. In addition, Mr. Nardo has produced volumes about ancient Egypt and Mesopotamia. He lives with his wife, Christine, in Massachusetts.